Diplomacy

The World of the *Honest Spy*

By Peter Barber

THE BRITISH LIBRARY

BL

© 1979 The British Library
ISBN 0 904654 29 X *cased*
ISBN 0 904654 30 3 *paper*
Published by the British Library,
Reference Division Publications, Great Russell Street,
London WC1B 3DG

British Library Cataloguing in Publication Data

Barber, Peter
    Diplomacy.
    1. Diplomacy – History – Pictorial works
    I. Title II. British Library.
    Reference Division
    327'.2'0222   JX1635

Designed by Ivor Claydon

Set in Monophoto Photina and printed in England
by Balding + Mansell, London and Wisbech

Contents

Introduction   6
I The Evolution of Modern
   Diplomacy (1–63)   8
II The Practitioners (64–93)   60
III The Mission (94–168)   85
   Suggestions for further reading   141
   Acknowledgements   143

Colour Plates (between pp.96 and 97)

I The Sardinian envoy's chapel in London,
   1808 (**32**)

II The state entry of Emperor Mathias I into
   Dresden, 1617: Detail showing the Imperial
   coach (**10**).

III Letter of James I to an unnamed oriental
   ruler, 1610 (**57**)

IV The state entry of Emperor Mathias I into
   Dresden, 1617: Detail showing Saxon
   trumpeters (**10**)

V Sir Thomas Roe at the court of the Mughal
   emperor, Jahangir, 1615 (**58**)

VI British ratification of an Anglo-Mexican
   convention, 1867: Detail showing the seal
   skippet (**133**)

VII The solemn entry of the British Ambassador
   into the Doge's Palace, Venice, by
   Carlevaris, 1707 (**110**)

VIII Ambassadors taking leave of their master,
   by Carpaccio, 1495 (**107**)

IX Badge of a British Queen's Messenger,
   1854–5 (**122**)

X Gold pendant badge of the Order of the Bath
   (**164**)

XI The arrival and first audience of ambassadors at an Italian court, by Carpaccio,
   c.1495 (**111**)

XII Henry VIII's confirmation (1523) of the
   Anglo-Danish treaty of 1490 (**138**)

XIII Patent of Knighthood of Constantijn
   Huygens, Dutch envoy in England, 1622
   (**158**)

XIV Protocol of the Anglo-Dutch treaty of
   Alliance and Defence, 1701 (**131**)

Cover Letter from James II to the Ottoman Grand
   Vizier Azem, 1685: Detail (**154**)

INTRODUCTION

Diplomacy, or the peaceful management of international relations, is an ancient and important field of human activity which has always tended to be shrouded in secrecy. Dimly remembered names of meaningless treaties or passing headlines in newspapers are often all that people know of its fruits. Of the practitioners and the work itself still less is generally known. The diplomat of the popular imagination seems to be almost totally evil or almost totally good. Some picture him as a heartless schemer, liar, and spy, who spends his time negotiating military alliances and engineering wars between the peoples of the world at his master's behest, or, at any rate, as one who blithely flaunts national customs' duties and local parking regulations by virtue of his 'CD' plate. Others portray the diplomat as an honest and very dignified gentleman who is for ever striving for international peace – the very antithesis of a warrior. He is to be seen entering Buckingham Palace in a black coach, and seems to do most of his work while attending endless receptions, cocktail parties, or balls. A worthy representative of his country abroad, he occasion-ally reaches the status of a romantic hero, as for example in Greta Garbo's film, *Queen Christina*. The only common ground between the two views is their acknowledgement of the diplomat's almost excessive polish, his charm, tact, and skill at persuasion which has given the word 'diplomatic' a second meaning unrelated to its actual origin.

The British Library's Department of Manuscripts is rich in the private papers of diplomats and English politicians, and in diplomatic documents. These enable a more accurate, and human, picture to be drawn and the objective of this study is to give the reader some idea of the range of the Department's holdings of such material. The study is divided into three parts. The first is intended to give an impression of the development of the best-known features of modern diplomatic practice – such as resident ambassadors and embassies, diplomatic immunity, and congresses – from about 1400 until about 1900, with a brief glimpse backwards to the earliest times. The second part gives an idea of the sort of people who served as diplomats before 1900 and looks at certain remarkable practitioners. Some are already known for their skill in this field, but most are not. We find Rubens acting as a political prophet, Thomas More engaged in outmanœuvring other ambassadors, Caxton printing an oration given by a fellow-diplomat – not to mention the unhappy Chevalier d'Eon begging permission to revert to being a man, and Metternich and Palmerston doodling in bored moments. The third part illustrates the work of the diplomat in a way which emphasises its basic immutability over the centuries, and its excitement and frequent splendour. At the same time the opportunity has been taken to illustrate the variety of treaties and other official 'diplomas' which were, apparently, the root of the word 'diplomacy'. Again the universality and immutability of their contents, despite their ever-changing external appearance, is noteworthy. An effort has been made throughout the study to demonstrate that diplomats were very human individuals, as well as the observers *par excellence* of their worlds, and this springs to life in their letters. Lack of space has regrettably forced the exclusion of many important aspects of diplomacy – particularly international organisation, methods of negotiation, non-European diplomacy before about 1700, the vital rôle played by consuls, and the developments since 1900. It is nevertheless hoped that the study will help to recreate the work and the world of diplomacy as it was until the dawn of the modern age.

While the prime purpose of this volume is to serve as a catalogue of an exhibition on the subject at the British Library in the summer of 1979, the degree of illustration and the extent of the text on each item is designed to present a coherent survey of the subject which stands quite independently of the exhibition.

Peter Barber

Note
The references in small italics under the headings refer to the pressmarks or manuscript numbers in the British Library. Underlinings and expansions of abbreviated words in the documents quoted are indicated in the text by italics.

Allegorical picture of the first audience of James II's Ambassador to the Holy See, the Earl of Castlemaine with Pope Innocent XI, 8th January 1687. Drawn by A. Cornelii and G. B. Lenardi, engraved by A. van Westerhout.

I THE EVOLUTION OF MODERN DIPLOMACY

1. EARLY DIPLOMACY

The earliest records deal primarily with four subjects: law, economics, war, and diplomacy (1). Even by then the practice of diplomacy must have been ancient. It had reached a level of considerable refinement in Mesopotamia and India (2, 3, 4). However, the practices that were directly to influence the evolution of post-medieval West European diplomacy, and through it the diplomacy of the world of today, stemmed from Ancient Greece, Rome, and the Byzantine Empire (5, 6, 7).

1 Sumerian clay nail of about 2400 BC
British Museum: Department of Western Asiatic Antiquities: 136843

Inscribed clay nails were originally inserted into the walls of Sumerian temples as a form of foundation document. The inscription under the head of this nail records the building of a temple for the goddess Inana and her consort by Entemena, ruler of the city-state of Lagash. It also mentions a 'brotherhood agreement' that had been concluded between him and Lugal-Kinishe-dudu, ruler of the city-state of Uruk. It is only a generation more recent than one of the earliest surviving historical documents of the Sumerians, the 'Stela of the Vultures' in the Louvre, which records the text of a treaty between Entemena's uncle Eannatum and the ruler of the city-state of Umma.

Sumer (in modern southern Iraq) contained many ambitious and contending states as did ancient Greece and medieval and renaissance Italy, where sophisticated diplomatic systems developed.

2 Letter of Tushratta, ruler of Mitanni, to Amenophis III of Egypt, *c.* 1390 BC
British Museum: Department of Western Asiatic Antiquities Amarna Tablet 29792

Tushratta informs the Pharaoh of his recent victory over the Hittites and sends him part of the booty, with personal gifts including five chariots and five teams of horses for him, and jewellery and trinkets for his wife, Tushratta's sister. He asks Amenophis to pass his news to the messenger, Gilia, and to Tunip-iwri, and to send them back speedily.

The kingdom of Mitanni, centred in northern Mesopotamia, had long been in alliance with Egypt against the Hittites, who threatened Mitanni from the west. This letter is an attempt to reaffirm the traditional alliance, ruptured a few years earlier following the anti-Egyptian coup which had placed Tushratta on the throne. The letter is accordingly full of assertions of friendship for the Pharaoh. Despite the re-establishment of the alliance, however, Tushratta did not succeed in stemming his kingdom's decline.

The tablet illustrates the envoy's earliest known function: that of conveying messages. The German word for ambassador (Botschafter) and a traditional title for a Papal envoy (Nuncio) both stem from this rôle (Botschaft means message, annunciare to announce). The convention of exchanging gifts through envoys dates from the earliest times and still continues.

3 Detail of an Assyrian relief showing envoys, 653 BC
British Museum: Department of Western Asiatic Antiquities

The short men in the tasselled caps are envoys from Assyria's northern neighbour Urartu which lay around Lake Van in Turkey. The pair of men on the right are envoys from Elam (southern Iran). Previously, war had broken out between Assyria and Elam, the Elamite envoys had been detained in Nineveh, and the Elamites had been decisively defeated and their King Teumman slain at the battle of Til-Tuba. In the incident depicted here the Elamite envoys are obliged to show to the Urartians the insulting message which they had brought from Elam before the war started. The Assyrians evidently hoped to deter the ruler of Urartu from repeating Teumman's mistake.

The scene is one of the earliest portrayals of ambassadors representing their masters. The atmosphere is remarkably close to that shown in the French medal of 1662 (146). In ancient times at least two envoys were customarily sent on missions and they were generally expected to return to their courts as speedily as possible, unless forcibly detained.

4 Kautalya's Arthaśāstra (translated by R. Shamasastry, Mysore, 1967)
Department of Printed Books

The Arthaśāstra is said to have been written between 321 and 296 BC by the Brāhman (priest) Kautalya, also known as Vishnugupta or Chandragupta. Like the works of other early political theorists, such as Plato, it embraces the whole field of domestic government and external relations, with a single chapter, the one shown, devoted to envoys.

3

The text reveals the sophistication attained by early North Indian diplomacy. Diplomatic immunity seems indeed to have been more limited than it is today, but various grades of envoy are distinguished: dūta (envoy), nisrishtarthah (chargé d'affaires), parimitārthah (agent), and sāsanaharah (conveyor of royal writs), while the tone of the advice is much more akin to secular post-medieval European theory than to that of the earlier European writers, such as the clergyman Bernard du Rosier (12). In this context Kautalya's stress on the envoy's duty of unconditional obedience to his master's orders, his distinction between envoys and spies and his definition of the envoy's duties ('transmission of missions, maintenance of treaties, issue of ultimatums, gaining of friends, intrigue, sowing dissension among friends, fetching secret force, carrying away by stealth relatives and gems, gathering information about the movements of spies, bravery, breaking of treaties of peace, winning over the favour of the enemy and government officers of the enemy') are particularly significant. The text of the Arthaśāstra only became widely known in this century.

5 Coin: Silver tridrachm of the Maritime League from Samos, 397–394 BC
British Museum: Department of Coins and Medals (electrotype)

This coin was probably issued following the liberation from Spartan domination of Greek cities in or near Asia Minor in the wake of the Battle of Cnidus (in 394 BC). Several coastal cities formed the so-called Maritime League and issued three-drachma pieces with their own standard obverse types (in Samos's case, a lion's scalp) but with a common reverse showing Heracles struggling with serpents and the letters ΣYN, an abbreviation either for $\Sigma YNMAX\Omega N$ ('of the allies') or $\Sigma YNMAXIKON$ ('allied' (coin)).

It is fitting that a diplomatic event should have been commemorated numismatically by the Greek city-states, since numismatics and diplomacy underwent precocious development in their world.

Concepts such as arbitration, neutrality, and diplomatic immunity for heralds were formulated, and their envoys were furnished with credentials and took public audiences on leave-taking, arrival and return. Copied by the Romans and noted by renaissance humanists, these concepts have influenced the development of modern diplomacy.

6 Coin: Sestertius of Trajan, AD 116
British Museum: Department of Coins and Medals: BMC 1046

The inscription REX PARTHIS DATUS means 'a King given to the Parthians' and Trajan is seen, seated, on a high platform, placing a diadem round the head of the new King, Pathamaspates, who stands before him. A Roman officer stands behind the Emperor, and on the ground before him kneels Parthia, wearing the Parthian pointed cap, who holds out both hands.

The inscription summarises the view of international relations held by the Romans at the height of their power. Earlier, however, they had shown greater humility towards their neighbours and had evolved a theory of diplomatic immunity for ambassadors and their accredited staff, who were returned to their masters for punishment if accused of any crime during their mission.

7 Coin: Follis of Romanus I Lecapenus, AD 919–944
British Museum: Department of Coins and Medals: BMC Constantine VII no. 15

The Emperor is seen full-face in his jewelled robes, crowned, and holding an orb and sceptre, as an envoy would have seen him at the first audience. The coin gives a good impression of the splendour and formality of the Byzantine court, where many of the rituals and ceremonies associated with diplomacy, such as the formal entry, originated. The Eastern Empire also had a department of state for foreign affairs staffed by a corps of professional negotiators, with a 'skrinion barbaron', an official responsible for the reception of ambassadors.

5   6   7

2. THE SPECIAL MISSION

The most ancient form of diplomacy is the special mission. The envoy was sent abroad with a certain limited objective or set of objectives and was expected to return home as speedily as possible. The mission could be for ceremony (9, 11) or for negotiation (8, 10) and it could be to one court (9, 10) or to several (8, 11), but it was never anticipated that the envoy should reside in one place for an extended period.

This system worked well in a stable system of states where crises were intermittent and where each state's right to survival was accepted by the rest. In the world of insecurity and permanent crisis that characterised post-medieval Europe, however, where alliances were ever-changing and there was a need for a constant supply of information from each foreign court, it soon became clear that a reliance on special missions alone would be insufficient if a state was to survive.

8 John of Gaunt's passport for Niccolo da Lucca of Florence, Calais, 18th May 1394

Additional Charter 7487

John of Gaunt, Duke of Lancaster, a son of Edward III of England, requests free passage for Niccolo on his journeys through Italy, Germany and elsewhere to undertake 'certain negotiations' on the Duke's behalf. John of Gaunt's seal was once appended.

The passport takes the form of an open letter with an official seal, or 'letter patent', like most official diplomatic documents to this day. In the Middle Ages, the right to send ambassadors was not confined to sovereign rulers or republics as it is today. As late as 1481 commissioners of the Spanish province of Guipúzcoa negotiated a commercial treaty with England. Until the late seventeenth century Italians were often employed as diplomats, as here, on account of their skill in that field and presumed personal loyalty to their master.

9 The ambassador of England presents a letter to the King of Brittany. From a fifteenth-century series of paintings depicting the legend of St Ursula

Courtesy of the Groeninge Museum, Bruges

In this version of the legend, the ambassador of England, shown as a fifteenth-century English herald, is given a letter by his pagan master, the King of England, requesting the hand of the Christian King of Brittany's daughter, Ursula, for his son Etherius. The Ambassador is seen travelling and, in the background, delivering the letter to the King of Brittany, next to whom stands Princess Ursula, with a halo and flowing blond locks.

Heralds have been involved with diplomacy since antiquity and played an important rôle in ancient Greece. In modern times, however, their contribution has been minor, and almost entirely confined to ceremonial missions (73), the delivery of formal

8

messages and, before 1701, the official declarations of war. In the rare cases where heralds undertook negotiations, they seem to have been selected because of their personal qualities rather than their status as heralds.

For pictures illustrating a different version of the legend, see 107 and 111.

10 The solemn entry of the Holy Roman Emperor Mathias, King Ferdinand of Bohemia, and Archduke Maximilian III into Dresden, 25th July 1617 (see plate nos II, IV)
Additional MS 21601

The inscription in the cartouche records that the 'triumphal' procession went from a meadow outside Dresden to the Elector of Saxony's palace inside the town at six o'clock in the afternoon. First comes a troop of Saxon bodyguards, all wearing the black and yellow colours of Saxony, led by their captains. Then follow the Saxon and, on the white horse, the Imperial court jesters, a Saxon drummer and trumpeters, and the Saxon chamberlain accompanied by courtiers. Behind another drummer and a few trumpeters trot a group of aristocrats including the Counts Mansfeld and Schwarzenburg. The Dukes Francis of Saxe-Lauenburg, and John Philip and Frederick of Saxe-Altenburg, do not wear the Saxon colours. Behind them march Saxon footmen with black and yellow breeches, escorting the Elector, John George III. He is clearly distinguished from the rest of the procession, mounted on a white horse and wearing green breeches, a splendid gold-embroidered white jacket, and a high white hat with a large black plume. Above he is described as Elector of Saxony and Duke of Cleves, Mark, and Jülich, though he never succeeded in making good his disputed claim to these three duchies. Behind the Elector ride mounted pages with pikes and helmets and officers of the Saxon Chamber. Then follows the Imperial procession, preceded by Imperial footmen, wearing red breeches, and the coach carrying the Emperor, sitting at the back, with his cousin Ferdinand, the newly elected King of Bohemia (facing by the door) and, seen from behind, his brother Archduke Maximilian, ruling Count of Tirol and Grand Master of the Teutonic Order. In the next coach under the red embroidered canopy are the Emperor's first minister, Cardinal Klehsl, and Count Fürstenberg. The third coach, with the black canopy, holds Bohemian councillors, though the man facing, by the door of the carriage, wears a Hungarian hat. A Bohemian page runs in front of them. Mathias, Count von Thurn, and Albert, Duke of Wallenstein, ride in the last coach.

The Emperor undertook the mission depicted here in order to secure the support of the Elector of Saxony for the election of his cousin, the recently elected King of Bohemia, as 'King of the Romans' and thus next Holy Roman Emperor. The mission was a success but within a year the Thirty Years' War had broken out. Many of the leading protagonists in that conflict, which was to devastate large tracts of central Europe, can be seen in this picture.

State visits by one ruler to another are one of the oldest forms of diplomacy and the ceremonial surrounding them was the origin of that which used to accompany ambassadors.

11 Petition for additional expenses for the Russian envoy extraordinary, October 1687
Additional MS 41842, f. 189

In the autumn of 1687, Vasili Timofeyeovich Posnikov was sent to London and Italy on behalf of the young joint Tsars Ivan and Peter (Peter the Great) to announce the conclusion of a Muscovite-Polish peace treaty. Here the payment of an additional subsistence allowance is requested from the English Government while, in the right-hand corner, Posnikov's secretary, Michael Larionov, acknowledges receipt of £100 for two weeks' ordinary subsistence and for subsistence for nine accredited members of the envoy extraordinary's suite. The Muscovite request was refused, the Russians left England in December aboard ships provided for them by Samuel Pepys.

In classical times it became customary for the host government to pay all the expenses of an ambassador and his accredited suite from the moment he handed over his credentials to the time of his departure. Until about 1800, non-western envoys, like Posnikov, continued to receive this treatment and after their public entries western envoys with the rank of ambassador were usually given vestigial hospitality, such as three days' free lodging in Paris, by their hosts. Generally, however, the coming of resident envoys, and rulers' growing reluctance to allow their representatives to be paid by foreign powers, led to the virtual disappearance of the custom after 1500.

The document comes from the papers of Charles Middleton, second Earl of Middleton, who was a secretary of state from 1684 until the time when James II fled from England in 1688.

12 Bernard du Rosier: *Ambaxiator Brevilogus,* **1436 (from V.E. Hrabar,** *De Legatis et Legationibus Tractatus Varii,* **Dorpat, Livonia, 1905)**
Department of Printed Books

Bernard du Rosier frequently served as an ambassador, his background as a lawyer and a cleric (he later became Archbishop of Toulouse) making him highly suitable in the eyes of his contemporaries for such a post. His 'Short Treatise on Ambassadors', which was probably written in the course of a mission to Castile, is the first western European tract to deal exclusively with the envoy and his duties, and does so generally in a practical way.

Much of the advice given and the forms and procedures described remain valid to this day, but the framework and spirit of the tract is that of medieval Europe with its assumption that Christendom was united and was governed by a common moral code based on Christian ethics tempered by custom and Roman law. Du Rosier repeatedly stresses that the ambassador works for the general welfare ('pro utilitate publica') because his business is peace. Anyone obstructing him in the execution of his duties therefore obstructs the 'public good . . . peace and tranquility' of Christendom as a whole. However, should the ambassador, for whatever reason and regardless of the impulse, transgress the moral code either through his objectives or his methods, he himself should be severely punished by the authorities wherever he happens to be.

This was the medieval theory of the ambassador's duty and diplomatic immunity. By the end of the century the diplomat's view of his world and his duties had undergone a revolutionary change. For another two centuries, however, du Rosier's views remained those of the majority of theorists.

10

3. THE COMING OF RESIDENT DIPLOMACY 1378–1559

The idea of sending envoys to reside at foreign courts is ancient and was being discussed, and dismissed, as early as 1380 BC in the Amarna letters. Though there had been several precedents since the days of the Greek City State (13), it was the circumstances prevailing in early renaissance Italy (14–20) that led to the first appearance of accredited resident envoys in the late fourteenth century. Outside Italy, competitive, relatively centralised, states later evolved, headed by dynastically and territorially ambitious rulers (23). These rulers came to have knowledge of Italian resident envoys, particularly those at the Papal Court in Rome (20, 22). King Ferdinand of Aragon appointed the first non-Italian resident envoys outside Italy in the 1480s (23, 24). The diplomatic pressures associated with the Italian Wars, after 1494, encouraged the spread of resident diplomacy, which existed throughout western Europe by 1559 (22). The first residents to be employed outside Italy by the English were appointed by Henry VII in the last year of his reign (25). Two further changes were inseparably connected with the evolution of resident diplomacy: the development, particularly in Italy, of officials and chanceries capable of supporting rulers in their execution of foreign policy (21, 25), and a new ethos which made the resident primarily responsible to his ruler and not to Christendom in general (26).

13

13 Seal of a Venetian bailo in Constantinople, c.1310
Detached Seal CLXVII.37 (cast)

The lion of St Mark, the symbol of Venice, is seen rising from the sea, clasping the gospel in its paws. The inscription reads S. IOHIS DELFIN. BAIUL. VENETI COSTATIOPOL. Z. TOTO DISTRITU D.N. IMPAT. MICH. or, when expanded and translated, 'seal of Giovanni Delfino, Venetian Bailo in Constantinople and all its region under our Lord Emperor Michael' (Michael IX reigned from 1295 to 1320).

Many precedents for resident diplomats have been discovered ranging from the 'proxenoi' of ancient Greece, who cared for the natives and interests of one city state in another, to the procurators, the resident lawyers who championed the interests of secular rulers in the papal courts of Rome and Avignon or those of the Kings of England as Dukes of Aquitaine at the French Court in the early fourteenth century. Medieval banking agents too anticipated the later practices of resident diplomats in reporting regularly to their masters, who frequently held influential positions in the government of their cities (see also 132). It was the consular officials such as the Venetian bailo who provide the closest precedents however – and, like the banking agents, their work and their rôle were familiar to the first people to make extensive use of resident diplomacy, the rulers of renaissance Italy.

The word bailo is connected with the English word bailiff and, as 'governors' of the Venetian merchants in Constantinople the bailos originally represented the merchants' interests to the Byzantine Emperor and adjudicated in disputes that broke out within the mercantile community. For medieval theory held that consuls and bailos carried the law of their land with them wherever they went. Eventually, in response to the Venetian need to maintain continuous contact with Constantinople whose trade they had come to dominate, the bailo's rôle expanded. He was appointed by the Venetian Government, became responsible for sending it regular information and occasionally undertook the minor negotiations that did not warrant the expense of sending an embassy. His special position, too, was acknowledged by the Byzantine authorities, and just as centuries later, young western European aristocrats served as resident envoys at the start of brilliant careers (94), so young patricians seem to have served as bailos in Constantinople. Giovanni Delfino (1280–1361) later served as ambassador to Constantinople in 1350 and 1355, and was eventually elected doge in 1356.

However, unlike the resident agents of renaissance Italy, proxenoi, procurators, bailos, consuls, and banking agents were not regarded by contemporaries as in any way enjoying the special status of ambassadors (12) and, as this seal shows, the bailos acknowledged the suzerainty of the Byzantine emperor.

14 Letter from the Republic of Lucca to the Republic of Siena, Lucca, 7th July 1437
Additional MS 16163, f.8

In 1437 Lucca was allied with Milan and other smaller Italian powers against a league including Florence and Venice. In this letter the Luccan leaders try to recruit Siena to their side. Lucca, they write, is determined to preserve its liberty, cost what it might, and they believe they will succeed, with God's help, if the Sienese too have their own liberty at heart. A few years earlier, Lucca reminds Siena, the whole of Tuscany nearly fell into the hands of the Florentines, 'the most rapacious ('rapacissimis', line 6) of all the Tuscans, following the surrender of Pisa (1406) whose defence had been neglected by its neighbours. 'Look to your own affairs then . . . Consider that in the long run it is better and wiser to confront the rapacity of the Florentines in time than . . . to repent in vain afterwards . . . Bestir yourselves' ('Advertat igitur . . . ad rem suam. Cogitet*que* longe melius ac sapientius esse florentino*rum* rapacitati in tempore occurrere *quam* post tempus . . . frustra penitere . . . expergiscantur', lines 7–11).

This appeal by one city to the civic patriotism of a second against a third, all in the same region, is typical of late medieval and renaissance Italy, though the letter's humanist hand and classical Latin are characteristic of the fifteenth century. The civic patriotism of the north and central Italian cities burnt all the fiercer because in most cases it was illegitimate. From the eleventh century onwards they had increasingly arrogated to themselves an independence to which they lacked a legitimate title. The communes of Lombardy had been encouraged by the Papacy in their struggle against their legal suzerains, the Holy Roman Emperors. Later the Papacy itself proved unable to maintain its hold over its lands in central Italy, particularly between 1309 and 1377, when the popes were in exile in Avignon, in France, and 1378 to 1417, when there were rival popes in Rome and Avignon. The greater cities of northern and central Italy struggled for domination over the towns and lordships of the peninsula. Many of the towns had to submit to their more powerful neighbours. Aided by the absence for long periods of great power intervention in Italy, three extensive 'empires' (Milan, Venice and Florence) were emerging by the end of the fourteenth century, though at this time many other cities still retained their independence. By 1400 the pressures had become too great for forms of government and diplomacy that were still to be found in the sprawling kingdoms north of the Alps a couple of centuries later.

14

15 Portrait medallion of Sigismondo Pandolfo Malatesta by Matteo de Pasti, 1446

British Museum: Department of Coins and Medals: Hill Corpus 164

15a

15b

Malatesta is seen in profile with the fortress of Rimini, which had been expanded by him, on the reverse. The inscription reads 'SIGISMONDUS PANDULFUS DE MALATESTIS, S. RO. ECCLESIE C. GENERALIS' ('Sigismondo Pandolfo Malatesta, Captain General of the Holy Roman Church') and 'Castellum Sismondum Ariminense M.CCCC.XLVI' ('Si(gi)smund's Castle in Rimini 1446').

In the course of their struggles against each other, many Italian cities came to be dominated by one family, whether from behind the scenes, like the Medici of Florence, or openly, as despots, like the Gonzaga of Mantua, the Este of Ferrera and the Malatesta of Rimini. The despots were able to make full use of the resources of their states, unrestrained by the fetters of constitutional propriety. Threatened from within and without, their survival often hinged on their ability to take quick and effective action. Accordingly, it was the despots who made the most daring institutional and political innovations.

Sigismondo Malatesta (1417–1468) came of a family which had dominated Rimini since the thirteenth century. Dissatisfied with the opportunities and revenue offered him as ruler in Rimini, he early became a mercenary soldier, or *condottiere*. He served and deserted the Popes, Venetians, Milanese, Neapolitans, and Sienese, before serving the Venetians and finally the Papacy again. He managed throughout to maintain his hold over Rimini, but only with difficulty and at one point, accused by Pope Pius II of incest, assassination, heresy, treachery, and other crimes, he was excommunicated and sentenced to be deprived of Rimini and burnt. Malatesta was also a poet and a patron of the leading architects and sculptors of his age. Malatesta's interests, career and methods were typical of those of many despots, though he was more colourful than most.

16 Letter of Antonio degli Arrighi, Captain General of the Florentine Army, to the Balia (Governing Council) of Florence, Volterra, 19th May 1432.

Additional MS 16163, f.6

This letter was written during one of Florence's attempts to conquer Lucca. The war had gone badly, however, and Siena had joined Lucca. Arrighi complains here that the position of the Florentine forces is worsening daily because of shortages. He begs for food, infantry and munitions for fortresses on Florence's borders and warns that morale is in danger of collapse. 'The fortress of Montecatini needs infantry, cross bows and provisions because men are deserting through hunger. Jacopo da Modigliana . . . says there is not enough infantry to keep that place. Therefore I recommend its safety to you. Sharp darts, infantry lances, bows, cross-bows, arrows and bowstrings are needed here. For heaven's sake send us them, your lordships, because nothing can be done without them.' Arrighi himself is hourly expecting to be replaced and asks for money, to enable him to return to Florence without having to pawn his own things.

As this letter forewarned, the Florentines were unable to achieve their ambitions, Lucca remaining an independent state until 1847. A direct result of this defeat was that the Albizzi family which had dominated Florence since the end of the previous century was overthrown and replaced by Cosimo de' Medici and his followers.

Italian rulers were generally reluctant to embark on wars which tended to be inordinately wasteful of men and money, both being in short supply. The existence of strong modern fortresses such as that in

Rimini (15) increased the tendency of wars to be static and to end in deadlock. The hire of *condottieri* was risky. They tended to reach agreements between themselves at their employers' expense and to avoid serious battles. Militarily unsuccessful rulers, as here, were also apt to be overthrown. Diplomacy, however, enabled rulers to pursue their objectives through loyal agents at a relatively low cost and with less danger of open defeats. Many renaissance rulers, influenced by the examples of Cicero and other orators of antiquity, were also convinced of the efficacy of eloquence as an instrument of policy.

17 Sigismondo Pandolfo Malatesta's credential for his envoy to the Florentine Priori, Rimini, 5th March 1448

Additional MS 24213, f.30

Malatesta, then commanding the Neapolitan forces against Florence, introduces his councillor, Luca, who has been ordered to represent 'certain things' to the Florentines in Malatesta's name. He begs the Florentines to believe and lend full faith to Luca, as though he were Malatesta himself. The seal on the reverse, authenticating the credential, shows a renaissance portrait, possibly of Malatesta himself.

The letter is couched in the standard terms used through the ages for credentials, but there are other features which make the document peculiar to renaissance Italy: apart from a few words at the start and close, it is written in Italian and not in the Latin that was customary in most of Europe outside Italy until the eighteenth century; its seal, though personal and official, is not the usual heraldic one. The credential shows the way in which Italian despots experimented with the forms and methods of diplomacy.

18 Uniface plaque portraying Giangaleazzo Visconti, ruler of Milan from 1378 to 1402. Milan, late fifteenth century

British Museum: Department of Coins and Medals: Hill Corpus 638

This portrait, although posthumous, closely resembles contemporary depictions, in word and picture, of Giangaleazzo Visconti, created Duke of Milan by the Holy Roman Emperor Wenceslas in 1395.

17

Magnifici et excellentes dni domini mei singularissimi. post debitam recomendatione. Ho comesso a Ser lucca mio canc^ro pnte exhibitore quale a mando la / che in mio nome expona alcune cose ale vre excelse Signorie: pero supplico quelle se digneno creder li et darli piena fede quanto ala mia propria persona. Arimini die v^ta Martij Mccccxlviij.

Servitor Sigismundus pandulfus de Malatestis

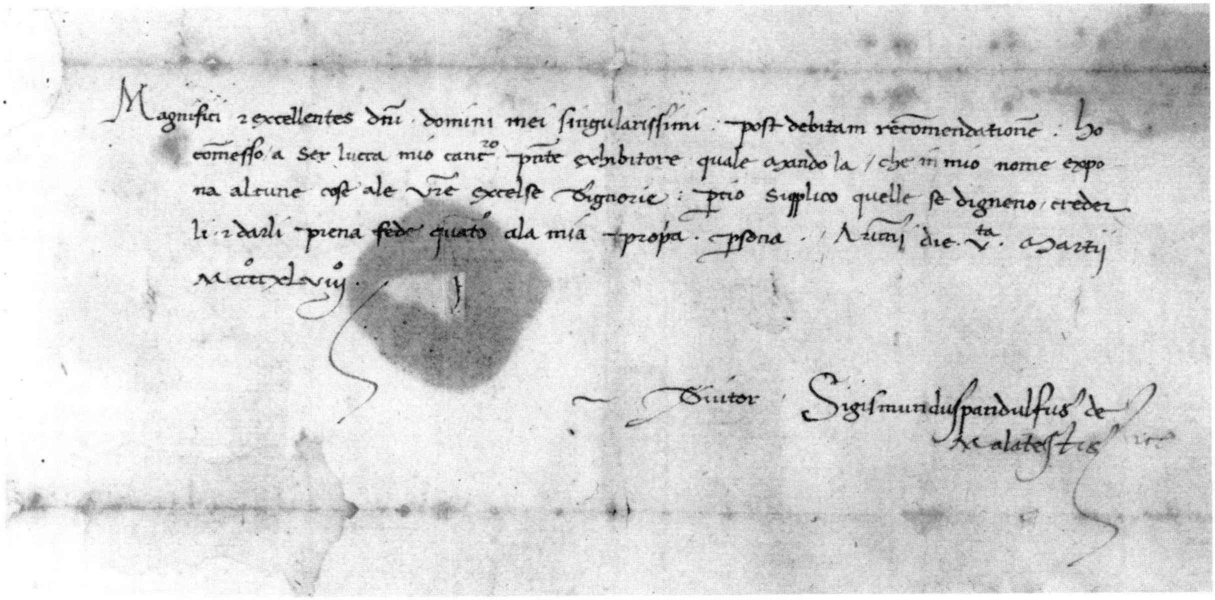

Visconti attempted to create an Italian kingdom based on Milan. In the process he became the first ruler to make extensive use of resident agents, several of whom apparently had a form of official diplomatic status. He employed the agents to maintain alliances and sometimes, as in the case of Pisa and Siena, to turn allies into subjects by subverting their courts. Giangaleazzo was given invaluable assistance by his well-ordered chancery, staffed by experienced diplomats under his secretary, Pasquino Capelli, and later his chamberlain, Francesco Barbavara. This acted as a fledgling foreign office, dealing with routine correspondence and communication with foreign envoys in Milan, leaving the Duke free to concentrate on major issues. By 1402 Giangaleazzo appeared to be on the verge of realising his ambitions, his realm extending from the St Gotthard Pass in the north to Assisi in the south, and from Genoa in the west to Padua in the east. On his death, however, his 'empire' underwent a collapse from which it never fully recovered.

Giangaleazzo was not the first to use resident agents – Luigi Gonzaga of Mantua employed one at the Court of Louis the Bavarian before 1341. He probably was the first Italian to give his agents a semi-diplomatic status, though they never seem to have enjoyed a formal title, contemporaries knowing them as 'the Duke's man', 'the Duke's agent', and even 'the Duke's spy'. But yet the Byzantine Emperor Manuel II (1391–1425) kept an accredited ambassador resident at the Ottoman Court in about the same period. The Duke's significance in the story of diplomacy, however, lies in the example which he set to other Italian rulers, among them his son, Filippo Maria Visconti, who between 1425 and 1432 became the first ruler to exchange a series of residents with another ruler, his ally the Holy Roman Emperor Sigismund.

19 Coin: Venetian zecchino struck in the name of Doge Francesco Foscari (1423–1457)

British Museum: Department of Coins and Medals: 1963–11–15–2

The Doge is seen kneeling before St Mark. Only the lettering identifies him as Francesco Foscari. The design of the zecchino, otherwise known as the sequin or ducat, remained unaltered from its introduction in 1284 to the fall of the Republic in 1797.

The formality and impersonality of the Venetian coinage reflect the order and constitutionality to which it and the other Italian republics aspired. These very ideals made it difficult for them to experiment with agents that were neither fully official nor completely unofficial, as the semi-official resident agents employed by the Gonzagas and Viscontis were. Conversely, however, once the decision to utilise resident diplomats had finally been taken, the republics felt compelled, as the despots until then never had, to give their residents a clear and undoubtedly official, accredited, status. Thus, while the despots were the first to use resident agents, it was the law-bound republics that made them respectable by giving them a place in accepted diplomatic practice.

Venice was the first Italian republic to make use of a resident agent, doing so in 1435 when, during its war against Filippo Maria Visconti of Milan, Zacharias Bembo was sent to reside in Rome as official Venetian 'Orator' – the accepted renaissance designation for an ambassador. From then onwards there seems always to have been a Venetian envoy in Rome, except in wartime, until 1797. But, official though his status was, Bembo and his immediate successors were still primarily merely agents responsible for the maintenance of an alliance.

20 Medallion showing Pope Paul II (1464–1471) in public consistory, c. 1467

British Museum: Department of Coins and medals: Hill Corpus 775E

The Pope is shown wearing the double tiara and seated on the throne surrounded by cardinals, with spectators and officials at the sides and in the front. The inscription reads 'SACRUM PUBLICUM APOSTOLICUM CONCISTORIUM PAULUS VENETUS PP (*Papa*) II'. By 1467 several of the spectators were certain to have been resident envoys from the Italian states, while many of the cardinals would have been unaccredited 'protectors' of the interests of other European countries in Rome. Neither the occasion for the striking of the original gold medallion, of which this is a contemporary bronze cast, nor its engraver are known for certain, though it might represent a stage in the ex-

18

communication of the King of Bohemia, George Podiebrad, and be the work of Emilio Orfini, the engraver to the Roman mint.

The papacy's contribution to the development of modern diplomacy has been immense. The form and phraseology of the public documents of diplomacy, such as credentials, full powers and ratifications, derive from the practice of the twelfth century papal court. In the mid-fifteenth century Nicholas V (1447–1455), wishing to mediate in the War of the Milanese Succession (1452–4), persuaded all the major participants in the two rival leagues, which covered most of Italy, to send agents to Rome. Thus for the first time official resident envoys were sent to the court of a neutral. By 1454, when peace was concluded, most rulers had come to appreciate the advantages of having a permanent agent in a neutral court to pass on a steady flow of information and to make or thwart alliances speedily and secretly, as required. Accordingly the Peace of Lodi was followed by the spread of resident diplomacy throughout Italy as former enemies exchanged resident envoys. The resident thus ceased to be simply the agent of an alliance.

The largest single group of resident envoys continued to be found in Rome and this had two further repercussions. First it meant that at Rome, under Pius II (1458–1464) the earliest known rules for diplomats as a body of men, a 'corps diplomatique', were drawn up. Previously, when all diplomatic missions had been temporary, there had rarely been more than one set of envoys at a court at any one time, and consequently no need to distinguish between them or to legislate for them as a group. Secondly, non-Italian states had their first experience of resident diplomacy at Rome. From 1460, undoubtedly under the impact of the appearance of Italian resident envoys in Rome, the status of national representatives in the papal court began to alter. John Shirwood, Bishop of Durham, after an initial period after 1477 as English Procurator and officially simply a lawyer in the papal court charged with English affairs, seems to have been appointed 'Orator-Procurator'. This was the title formally contained in the credentials of Giovanni de Giglis, Bishop of Worcester, in 1490. They thus became the earliest resident envoys appointed by an English ruler, though the haughty Christopher Bainbridge, Cardinal Archbishop of York, the first man to be officially termed 'Orator' and not 'Orator-Procurator', was only appointed in 1509.

Surprisingly, the popes themselves only began to make use of formally accredited resident envoys, styled *nuncii*, to distinguish them from the residents sent by secular rulers, in the 1490s. Since then, however, nuncii have enjoyed precedence before the envoys of all other countries in Roman Catholic courts.

20a

20b

21 Letter of Alfonso, Duke of Calabria to Benedetto Dei, Capua, 5th November 1489

Additional MS 24213, f.65

Alfonso, the heir of Ferdinand I of Naples (1458–1494) whom he was to succeed briefly in 1494 as King Alfonso II, acknowledges receipt of recent letters from Dei, who at this time was apparently his semi-official resident in Florence. He excuses himself for not having replied earlier on account of illness and, after stressing how he appreciates the news contained in the letters, he orders Dei to continue keeping him informed of what he hears. The letter is signed by Alfonso and was originally sealed with his personal heraldic seal, traces of which can be seen. The letter is counter-signed and thus authenticated by Alfonso's councillor and secretary, Bernardino de Bernaudo.

Benedetto Dei (1418–1492) was a member of an old-established family. For, unlike many of the first non-Italian residents such as Dr de Puebla (**24**), the first official Italian residents were usually well-born like Ermolao Barbaro (**26**). Dei served the Medici on diplomatic missions in Constantinople and France before becoming official 'Orator' of the Florentine Republic in Milan in the early 1480s. While in Florence he also acted as agent ('mandatario') for the Neapolitan-born *condottiere*, Roberto di San Severino, and, less officially, he undertook commissions of a diplomatic nature on behalf of the rulers of Milan, Ferrara and Bologna. Until the seventeenth century it was quite common for a resident to serve more than one master simultaneously (**24, 64**).

This letter has the typical appearance of fifteenth-century Italian diplomatic instructions (for a fifteenth-century ratification, see **132**). It indicates the increasing part played by royal officials at the head of well-organised chanceries in the execution of foreign policy, while the letter's contents highlight the primary responsibility of the earliest residents: the transmission of a steady flow of reliable information.

22 Philippe de Comines to Lodovico 'il Moro', Duke of Milan, Venice, 9th March 1495

Egerton MS 1963, f.1

This letter was written when resident diplomacy had begun to spread throughout Europe. It is an attempt by Comines, who was on a special mission to Venice on behalf of Charles VIII of France, to dissuade Lodovico from allying against France following the French King's conquest of Naples in February 1495.

Lodovico had written complaining of the King's ingratitude. After exonerating himself and Charles from any blame, Comines gives instances of French gratitude in the past. For example (paragraph 2) Charles had always refused to take action against Aragon in gratitude for the kindness of Alfonso V (I of Naples and Sicily) in not invading Languedoc from Catalonia, when Charles VII was being hard-pressed by the English. Similarly (paragraph 3) Louis XI had always held Lodovico's father 'en aussi grant Reverence com*me* sil eust este son pere' ('in as great reverence, as if he had been his father') (lines 23–4) because of his help with mercenaries and good advice. Yet these favours could not be compared with those Lodovico had rendered and Comines hopes King Charles will not be any less grateful than his predecessors. Indeed 'il aura plus affaire de v*ou*s pour luy aider agarder le Royaume de napples quant il en sera party quil na eu a le conquerir' ('he will have more need for your help in keeping the kingdom of Naples, once he has left it, than he had in conquering it') (lines 28–30). In a postscript Comines adds that he is not sending any news from Venice 'p*our* ce que mess*ieur*s les ambassadeurs que vous y avez vous advertissent de tout' ('because your ambassadors here keep you informed of everything') (lines 34–36).

In 1494 Lodovico, to counter a Florentine-Neapolitan alliance against Milan, had urged the French king to make good his long-standing family claim to Naples. Charles VIII, young and head-strong, had responded with excessive alacrity and in March 1495, alarmed at his consequent success, Lodovico joined Venice, Pope Alexander VI, the Emperor Maximilian, and Ferdinand of Aragon in a counter-league. The French were rapidly expelled from Italy, but the balance of power inside Italy had been irreparably upset. Thenceforward the peninsula became the principal battlefield in a conflict between the Habsburgs and the Valois rulers of France that was to last, with few pauses, until 1559. The Italian states with the exception of the Papacy and Venice became mere pawns in the struggle, one of the earliest casualties being Lodovico himself. Stripped of his duchy by the new French king, Louis XII, in 1499, he died a prisoner in France in 1508.

Philippe de Comines (1445–1509) served Charles the Bold, Duke of Burgundy and after 1472, the French kings Louis XI and Charles VIII as a counsellor and envoy. Although never a resident himself, he had direct experience of them. Between 1463 and 1475 Milan had sent a series of residents to the French court, and from 1470 Venice had maintained rival residents at the Burgundian court and later with the King of France, while before 1490, when all the main Italian courts began sending residents beyond the Alps, Comines had seen them at work in Italy. Like most of his contemporaries he was baffled and worried by them. Pius II, Louis XI, and Henry VII of England had tried to prevent envoys from residing at their courts, while, in 1482, Venice forbade its natives to pass on information to foreign envoys on pain of a fine of 2000 ducats. Comines summed up the fears and confusion that lay behind these measures by describing the resident as 'an honest kind of spy'.

Nevertheless the pressures associated with the Italian wars led even the most conservative rulers to avail themselves of resident envoys who, by 1559, were present in considerable numbers in all the major European courts.

Dux Calabrie ec

Benedicto nro dilecto: In questi di havemo recepute alcune lre vre, Alequale se purria non e stato resposto, ne stata causa, questa nra indispositione: Con la pñte ve adiu samo dela recepta de dicte lre, et ve diremo, che ne so state carissime, p havere inteso li adui, che p qlle ne havete dati: Confortandove, ad volerne aduisare de qllo piu intenderete: che ce ne farete piacere acceptissimo: Dat p in Castello Capuane Neap in Nouembris MCCCCLXXXVIIIJ : Alfonso.

B. bernardus p

23 Queen Isabella's Breviary

Additional MS 18851. ff.436ᵛ–437ʳ

This prayerbook was written and illuminated in Bruges in the 1490s. In 1496 or 1497, the left-hand page was inserted and the right-hand one altered when the book was presented to Queen Isabella of Castile, wife of Ferdinand of Aragon, by its owner, Don Francisco de Rojas, Spain's resident envoy with the Emperor Maximilian I. The dedication can be seen in the panel next to de Rojas's coat of arms in the bottom outer corner of the right-hand page. The occasion was the double betrothal, which de Rojas had helped to negotiate, in December 1495, of Isabella's son and one of her daughters, Juan and Juana, with Maximilian's offspring, Margaret and Philip. The left-hand page contains the royal Spanish coat of arms crowned and supported by an eagle with outstretched wings and underneath, the coat of arms of John, who died in 1497, and the coat of arms, surmounted by the archducal crown of Austria, of Philip. The inscriptions on the scrolls invoke God's protection for Spain and predict the power the offspring of the marriages would wield over the earth. The prediction was fulfilled; the son

of Philip and Johanna, Charles V, Holy Roman Emperor, King of Spain and Duke of Burgundy ruled one of the largest empires known in European history.

The rulers of Aragon had long been involved with Italian politics as Kings of Sicily and, intermittently, of Naples. Ferdinand was the first non-Italian monarch to employ resident diplomats outside Italy. Among them was Don Francisco de Rojas, a gentleman of distinguished family and a veteran of the Granadan wars. In the winter of 1487 and 1488 he had been sent to Brittany, to quote his credentials, 'for as long as Your Grace (the Breton Duke, Francis II) pleases' to help the duchy maintain its independence from France. Withdrawn after the new duchess Anne's marriage to Charles VIII of France in December 1491, he was sent to Maximilian's court following the French invasion of Italy and did not return for several years. He finished his career as resident in Rome, the principal Spanish post in the peninsula.

The change that came over western Europe from the late fifteenth century is well illustrated here. Nominally Christian, the prevailing political ethos

became that of dynastic self-interest. Still theoretically a united Christian republic, western Europe was dissolving into a community of ever more secular and increasingly internally pacified states centred around rulers who, like the Italian despots they frequently resembled, were engaged in an intensifying struggle for dynastic and territorial advantage at the others' expense. Just as in mid-fifteenth-century Italy, as the pace increased, so resident diplomats became more common.

24 Dr Roderigo Gonsalez de Puebla to Ferdinand and Isabella of Spain, London, 11th January 1500

Egerton MS 616, f.25

Dr de Puebla, a lower middle-class lawyer of undistinguished appearance and with a limp, was more representative of the earliest non-Italian residents than the aristocratic de Rojas. The first resident diplomat to appear at the English court, he was sent to London in 1487 and continued to reside there, except for a three-year interval after 1492, for over twenty years. Throughout this period he strove with untiring energy and a modicum of show to strengthen the Anglo-Spanish alliance against France. The marriages of Catherine of Aragon, another of Ferdinand and Isabella's daughters, with Arthur, Prince of Wales and, after his death, with Henry VIII, were largely the fruit of his labours. Formally created Resident Ambassador, a new grade, in 1495 and for a period also the Emperor Maximilian's representative in England, he was consistently neglected and deceived, frequently derided, and almost permanently left without pay by his master. Ferdinand was also wont to send higher-born ambassadors to negotiate with and spy on him, and in 1508 the latest of them secured his dismissal. He died in London ten months later.

This letter was written following the marriage by proxy of Arthur and Catherine and the conclusion of an Anglo-Spanish treaty in 1499. The Yorkist pretender, Perkin Warbeck, and Richard, Earl of Warwick, the senior Yorkist claimant to the English throne, had recently been executed and de Puebla writes that England had never before been so peaceful and obedient. For the undoubted blood royal flowed only through the veins of the English King and Queen, and above all, of the Prince of Wales. He reports that, after much haggling over the size of the dowry, James IV of Scotland had agreed to wait four or five years before marrying Arthur's sister, Princess Margaret, who would then be of marriageable age. So, de Puebla considers 'la cosa es fecha' ('the thing is done') (line 23). He asks for the ratification of the Anglo-Spanish treaty to be sent to him as speedily as possible because King Henry had

24a

24b

assured him things would be very different for Spain at his court once the ratification and Catherine had arrived. Indeed he needs to know the Princess's time and place of departure from Spain, since elaborate preparations were being made for her reception in England. Finally he says he does not want to accept the bishopric or noble marriage offered him by Henry VII because it seems improper for a true servant of the Spanish rulers to do so. He would, however, like to be paid his salary . . .

The letter is in de Puebla's hand. He uses a code substituting numbers for names but leaving the context in plain writing (eg: DCCCCXXI (line 23) = King of Scotland), which is so simple as to be useless. His cipher could be more sophisticated, but also more cumbersome. De Puebla's refusal to accept preferment at the hands of a foreign ruler reflects the quality of the envoys selected by Ferdinand and of the Spanish chancery that came to be staffed by them. It was far in advance of their non-Italian contemporaries. The marriage of James IV and Margaret took place in 1503, their great-grandson being James VI of Scotland and I of England. De Puebla's appeal for pay has been echoed by ambassadors down the centuries.

25 Private letter of Thomas Spinelly to Cardinal Wolsey, Saragossa, 29th November 1518

Cotton MS Vespasian c.i., ff.224ᵛ–225ʳ

Thomas Spinelly, a Florentine of humble birth, was one of the first English residents to be employed outside Italy. In 1508 Henry VII appointed him his semi-official agent in the Netherlands and shortly afterwards Henry VIII gave him formal credentials. He continued serving in the Low Countries until 1516 and then worked there and intermittently in Spain where he died in 1522. In his last years, frequently overshadowed by more aristocratic special ambassadors, he also came to be Cardinal Wolsey's special agent. Although writing regularly to the King, he left his most important information for the Cardinal. In this he anticipated the practice of later envoys who corresponded primarily with their ruler's most trusted minister, who was often his secretary.

Here Spinelly informs Wolsey, in cipher, of the Pope's private approval of the recently concluded Anglo-French Treaty of London. He had not mentioned this in his letter to the King and he begs Wolsey to keep it secret 'or ellis som frende of myne

25a

25b

mygt . . . henstorthe absteyn hymself to declare me anything'. A Spanish minister has also promised to provide Wolsey's Spanish pension for half-a-year, saying that Wolsey 'hathe deserved moche more' from King Charles of Spain. The transcription at the side was made by an English clerk in London.

Finally Spinelly turns to his own affairs. The English ambassadors had told him of their forthcoming departure 'and that I shall remayne here'. But, while assuring Wolsey 'that towarde my *master's* causes I shalbe trwe and dyligent, in your grac*es* particulers affeyres . . . a fatyphull and bownding servant', he beseeches 'my allways good Lord . . . that my dyete be augment(ed) to xx shalyns a day and my monney avansed ever(y) half yere for otherwise I may not lyve here and am compelted to borow to my great displeasor.' Moreover, the cost of entertaining members of the Spanish court 'to disner and soupper . . . putte me to extraordinary charge'. He also begs Wolsey 'that by your meanis I may have some park or domycyle about London of the king*es* gyft to the intente that whan I shall cume in england that I may have a lytel hol for to lyve in the resydu of the tyme that shall please god to kepe me in this world'.

It should be added that by 1518 Spanish officials could probably read the secret part of Spinelly's letters without difficulty, since he had been using the same cipher for ten years and was never to change it. The 'lytel holes' near London coveted by Spinelly and his more successful contemporaries tended to expand in reality into large stately homes such as Penshurst Place or Knole.

26 Portrait of Ermolao Barbaro (1453–1493) with an extract from his 'De Officio Legati'. Published in V. Branca *Nuova Collezione di Testi Umanistici Inediti o Rari* **vol. xiv (Florence, 1969)**
Department of Printed Books

Ermolao Barbaro was the first person to write a tract devoted solely to resident envoys, a class of diplomat that had been unknown to du Rosier. But, being a student of antiquity, Barbaro felt compelled to call them by the classical Latin name for ambassador, 'legatus', literally 'one delegated'. A Venetian patrician, better known as a leading humanist, he had diplomatic experience himself. After being sent on a special mission to the Emperor Frederick III he became Venetian resident in Milan and later Rome, where his short tract 'on the office of ambassador' ('De Officio Legati') was written in 1490.

The tract takes the form of a letter to a friend entering the Venetian diplomatic service. Much of the advice it contains is similar to that given by du Rosier, whom he had not read. He argues that the resident should be diligent, virtuous, tactful but firm and honest, and he condemns fraud, bribery, assassination and spying, on moral grounds and on practical grounds, as counter-productive, for it destroys the envoy's reputation with those whom he should seek to influence. However Barbaro's spirit is as secular as du Rosier's is Christian. Du Rosier's stress on the ambassador's duty being to serve the public good of Christendom is replaced by Barbaro's insistence that his 'first duty, exactly like that of any other servant of a government . . . is to do, say, advise and think whatever may best serve the preservation and aggrandisement of his own state' ('Finis legato idem est qui et caeteris ad Rempublicam accedentibus; ut ea faciant, dicant, consultant et cogitent quae ad optimum suae civitatis statum et retinendum et amplificandum pertinere posse iudicent', section 7). A few years later Macchiavelli wrote his study, *The Prince*.

Barbaro expressed the credo of the modern diplomat, but for the next century and a half most theorists continued to write of the ambassador in the terms used by du Rosier.

The portrait of Barbaro, holding a papal robe forms part of Vittore Carpaccio's painting, 'The Meeting of St Ursula with St Syricius', in the Accademia in Venice. It contains portraits of many prominent Venetians of the late fifteenth century in the guise of participants.

4. THE DEVELOPMENT OF MODERN DIPLOMATIC IMMUNITY, 1500–1720

By the early sixteenth century, medieval theories of ambassadorial immunity (12) were usually being ignored since they were unable to give resident diplomats effective protection in the execution of their duties (27). As the social class of resident ambassadors rose and their representational function became more important they demanded greater privileges and in particular the right to worship God after their master's manner (28). This was often unpalatable to the rulers of post-Reformation Europe who were becoming increasingly insistent on the observance of their creed by everyone within their dominions (28, 29). The refusal to accept embassy chapels, and the increasing support lent by monarchs and their envoys to rebels in other states (30, 31), precipitated the virtual severance of links between northern and southern Europe in the late sixteenth century. The rôle of the envoy became distorted and the development of diplomacy and diplomatic privilege was halted. A few years later all rulers had to accept the right of envoys to their own chapels as the price for the renewal of diplomatic relations which each had his own reason for desiring (32). Despite occasional storms (33), the privileges of ambassadors and their suites steadily increased in the seventeenth century and in some capitals even took the grotesque form of the *franchise de quartier* (34). In Great Britain the rights of diplomats were regulated by statute, but this was exceptional, the rulers of most countries adopting a more autocratic and informal approach (35). At the turn of the sixteenth and seventeenth centuries, Ayrault and Grotius developed the new theory of extra-territoriality to provide a conceptual framework for the immunities that had already evolved in practice (36, 37).

Most of today's diplomatic privileges were in existence by 1720.

27 Letter of Don Guerau Despés, Spanish Ambassador to England, to the Privy Council, London, 16th January 1569
Cotton MS Galba c. iii, f.156

The medieval theory of ambassadorial immunity did not extend to any unethical acts committed by him during his mission (12). Until about 1450 this created few problems, missions generally being very short and residents having little occasion to displease their hosts since they were usually agents of an alliance. Moreover, if they did commit a crime, they could be tried anywhere since Christendom shared the same ethical standards. By the sixteenth century, however, medieval theory if strictly interpreted could prevent a resident from properly executing his duty, as in this instance.

In January 1569, Queen Elizabeth I's Principal Secretary of State, William Cecil, later Lord Burghley, had Despés placed under house arrest, partly in retaliation for Spain's seizure of English goods, and certain individuals, in the Netherlands, and partly as a warning to the ambassador not to intrigue with Catholic malcontents, as he was known to be doing. The reason officially alleged, however, was the 'very slanderous' language of two of Despés's letters which, by trickery, had come into Cecil's hands. In them Despés had accused Cecil of insincerity and malevolence towards Spain and described Elizabeth's rule as unpopular with the nobility and people of England. The Privy Council judged this proved that, far from working for amity between England and Spain as an ambassador should, he was maliciously sowing dissension between the two. Accordingly, while professing their desire to increase the amity between Philip and Elizabeth, the Privy Council informed Despés on 14th January that he was unworthy to hold the office of ambassador, banished him from court, and placed him under house arrest.

Here Despés indignantly chides the Council for replying to letters that were not addressed to it, and denies the charges levied against him. Since the Council's knowledge of Spanish was clearly defective, he offers to send it native Spanish speakers, to translate the letters correctly and prove the zeal with which he had always tried to conserve peace and friendship between Spain and England, 'while serving the King as I ought'. His differences with Cecil, he concludes, are personal and of a kind that arise in the course of negotiations and do not imply that Cecil is not a very good servant of his mistress and even, perhaps, not Despés's enemy.

The ambassador's arrest was undoubtedly justified from the standpoint of medieval theory. The ambassador's duty of loyalty to his master, which Despés expresses as a qualification, tended in

Vra carta de xuij del corriente tengo recibida y me marauillo mucho que tales
personas ayan asi respondido a cartas mias, y que no y ban para ellos, sin en-
tenderlas bien primero / quen Español quando se han de significar los señores
se dizen grandes absolutamente y grandes y pequeños, o de otra manera /
cho significa otra cosa differente mucho de aquel sentido / y por esta me-
ma falta de no entender los terminos de la lengua / no saueys enten-
de la carta mia familiar para Gerº de Curiel / la qual dize todo
contrario de lo que en Vra carta señalais / como si fueredes contentos
ay facultad para ello os lo hare entender por personas a las qua
sera natural la lengua Española / y asi tambien la claridad y verd
de mis progressos y el Zelo que he temido y tengo de conseruar en
paz y amistad los estados del rey mi sºr y estos / guardando el re-
to que deuo a su seruicio / A las otras partes de Vra carta como
nascidas deste fundamento no ay mas que responder / y si qua
estuuieredes Informados / todauia os pareciere que aueys deshaz
comigo / corresponder en aquello como deuiere de hazer. Dexa
aparte las controuersias quel secrº Cecil parece pretender comi
no participan en parte alguna con los señores desta tierra, ques
como cosas que acontecen entre personas que tratan negocios, ella
Zen su curso y no por esso puede dexar de Ser el muy buen seruido
de su Señora y hombre honrrado y por Ventura no mi enemigo
Londres a 16 de Henero 1569

Don gueran despes

27

practice however to relegate medieval diplomatic
theory to the sidelines. For a resident envoy could
not satisfy his master unless the ruler to whom he
was accredited accepted that the envoy worked on
his master's behalf and should be allowed to operate
freely, even though his instructions might be vil-
lainous and seditious and his reports untrue.

Since such freedom from interference was of
mutual advantage to rulers and contained no
ideological or spiritual undertones, an ambassador's
immunity from prosecution for treason and political
offences was informally conceded, on a reciprocal
basis, at a very early date. Normally the worst that
could happen was that an envoy was declared
unacceptable ('persona non grata') at court and his
master was requested to recall him. It being rare for
an ambassador to indulge in robbery or murder, his
immunity from criminal prosecution caused little
trouble. Medieval theory was rarely invoked after
1500 and then only *in extremis*, half-heartedly and
with some embarrassment, to justify a course of
action that had been decided, as here, on quite

different grounds. This letter was singed, with many
other manuscripts in the Cotton Collection, during a
great fire at Ashburnham House, Westminster (now
part of Westminster School) in 1731.

28 Letter of Dr John Man, Dean of Gloucester, English Ambassador in Spain, to Philip II, June 1567 (*draft*)

Cotton MS. Vespasian c.vii, f.299

By the mid-sixteenth century, resident ambassadors
were generally of a higher social class than their
earliest predecessors. From being their masters'
messengers, 'honourable spies', and negotiators,
they came to regard themselves and to be regarded
as representing their masters' dignity. Since the
Reformation a vital element of sovereignty had been
the rulers' prerogative of worshipping God in their
own way. When this right was demanded by
ambassadors, the princes to whom they were
accredited, if of a different creed, were invariably
placed in an embarrassing position. Refusal might
involve the alienation of a potential ally. Acceptance, however, could open the door to serious evils.
The religious prince feared eternal damnation
if he tolerated heresy in his dominions. The
more secular-minded monarch feared a large-scale
threat to hard-won internal order. For in almost all
states, creeds other than the monarch's own were
proscribed by law. Embassy chapels thus became
flagrant examples of successful law-breaking in the
very heart of the kingdom, not only by the ambassador, but also by his staff which might include
natives of the host country. The chapels also acted
as magnets for disaffected elements in the state, and
it soon proved impossible to bar these permanently
from attending services in the chapel without
infringing the ambassador's rights. At the height of
the Protestant–Catholic confrontation in sixteenth-
century Europe, some rulers such as Philip II felt the
embassy chapel was too high a price to pay even for
the maintenance of diplomatic relations with
'heretical' rulers.

Dr John Man arrived in Spain as English
Ambassador early in 1567. By the time this letter
was written a few months later, he had already been
banished from court because of his rude comments
about the Pope, and his servants compelled by the
Inquisition to attend Mass. Here he requests
permission to keep an Anglican priest and to hold
Anglican services in his house, reminding Philip
that the Spanish Ambassador in England had long
been allowed by the English Queen to employ a
Catholic priest and celebrate Mass in his house
in London. He also asks that no member of his
household be forced to celebrate Mass.

To modern ears, this may sound eminently reasonable. Philip II however refused to accede to the requests and shortly afterwards he imprisoned the ambassador who had defiantly continued to hold Anglican services in his house. Within the year Dr Man had been recalled to London. There was not to be another English ambassador in Spain until after the death of both Philip and Elizabeth more than thirty years later, though a Spanish envoy continued to reside in London until 1583.

28

29 Letter of Edwin Sandys, Bishop of London, to Robert Dudley, Earl of Leicester, Fulham, 4th March 1572/3
Additional MS 32091, f.266

Hostility to embassy chapels was not confined to Spain and its ruler. The Portuguese Ambassador in England had to withstand repeated attempts by the local authorities to force the closure of his chapel. One of the fiercest occurred in early 1573 when, having failed to prevent known English Catholics from entering the Catholic chapel in his house, the London magistrates issued warrants for the arrest of the Ambassador and his priest. The Ambassador, Giraldi, was compelled to go to Court to ask for their

release. While he was en route, in Fulham Palace the Bishop of London, who was notorious for his extreme Protestantism, 'scribled in hast' this diatribe against Giraldi and his chapel, and addressed it to Leicester. In it Sandys repeats most of the main arguments against resident envoys and their chapels and, after a fleeting reference to Dr Man 'who could fynde nether suche favor neither such tolleration in spayne', he calls for Giraldi's punishment or at least expulsion:

'Geralde the portingale . . . hath bene evil suffered. Goddes cause is not negligently to be handled but zealously to be maintained . . . Happely he alledgith that he is an Ambassador . . . is he therfor priveledged to Committ treason agaynst hir Matie? . . . No christian prince ought to suffer him within his dominion to Committ such treason against the Matie of the Almightie god the king of all kinges . . . for wittingly to tollerate that were to procure goddes . . . spedy vengiance . . . This idolatrouse proude portingale hath dayly sondays and holydays had Masse in his house this Twelvemonth . . . whereunto hath resorted from tym to tym 20 at the least of hir

29

Maties subiectes . . . in the dispite of god, her Matie and . . . to ye great offence of goddes good people . . . This open fact openly knowne and not openly punished wold give a dangerouse example . . . it were convenient . . . to send home both franceys Geralde and Anthony Guarres who lurke here . . . as spies to practise mischiefe and to intise hir Maties subiectes to Idolaterie.'

Despite Sandys' eloquence, Elizabeth speedily complied with Giraldi's request. For Portugal was an old ally (130) whose friendship was particularly important in the 1570s in face of the growing threat from Spain. The chapel continued to exist until Philip II inherited the Portuguese crown in 1580.

30 Philip II to the Constable de Montmorency, Madrid, 13th June 1561
Harley MS 7016, f.15

In the second half of the sixteenth century, the rôles of Catholic ambassadors at Protestant courts and of Protestant ambassadors at Catholic courts radically altered. Under the impact of growing religious partisanship on both sides, they became agents of war and discord as leaders of conspiracies against the rulers to whom they were accredited, and disseminators of false information. Suspect from the moment of their arrival and frequently banned from court and contact with ministers, as Man and Despés had been, the ambassadors, if they were to have anything to report, were forced to get involved with and to rely on information, grotesquely distorted though it often was, from discontented elements, such as Catholic nobles in England. The ambassadors' masters were largely responsible for this state of affairs for they increasingly found themselves playing the rôle of religious zealots and ordered their representatives to do likewise.

This letter illustrates the point. It was written at the start of the French Wars of Religion and is addressed to a leader of the French Catholics, the Constable de Montmorency, who was then in alliance with the French Queen-Regent, Catherine de' Medici. Philip writes of his satisfaction at hearing from his ambassador of Montmorency's great desire and determination to support the royal authority and (Catholic) religion in France. Philip has learned further particulars about the state of (the Catholic) religion there and the need for a 'speedy remedy' ('breve remedio', line 9). Because of his duty as a Christian prince and his love for the French King, he wishes to help as much as he can 'with the same will as if my own kingdoms were concerned' ('con la misma voluntad que si a mis reynos proprios tocasse', lines 12–13). Accordingly he has ordered his ambassador to inform the Constable of his

30

thoughts as to how matters should proceed. Montmorency should believe what the ambassador says and if he does his duty to God, Christendom and his Prince, he will place Philip under a great obligation. Philip signs the letter, in the traditional Spanish manner, 'Yo El Rey' ('I, the King'), and it is countersigned by his efficient and increasingly influential secretary of state, Gonsalvo Perez.

The letter is replete with standard expressions of esteem for the French King, but its most striking feature is the emphasis Philip places on his Christian ardour and his readiness to intervene for religion's sake in French domestic affairs. By 1589 his ambassador Bernardino de Mendoza was playing a large part at the barricades in holding Paris for the Catholic League against the legitimate but Protestant French King, Henry IV. A few years earlier Mendoza had been expelled from England because of his involvement, at Philip's orders, in the Throckmorton conspiracy for a Spanish invasion of England and the replacement of Elizabeth I with Mary Queen of Scots as English Queen. Mendoza's conduct was, by then, not untypical of ambassadors, and he was esteemed by Philip II. However, such open dabbling with treason by a succession of ambassadors eventually became intolerable to the host rulers, and destructive of diplomacy. For most of the 1590s diplomatic contact between Catholic and Protestant states in Europe was virtually non-existent and most resident envoys reverted to their original rôle as mere agents of an alliance.

31a   31b

31 Medallion commemorating Elizabeth I's support for Protestant rebels in the Netherlands, 1587

British Museum: Department of Coins and Medals: George III Fl. + D. 42

On the obverse the Earl of Leicester, who had been created Governor and Captain-General of the United Provinces in the previous year, is seen interceding with the Queen on behalf of the provinces of Guelderland, Holland, Zeeland, Utrecht and Friesland. The inscription reads DEO. OPT. MAX. LAVS. ET. HONOR. IN. Œ. ÆVVM. QVOD. 1587 ('To the best and greatest God be praise and honour for ever, because. 1587'). On the reverse the Pope, bishops and other ecclesiastics, with chalices, wafers and other sacramental items, are seen falling from heaven, where appears the name of Jehovah in Hebrew. The legend reads QVEM. DEVS. CONFICIET. SPIRITV. ORIS. SVI (Literally 'whom the Lord shall consume with the spirit of his mouth'). The medallion was struck in the Netherlands.

It serves as a reminder that Protestant rulers too played their part in dividing Europe along religious lines in the later sixteenth century, through their aid to Protestant rebels in countries with Catholic sovereigns. Elizabeth I was more discreet than Philip II, but her ambassador in France, Nicholas Throckmorton (120), was imprisoned by Catherine de' Medici in 1563 on a trumped-up charge, because of his support for the French Protestants.

32 Rowlandson and Pugin: The Sardinian envoy's Chapel, Lincoln's Inn Fields, London. From R. Ackermann, *Microcosm of London*, 1808, plate 16 (see plate no. I)

Department of Printed Books

Designed in the 1760s by Jean-Baptiste Jaque, the secretary of Count Vizzi, then Sardinian envoy to the British Court, this chapel was erected at the King of Sardinia's expense. No longer part of the envoy's house, the chapel seems from the first to have been staffed by English priests and to have been open to the public, though English Governments had repeatedly condemned such practices. At one time the organist was Thomas Arne, the composer. The chapel was badly damaged in 1780 by anti-Catholic rioters instigated by Lord George Gordon. After 1797 it became independent of Sardinian support,

though it remained under Sardinian patronage until 1858. It was demolished in 1904–1905, but embassy churches and chapels are still to be found in capital cities throughout the world.

Following the deaths of Philip II and Elizabeth I, the Catholic and Protestant countries of Europe found it in their interest once again to resume diplomatic relations by exchanging resident envoys. A precondition for renewed relations was the recognition by all sides of each envoy's right to practise his religion after his master's manner. This was the most important step in the evolution of the practice of modern ambassadorial immunity, since nothing an ambassador could at that time have demanded could have been more injurious to a ruler's sovereign jurisdiction. Once accepted, the other privileges followed without excessive difficulty. In the course of the seventeenth and early eighteenth centuries, the remaining problems of ambassadorial immunity, mainly in the field of civil law, such as freedom from prosecution for debt and immunity from excise and other duties, were settled on a pragmatic basis. The result varied slightly from court to court, depending on reciprocity, the power wielded by the envoy's master, and the envoy's own ingenuity and strength of character.

The reappearance of embassy chapels on a permanent basis resurrected other more thorny problems, however, particularly that of the immunity to be enjoyed by the ambassador's chaplain and hence the rest of his staff – including 'natives' such as Arne. Unlike the ambassador's personal immunity this affected large sections of the native population as victims, or creditors of the ambassador's staff and was – and is – much resented by them. To this day the full extent of this immunity has not been agreed upon.

Another associated problem was the immunity of the ambassador's residence, which was disregarded whenever guards acting on behalf of the court to which the ambassador was accredited invaded his chapel to seize natives who were worshipping there. Such invasions frequently occurred in England before 1660, and caused consternation to the ambassador and his master. Failure to take this action, however, infuriated the native law-abiding population (29). Accordingly ambassadors and host governments were forced to negotiate over the issue and by 1700 the broad lines of agreement had been reached throughout Europe – mainly to the ambassador's advantage. Nevertheless the precise extent and nature of the immunity of diplomatic buildings remains in dispute to this day.

33 Medallion commemorating the destruction of the Portuguese Embassy Chapel, December 1688

British Museum: Department of Coins and Medals: 1837–10–30–72

33a

People are seen rejoicing around a bonfire in Lincoln's Inn Fields, and throwing emblems of Popery, looted from embassy chapels, into the fire. In the background the west side of the Fields is shown with the Portuguese chapel in Duke Street in ruins. The legend reads NEC. LEX. EST. IUSTIOR. ULLA ('Nor is any law more just').

Although the privileges of ambassadors and their suites continued to be subject to inter-governmental negotiation after 1604, it was only occasionally after 1660 that popular animosity to diplomatic immunity and Catholicism flared up with its old vigour. In December 1688 after the Catholic James II's precipitate flight to France in the wake of the invasion of England by William (III) Prince of Orange, the chapels of Catholic envoys throughout London were destroyed by the mob. In 1745, when Bonnie Prince Charlie was advancing into England, and again in 1780 during the anti-Catholic Gordon Riots, there were similar scenes. The stern measures against diplomats and Catholics which tended to follow these events were, however, soon ignored by all concerned.

33b

34 'Immunity' plaque on a parish church in Assisi, Italy

Photograph by the author

34

The translation runs 'Immunity and right of patronage of the King of the Spains'. Close by is the coat of arms of the Bourbon Kings of Spain. Since the Middle Ages Europeans had been familiar with the concept of sanctuary for law-breakers, usually in a church or on church land. At an early date this became associated with the jurisdiction in that area, of a third party, be it the Papacy or, as here, the King of Spain, exercising rights independently of the local authorities. These ideas were to have an important influence on the development of diplomatic privileges.

By the seventeenth century the most prestigious diplomatic posts were often filled by prominent aristocrats, accustomed to wielding power. An inflated sense of the ambassador's importance led them to make false deductions from familiar concepts such as sanctuary, independent or 'exempt' jurisdictions, the ambassador's immunity (12), and the independence of consuls from local law and their exercise of a certain limited authority over their fellow nationals abroad (13), in order to procure a grotesque extension of ambassadorial rights. From demanding immunity from civil and criminal law for themselves, their suites and their houses they came to demand immunity for the whole neighbourhood of their residences. Certain governments, particularly those of Spain and the Papal States, were too weak to resist. As a result large areas of Rome and Madrid became islands of lawlessness and anarchy where the native authorities dared not intervene for fear of provoking diplomatic incidents, but where the ambassadors were neither able nor in strict point of law entitled to exert any control. By the middle of the century these 'franchises du quartier' were widely recognised as scandals and in the 1680s and 1690s they finally disappeared as the powers involved were persuaded – not without difficulty – to renounce their self-claimed rights.

Since then the extent of diplomatic rights and immunities has largely remained unaltered, though where the central authority is weak, as in late nineteenth-century China, features akin to the 'franchise du quartier', such as the 'concessions', have tended to reappear.

35 *Act for Preserving the Privileges of Ambassadors,* 7 Anne Cap. 12, 1708–9
Department of Printed Books

In July 1708, while riding through the streets of London in his coach, shortly before he was to depart for Russia, Peter the Great's ambassador in Great Britain, Andrei Matveev, was arrested for debt and imprisoned. Similar and worse misfortunes had befallen envoys in London and elsewhere before, without any long-term repercussions. In this instance, however, the British Government could not avail itself of its usual expedient of apologising to and ordering the release of the Ambassador. It had to do all it could to assuage the enraged Tsar who, it was feared, might otherwise be provoked into joining France in its war against Britain and its allies. Peter proved to be extremely demanding. Matveev was released and fully compensated, a special mission was sent to Moscow to apologise formally for the affront the Tsar had received in the person of his Ambassador (144) – and this short law was forced through Parliament, receiving the royal assent in 1709.

The Act provides immunity from arrest, imprison-ment, and confiscation of goods for criminal and civil offences not only to all 'Ambassadors and other Publick Ministers of Foreign Princes and States' who had been 'authorised and received as such by Her Majesty', but also to their domestic servants, excepting only bankrupt merchants and traders who had put themselves under the ambassador's wing as protection against their creditors. So long as one of the British Secretaries of State was first given the name of any servant who had been a victim, those convicted under the act were to be punished as 'Violaters of the Laws of Nations and Disturbers of the Publick Repose'.

Britain, the Dutch Republic (1679), and Denmark (1708), were for long, and still may be, the only countries with laws relating to diplomatic immunity.

Most Governments have avoided the humiliation of enshrining immunity for law-breakers in their statute books by dealing with cases individually by decree on the basis of precedent following private application by the ambassador. But this particular law, which grants far wider diplomatic immunities than many governments would find acceptable even now, has remained the basis for diplomatic privilege in Britain to this day.

36 P. Ayrault, *L'Ordre, Formalité et Instruction Judiciaire,* enlarged and revised edition, Paris, 1588
Department of Printed Books c.82, d.8

The modern practice of diplomatic immunity evolved pragmatically and quite independently of medieval theory, which it often contradicted, and renaissance and post-reformation attempts to discover theories that squared with changed practices. It took many decades before a new theory became generally accepted as providing a satisfactory basis for modern practice. This was the theory of extra-territoriality.

It was first formulated by Pierre Ayrault, a French lawyer, in the second, revised, edition of his work *L'Ordre, Formalité et Instruction Judiciaire dont les anciens Grecs et Romains ont usé ès accusations publiques conferé au stil et usage de nostre France* ('the legal order, forms and instruction employed by the ancient Greeks and Romans in their public accusations, adapted to the style and usage of our France') first published in 1576. The appearance of the revised edition coincided with a renewed interest in diplomacy, no doubt a reaction to the religious wars then ravaging France and the Netherlands, which found expression in several new works on the ambassador and his duties.

Annæ Reginæ.

An Act for Preserving the Privileges of Ambaſſadors, and other Publick Miniſters of Foreign Princes and States.

 hereas ſeveral turbulent and diſorderly Perſons having in a moſt outragious Manner Inſulted the Perſon of his Excellency Andrew Artemonowitz Mattueof, Ambaſſador Extraordinary of his Czariſh Majeſty, Emperor of Great Ruſſia, her Majeſties good Friend and Ally, by Arreſting him, and Taking him by Violence out of his Coach in the publick Street, and Detaining him in Cuſtody for ſeveral hours, in Contempt of the Protection Granted by her Majeſty, contrary to the Law of Nations, and in Prejudice of the Rights and Privileges which Ambaſſadors and other Publick Miniſters, Authorized and Received as ſuch, have at all times been thereby Poſſeſſed of, and ought to be kept Sacred and Inviolable; Be it therefore Declared by the Queens moſt Excellent Majeſty, by and with the Advice and Conſent of the Lords Spiritual and Temporal, and Commons in Parliament Aſſembled, and by the Authority of the ſame, That all Actions and Suits, Writs and Proceſſes Commenced, Sued or Proſecuted againſt the ſaid Ambaſſador by any Perſon or Perſons whatſoever, and all Bail-Bonds given by the ſaid Ambaſſador, or any other Perſon or Perſons on his behalf, and all Recognizances of Bail given or acknowledged in any ſuch Action or Suit, and all Proceedings upon, or by Pretext or Colour of any ſuch Action or Suit, Writ or Proceſs, and all Judgments had thereupon, are utterly Null and Void, and ſhall be Deemed and Adjudged to be utterly Null and Void, to all Intents, Conſtructions and Purpoſes whatſoever.

And be it Enacted by the Authority aforeſaid, That all Entries, Proceedings and Records againſt the ſaid Ambaſſador, or his Bail, ſhall be Vacated and Cancelled.

5   Mm m 2   And

Only a few pages of Ayrault's work were devoted to the ambassador, and then only to his legal position and that of other foreigners in France. But significantly these were among the sections he radically revised in the 1588 edition. Here he argues, along traditional lines, that the person of the ambassador is sacred and cannot be violated. However he adds that the ambassador represents and is solely responsible to his prince, whose orders he executes – often as an 'honest' spy. One can take precautions to see he does no harm but, Ayrault deduces, if he commits a crime, even while he is on enemy soil, 'il y sera tenu pour absent & pour present en son pays' ('he will be considered as absent from there and as present in his own territory') (Book 1 section 4, folio 53 lines 25–6), and should therefore not be punished by anyone but his master.

Initially, the theory does not seem to have been much heeded. Only when espoused, on different grounds, by Hugo Grotius, did it become widely accepted.

This book has the feathers and motto of the Prince of Wales stamped on both covers, with the Tudor rose and royal crown alternating along the spine and may once have belonged to James I's eldest son, Henry Prince of Wales, who died in 1612, or his brother, later Charles I.

37 *The Illustrious Hugo Grotius of the Law of Warre and Peace with Annotations III Parts and Memorials of the Author's Life and Death* **(translated by Clement Barksdale), London, 1654. From the library of George III**
Department of Printed Books. E.1445

Hugo Grotius or Huig van Groot (1583–1645), a Dutch lawyer, diplomat, and philosopher, is generally regarded as the father of modern diplomatic theory. His most important contribution in this field was *De Jure Belli ac Pacis*, a three-volume work which appeared in 1625 when he was living in exile in Paris. This is the earliest English translation and has a portrait of the author as its frontispiece.

Most of Grotius's tenets were not new. However, unlike most previous theorists he accepted the existence of a world of equal sovereign states amenable mainly to considerations of their own self-interest and yet still argued for the continuing validity of the old maxims. His arguments, in contrast to his predecessors', were based not on Christian theology and custom alone but primarily on the exercise of reason, so framed as to appeal to rulers of sovereign states regardless of their religion. They were soon accepted in Europe, and remain so throughout the world.

Broadly Grotius argued that it was necessary and advantageous for sovereign states to abide by certain rationally founded ethical concepts or 'natural laws' in their conduct of international relations for the sake of their own long-term survival. One of these concepts was the 'extra-territoriality' of ambassadors which he based on custom as well as pure reason. In the sixty-seventh chapter of his second book, he argues that the security of ambassadors as a class is more useful and advantageous to mankind than their punishment as individuals for any crimes they commit – for ambassadors are the principal means by which governments remain in contact and therefore at peace with one another, and so merit their traditionally privileged position. At the same time, since they carry out their masters' orders, punishing them for their actions is not likely to prevent greater bloodshed and might even needlessly provoke a war. Moreover, in the words of this translation, 'The safety of embassadors is in a slippery place if they ought to render a reason of their actions to any other but him by whom they are sent'. They need protection from trumped-up charges aimed at preventing them from doing their duty. Therefore rulers should ignore their less important offences. But 'if the crime be cruel and publicly mischievous, the Embassador must be sent to his Master with a request that he would punish him or give him up' – for serious crimes must be punished. Thus, concludes Grotius, just as ambassadors 'are accounted by a certain fiction as the persons of their masters', so by a similar fiction, during their missions they should be considered as 'extra territorium' or 'outside the country' (where they are then residing). There are only three conditions: the ambassador must be accepted as such by the ruler to whom he is accredited, he may be detained for questioning if a national catastrophe can be avoided in no other way (but he must be released unharmed) and he may be killed in self-defence. Grotius also emphasises that the ambassador's suite and his residence are only immune in so far as this enables the ambassador to carry out his duties freely. Thus Grotius finally reconciled national sovereignty and diplomatic immunity.

RUIT HORA

Hugo   Grotius

God & Church
Warr & Peace
State & Church

See you not Learning in his Lookes?
See it more Lively in his Bookes.

Tho. Cross Sculpsit

THE ILLUSTRIOUS
HUGO GROTIUS
OF THE LAW
OF
WARRE
AND
PEACE
WITH
ANNOTATIONS.
III. PARTS.
AND
Memorials of the Author's
Life and Death.

Ὁ ἀδικῶν ἀσεβεῖ M. Antonin. Imp. l. 9.

LONDON,
Printed by *T. Warren*, for *William Lee*, And are to be
sold at his shop, at the signe of the *Turks-head*
in *Fleet-street*, M. DC. LIV.

37

5. THE CONGRESS

Congresses, arguably the most distinctive feature in the development of diplomacy in the later seventeenth and early eighteenth centuries, date back at least to the Olympic Games of Ancient Greece. They continue to be held, though taking the form of the 'United Nations', or called 'conferences'. The immediate precedent for modern congresses was the medieval church council which, although primarily concerned with the government of the church, was international in character and frequently discussed European political problems such as those connected with the Hussites. Under the impetus of rationalist pleas for the peaceful settlement of international disputes made by Grotius, Pufendorf (38) and their successors, and a general revulsion at the wars that had ravaged western Europe almost without cease for a century, congresses were frequently held after 1640.

Initially, and usually primarily concerned with the detailed settlement of European problems on a multilateral basis, and held towards or after the close of major wars, as were the congresses of Utrecht (39), Vienna (41) or Paris (44), they gradually became wider in their scope. Some have come to be devoted to the airing and peaceful resolution of international problems in the hope of avoiding war (42). This tradition is represented today by the United Nations and by many special conferences devoted to the settlement of acute and menacing international military and political disputes. Since the early nineteenth century, when a distinction began to be drawn between congresses (attended by ministers for foreign affairs) and conferences (attended by ambassadors) an increasing number of international gatherings have been devoted to the intergovernmental solution of international social, humanitarian and administrative problems, such as the treatment of prisoners of war (1899) or postal communications (1874). Since the seventeenth century the mechanism of negotiation has continually gained in sophistication (40).

Congresses have been of benefit to international relations and the development of diplomacy in several ways. If they assemble and negotiations commence in wartime, they imply the formal recognition by each of the other parties' right to exist. Even if the congresses then fail, this can help to moderate mutual suspicions and the ferocity of a conflict. Congresses have often also enabled national leaders to become personally acquainted and even personal friends (41).

Because of the number of participants and signatories and the formality and solemnity of the proceedings, agreements reached at congresses have tended to be more respected and longer lasting than bilateral agreements reached elsewhere. Congresses have thus become natural platforms for the discussion, official elucidation, and expansion of international law (44). At the same time congresses have played an important rôle in the training of young diplomats (43), in the development of a sense of professional unity among them (42), and in the evolution of diplomatic methods, customs and privileges (39, 40, 42).

Nevertheless the formality and publicity surrounding them (39, 40) have rendered congresses unsuitable for the genuine negotiation of major issues, even if informal discussions outside the conference chamber (41) have often enabled some progress to be made. Indeed, unless carefully prepared beforehand, as most successful congresses have been, the result has sometimes been the aggravation of international tension.

38 S. von Pufendorf, *De Jure Naturae et Gentium Libri Octo,* **2nd edition, Frankfurt-am-Main, 1684**
Department of Printed Books 1842 c.22

Samuel, Freiherr (Baron) von Pufendorf (1632–1694), a Saxon-born jurist and historian, spent most of his adult life in the employ of the rulers of the Palatinate, Sweden, and Brandenburg, and teaching in the universities of Heidelberg and Lund. His writings, which were much influenced by Grotius, reflect the optimism, revulsion at warfare, and belief in reason that characterised his age.

In his *De Jure Naturae et Gentium Libri Octo* ('Eight Books on the Law of Nature and Nations'), which first appeared in 1672, he postulated, unlike most of his predecessors, that man's natural state was peace. Conceding that war could not always be avoided, he attempted to define the conditions under which it was justified: in self-defence, to recover what is owed one but cannot be recovered by other means, and to secure compensation for unjustly inflicted losses and injuries and guarantees against similar conduct in the future. Before embarking even on justified wars, however, Pufendorf insisted, all rulers had a duty to attempt to settle their differences peacefully by arbitration.

Pufendorf's works were rapidly translated into the principal European languages, his *De Jure* becoming, in the words of Professor R.M. Hatton, 'The textbook of generations of foreign chancellery officials all over Europe'. Its concepts strongly influenced the conduct of war and peace in late seventeenth-century and early eighteenth-century Europe and can be linked to the increased frequency of congresses and the sophistication of attempts at the peaceful settlement of major international problems in the same period.

39 Engraving commemorating the Congress of Utrecht, 1712–1713. Published by A. Allard, Amsterdam [1713]

British Museum: Department of Prints and Drawings: 1882-8-12-458

The negotiations at Utrecht resulted in the conclusion of peace treaties between most of the participants in the War of the Spanish Succession which had broken out following the death of the childless Carlos II of Spain in November 1700. This was the third major congress to be held in the Dutch Republic since 1676. Its ceremonial and methods of negotiation followed the pattern set at Nijmegen (1676–9), Rijswijck (1696–7) and, indirectly, at Münster and Osnabrück (1643–8), the first important congresses of modern Europe.

The centrepiece of this engraving, which probably dates from the summer of 1713, shows Peace seated, with an upturned cornucopia representing Plenty, handing Europe (the crowned lady kneeling before her) the symbol of healing (and of peace, ambassadors, and heralds), the caduceus. In the background to the left is a monument to this peace, adorned with portraits of the major rulers and the lion of the United Provinces of the Netherlands. To the right, a sacrifice is being offered at the altar of peace. In the small inset squares, the

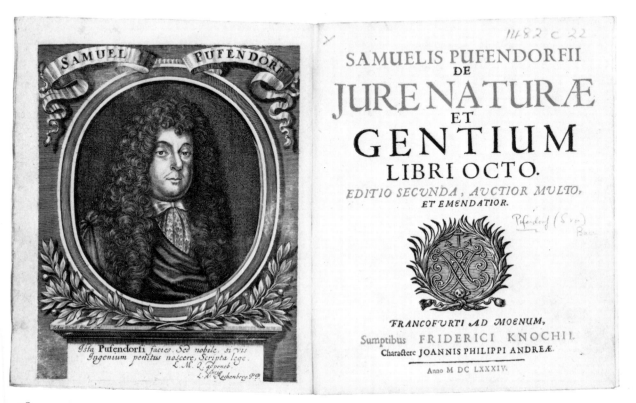

38

doors of the temple of Janus are being closed, as had been done on the Forum in Ancient Rome at the end of every war (left) and Mars, the god of war, is seen departing in his chariot (right). The Dutch and French verses celebrate the blessings of peace and the Dutch share in the creation of such a just settlement.

The surrounding engravings show different stages in the negotiations. At the top there is a view of the city of Utrecht. The formal negotiations at the earlier congresses took place in town halls such as the Utrecht 'Stadhuis', the tower of which is the third to the left from the big tower of the Cathedral ('Dom') in the centre. The two side engravings beneath show the plenipotentiaries of the Allies (left) and the French plenipotentiaries Huxelles, Polignac, and Mesnager (right) in their rooms at the Town Hall. This separation of the parties, who were still at war with each other, was customary. Formal contact took place through mediators – in this case

the British. For although a member of the anti-Bourbon Grand Alliance, Britain had reached a preliminary agreement with France over the broad terms of the peace and the holding of a congress. Such preliminary agreements and the signatories' ability to enforce their will on the other parties often accounted for the success of congresses, which otherwise tended not to progress through the intransigence of all concerned. Accordingly in the next engraving on the left are seen the British plenipotentiaries, Thomas Wentworth, Earl of Strafford (standing) and John Robinson, Bishop of Bristol and Lord Privy Seal (seated centre), with their secretary. The Anglo-French co-operation is also commemorated in the verses in the central panel. The signature of articles of peace between Britain, Portugal, Prussia, Savoy, the United Provinces, and France is shown in the corresponding engraving on the right. Although depicted as taking place simultaneously, these treaties were in

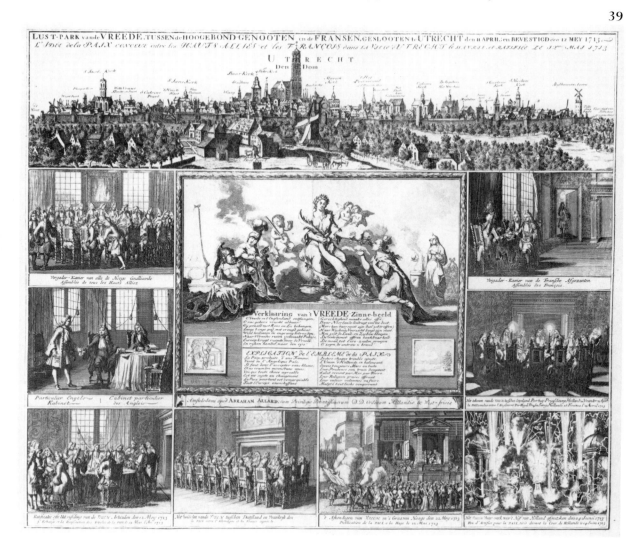

fact signed in a leisurely fashion, one after the other between 2 pm and midnight on 11th April 1713 at the Bishop of Bristol's residence (see also **129** for the signature of the Franco-Spanish treaty at Nijmegen in 1678). On the bottom row, far left, the exchange of the ratifications of these treaties on 12th May is shown. The plenipotentiaries at the left are checking the wording of the documents, while to the right, the oaths of ratification are being sworn (see also **135** by Ter Borch, for a similar scene at Münster in 1648). In the next panel the French and the Austrian plenipotentiaries, representing the Holy Roman Empire, are shown signing the peace treaty between the French and the Germans. No date is given, for no such treaty was signed at Utrecht. At the last moment, Vienna refused to accept additional French demands and recalled its ambassadors. After another campaign the Franco-Austrian treaty was signed at Rastatt in Germany and the Franco-Imperial at Baden in Switzerland in 1714. This engraving is modelled on conventional representations of the signature of peace treaties at other congresses. The next panel shows the proclamation of peace between France and the Dutch and the next the celebratory fireworks, both at the Hague on 22nd May and 14th June respectively. A few weeks later treaties were concluded at Utrecht between Philip V, the Bourbon King of Spain, and his former enemies, with the exception of Emperor Charles VI and the Holy Roman Empire. The Congress of Utrecht then dispersed.

These engravings, despite their inaccuracies and plagiarism, convey a good impression of the formality of negotiation at seventeenth- and eighteenth-century congresses.

40 Letter of the Bishop of Bristol and the Earl of Strafford to Lord Lexington. Utrecht, 24th January/ 4th February 1712/13. From the Lexington Papers
Additional MS 46547, ff. 32v–33

The British plenipotentiaries inform the British Ambassador in Spain that the Imperial (Austrian) ministers had agreed to start negotiations with the French but that the French had received the minutes of their initial demands 'very coldly'. The British, too, have met with French intransigence in their commercial negotiations. Meanwhile, Strafford and Robinson and the Imperial ministers need instructions and information from London and Vienna before much progress can really be achieved at Utrecht.

At the earlier congresses formal negotiations tended to proceed very slowly. The initial demands of one side, in writing, were answered by counter-

demands of the other. Answer was then met by answer. In the interim fresh instructions had usually to be requested and received from the plenipotentiaries' courts, and from a third court too, if there was mediation, as at Utrecht. Thus at least a month normally elapsed between the different stages of negotiations. Since the differences to be whittled down were often immense and there was frequently a complete refusal to compromise, negotiations had a tendency to continue for years.

By the nineteenth century, congresses and conferences usually lasted for only a few months or even weeks. Communications were swifter, the foreign ministers who attended congresses often had more freedom than seventeenth and early eighteenth century Plenipotentiaries to make concessions and the method of transacting business had changed. The matters for discussion were divided according to subject, which were often dealt with in detail by special commissions on which all parties were represented. Rapid progress could therefore be made on certain matters of general concern, despite difficulties over others. Moreover, the practice of keeping official and agreed records or 'protocols' of formal meetings and of the decisions taken at them became invariable, as it had not been at earlier periods. On the whole these facilitated negotiations. Difficulties and misunderstandings could be identified at an early stage and agreements or resolutions to defer further discussion of certain topics could be formally recorded.

Even so, congresses and conferences were, and have remained, unsuitable platforms for serious negotiation of any but the most apolitical and mundane issues. For the publicity and formality attendant on their every phase have always bred a fear among the plenipotentiaries of 'losing face' through making reciprocal compromises which might objectively be desirable and would perhaps have been possible in secret or informal negotiations. Thus congresses have often exacerbated and not reduced international tension.

41 Private letter of Viscount Castlereagh to the Earl of Liverpool, Vienna, 2nd January 1815
Loan 72 (supplementary Liverpool Papers) vol. 27, ff. 122v–123r

The Congress of Vienna assembled soon after the first abdication of Napoleon I in 1814 in order to settle the boundaries of post-Revolutionary Europe and regulate certain European-wide political and social problems. It quickly ran into difficulties. Great Britain and Austria strongly opposed Russia and Prussia's efforts to retain, respectively, large areas of Poland and all of the kingdom of Saxony. In order to get their way through French support, both sides began assiduously courting France. Talleyrand, the French Foreign Minister and representative in Vienna, however, insisted that France be first admitted to the deliberations of the great powers, from which Russia, Prussia, Great Britain, and Austria had originally agreed it should be excluded.

In this letter the British Foreign Secretary, and representative in Vienna, reports the latest news to his Prime Minister and particularly that the 'Auspicious and Seasonable' news of the recently concluded peace between Great Britain and the United States of America, at Ghent, had 'produced the greatest possible sensation here and will . . . enter largely into the calculations of our opponents'. After mentioning his recent long audience with Tsar Alexander of Russia, he adds that 'at the Ball last night at Court . . . he (the Tsar) address'd himself to Talleyrand and said he had declared that *He* would not negotiate without France. Talleyrand, who knew every thing that had pass'd, replied that he had understood England and Austria meant to Propose his admission and that it gave him great pleasure to find they would have HIM's (His Imperial Majesty's) support'. The day after this letter was

written Britain, France, and Austria concluded a secret defensive alliance against Russia and Prussia, to which the Netherlands, Hanover, and Bavaria later acceded. Shortly afterwards a compromise solution to the Polish-Saxon question was reached.

In what has become a famous *bon mot*, the elderly Prince Charles Joseph of Ligne, who was then living in Vienna, wrote that 'le Congrès danse et ne marche pas' ('the Congress dances and does not move on'). He misunderstood, however. For dinners, celebrations, and – as in this instance – balls gave diplomats almost their only chance to engage in informal negotiations which could result in progress being made at the Congress itself. The personal cost to ambassadors could nevertheless be high – Charles Whitworth's death in 1725 was at least in part caused by the over-eating and festivities he had been forced to endure at the Congress of Cambrai (42, 48, 144). This letter also illustrates one of the major, but less obvious, advantages of congresses. They gave foreign ministers the chance to become personally acquainted. This often exerted an important and usually beneficial influence on their later conduct of foreign policy, though not on the objectives thereby pursued.

41

42 *Réglement de Police pour le Congrès de Cambray,* **7th April 1724. From the papers of Charles, Lord Whitworth, second British Plenipotentiary at the Congress**
Additional MS 37394, ff.61v–62r

The Congress of Cambrai (1724–5) was originally intended to set the seal without further war on the reconciliation between the Emperor Charles VI and Philip V of Spain which had been arranged under the terms of the Treaty of Quadruple Alliance of 1718 (39). In this it would not have radically differed from the congresses that had preceded it. In the event Spain and the Emperor also tried to utilise the Congress for the peaceful settlement under Anglo-French mediation of issues that had consequently arisen but had not yet resulted in war. In this sense it, its successor the Congress of Soissons (1728–9) and the other peace-time congresses of Aix-la-Chapelle (1818), Troppau (1820), Laibach (1821), and Verona (1822), can be seen as predecessors of the United Nations. At the time, however, paralysis quickly resulted as none of the parties conceded the others' right to raise topical issues or showed any flexibility over the rest. Consequently the only formal agreement reached was this list of regulations for the conduct of plenipotentiaries and their suites. It was drawn up to avoid disputes over precedence and jurisdiction during the Congress, and was based on the code or *réglement* in force at the Congress of Rijswijck.

The first three points regulate the manner in which plenipotentiaries were to arrive at and sit round the conference table in the Town Hall; points four to six, how the plenipotentiaries' coachmen and servants were to pass each other inside and outside the town, such disputes having caused bloodshed in the past (146). Point seven forbids pages, valets, or any servants in livery to carry arms or to be out of doors, without authority, late at night; points eight to twelve deal with offenders. Unlike those of Great Britain (35), local magistrates are allowed to imprison any servants found in the act of committing a crime, so long as their masters are immediately informed and they are then released if the Plenipotentiary so requires. If, on examination, the Plenipotentiary consequently finds his servant's guilt established, he is to hand the malefactor to the civic authorities for punishment. Any servant found causing trouble or infringing these regulations is to be expelled from his master's household and employed in no other. Finally it is stipulated that this *Réglement* cannot be taken as a precedent. Two examples of the original were signed by the British and French Plenipotentiaries, the Lords Polwarth and Whitworth (48), and the Comte de St-Contest and the Marquis de Rottembourg,

handed to the local magistrates and deposited in the municipal archives as is certified at the bottom of the document.

Despite its final provision, the *Réglement* was later taken as a precedent. It highlights the way in which congresses, particularly the earlier ones where diplomats were clustered together in provincial towns, far from any court and independent of local jurisdiction, acted as forcing houses for diplomatic procedure, privileges, and immunities.

43 Letter from the Honourable Robert Trevor to his oldest brother, the Honourable Thomas Trevor, Haute Fontaine, near Soissons, 24th May 1729
Blenheim (Trevor) Papers F 1–39

Robert Trevor, the youngest son of the first Lord Trevor of Bromham, spent most of his twenty-third year, in 1728 and 1729, in the household of Stephen Poyntz, one of the British plenipotentiaries at the Congress of Soissons. Since the important negotiations took place at the French Court and not in Soissons, Poyntz had rented Haute Fontaine 'for the convenience of ye Country diversions and ye neighbourhood of the Court'.

Here Trevor tells his brother of his plans ('I believe my stay in this Kingdom will not be so long'), regales him with gossip ('There is an unphilosophical story of a Woman brought to bed t'other day at Paris of two young lions'), and gives him news of his activities and of the Congress. Relations between the envoys and the townspeople have improved and 'the time I have stay'd at Soissons has been spent more gayly than it was last year'. At Haute Fontaine 'besides the diversions of coursing, shooting, fishing etc. we have the pleasure of seeing a good deal of Company: few of the Foreign Ministers omitting to call here as they pass or repass from Soissons to the Court . . . I have known seventy people in it (the house) at once . . . indeed I am so used to an Ambassador's table, that it is awkward to me to be in a place where I have not that convenience'. He himself is about to leave for a couple of days hunting at Compiègne with Louis XV and the British Ambassador in France, Sir Robert Walpole's brother, Horatio.

Until the end of the last century, attendance at a congress as an unpaid member of an ambassador's household was regarded as an ideal introduction to diplomacy for young men of aristocratic or prosperous backgrounds. Robert Trevor (1706–83) eventually became British Envoy Extraordinary and Plenipotentiary in the Dutch Republic (1739–47), having previously served as secretary to Horatio Walpole when at the Hague (1734–6), and as Secretary of Embassy there (1736–9).

Later still he became Joint Postmaster-General (1759–65) and was to end his life as Viscount Hampden of Great and Little Hampden, Buckinghamshire. His time at Soissons was his first experience of diplomacy.

44 Austrian ratification of the Treaty of Paris, 1856
Public Record Office F.O. 94/451

The ratification has a velvet cover of dark violet with violet, black, and gold ribbons. It is attached to the silver-gilt skippet, embossed with the Austrian arms, and containing the seal, by a cord of entwined gold and dark violet threads ending in tassels. It closely resembles other nineteenth-century Austrian ratifications.

The Treaty of Paris, signed on 30th March 1856 by representatives of Great Britain, Russia, France, Austria, Turkey, and Sardinia, brought a formal end to the Crimean War. Much of the treaty is taken up with detailed provisions relating to the causes of the war, such as the protection of Christians in the Ottoman Empire, and the status of the Danubian principalities of Wallachia and Moldavia and of the Black Sea. In this it resembles most bilateral peace treaties. However the formal participation at the Congress and adhesion to the Treaty of the most powerful European states, except Prussia, and the less formal participation of so many others made this treaty into the most effective method then available of adding to the body of international law and making provision for matters of international importance unrelated, or little related, to the war. Thus article seven formally admitted Turkey to the international law of Europe and to the family of European powers ('aux avantages du droit public et du concert européens'). Article fifteen expressly declared for the first time that free navigation for merchantmen of all nations on all international rivers was part of European law and protocol; twenty-three contained the 'desire that states . . . should before appealing to arms, have recourse, so far as circumstances allow, to the good offices of a friendly power'. In a similar way treaties resulting from the Congresses of Münster and Osnabrück (1648) were able to regulate the constitution of the Holy Roman Empire and the Congress of Vienna produced declarations on a host of issues including diplomatic precedence and the slave trade (which Castlereagh mentions having discussed with the Tsar in his letter of 2nd January 1815 (41)). It also formulated the constitution of the Germanic Confederation. The conferences of Helsinki and Belgrade in the 1970s have continued this tradition.

The nature of documents concluding successful congresses has varied considerably. In addition to multilateral treaties, as at Paris, for instance, there have been a series of bilateral treaties between the participants, as at Utrecht, or a final declaration with binding force ('Acte Finale') listing the points of general interest that had been agreed, on the basis of the protocols of various conferences, and, in annexes, summarising or recapitulating the terms of the bilateral treaties concluded shortly before or during the Congress, as at Vienna. All, however, have had the same special status, in terms of content and validity, enjoyed by formal agreements reached at congresses.

6. THE GROWTH OF PROFESSIONALISM 1550–1900

Modern foreign ministries and diplomatic services are creations of the later nineteenth century but they can trace their roots to the chanceries of renaissance Italy (**18, 20, 21**). By the mid-sixteenth century, capable royal secretaries were aiding their masters in the administration of foreign policy, though they rarely exercised much influence over its formation (**45**). Their successors evolved over a period into foreign ministers, though often retaining the title of secretary, as in Britain and the United States. From the later seventeenth century the secretary's staff and particularly the under secretary (**47**) became more important. As the secretary of state's rôle became predominantly political, the staff took over the routine administration and formed the original foreign offices (**46**). From the time of the earliest residents there have been men who pursued diplomatic careers (**48**), but in the late seventeenth and eighteenth centuries their conditions of service improved. Rates of pay became related to rank and posting (**49**), a career structure developed as the number of diplomatic grades increased and a 'professional' ethos became more general among diplomats (**53**). The growing external pressures on European states which brought about these developments were further increased in the nineteenth century by the improvement in communications as a result of the Industrial Revolution. European resident missions rapidly appeared throughout the world, the size of foreign ministries and the staffs of embassies underwent enormous growth, and such features as permanent embassy buildings and diplomatic uniforms appeared (**51, 52**). Despite its enhanced size, efficiency, and quality, however, the British diplomatic service of 1900 was still in several respects non-professional (**52**).

45 Eighteenth-century engraving of a contemporary portrait of Sir Francis Walsingham, c.1530–1590

Additional MS 32091, f.261

Sir Francis Walsingham, by origin a lawyer with a small country estate, served as Queen Elizabeth I's Principal Secretary of State from 1572 until his death, but is better known as the head of the Elizabethan spy service. Convinced that 'knowledge is never too dear', he uncovered many of the Catholic plots against his mistress and managed to maintain a steady flow of reliable information from Catholic Europe, despite the breakdown of diplomatic relations. He was the first of the Queen's counsellors to know of Spanish preparations for the Armada. His patriotism, abilities, diligence, and diplomatic experience in France from 1570 to 1572 had led to his appointment as Principal Secretary, and while in office he was charged with further diplomatic missions to the Netherlands (1578), France (1581), and Scotland (1583). Although, as Principal Secretary, he was responsible for routine correspondence with English envoys abroad and was consulted by Lord Burghley and the Queen, his rôle was essentially that of a modern senior civil servant and he played little part in the formulation of foreign policy. He died a poor man, having received few rewards from Elizabeth I who disliked his forthrightness and zealous Protestantism.

This portrait gives a good impression of Walsingham's intelligence, watchfulness, and personal simplicity. In his origins, previous diplomatic experience, and minor rôle in the formulation of foreign policy, Walsingham was typical of English Secretaries of State, although there were brilliant exceptions such as Burghley and Robert Cecil (1st Earl of Salisbury) (**152**). There was also a growing tendency from the late seventeenth century onwards to appoint politicians such as the Duke of Newcastle or William Pitt the Elder to the senior Secretaryship.

In England there were almost invariably two Secretaries of State from the mid-sixteenth century. By the late seventeenth century one had become mainly responsible for relations with northern Europe and the other with southern Europe. Since one of the Secretaries was always the more dominant in fact if not in title, this division was not generally harmful. However both Secretaries also continued to have considerable responsibility for domestic affairs. Since foreign affairs was the last field over which rulers were ready to surrender control, the Secretaries generally exercised little influence on policy until well into the eighteenth century. It was only in 1782 that one of the Secretaries of State in the person of Charles James

Fox, was given exclusive responsibility for foreign affairs. Since then the Foreign Secretary's importance has depended on his personality and not on his office.

The development of the office of Minister for Foreign Affairs has followed a similar course in most European countries, and counterparts to the Cecils were Villeroy in France, under Henry IV, and Gonzalo and Antonio Perez under Philip II, in Spain (**30**). The first official Secretary responsible for foreign affairs alone was appointed in France, administratively the best-organised west European state, in 1626, but for many years afterwards French diplomatic relations with certain European countries remained the responsibility of other ministers.

46 Choiseul's foreign office, Versailles
Photograph by courtesy of the Amis de la Bibliothèque de Versailles

Although completed only in 1761, when the Duc de Choiseul (1719–85) was Louis XV's leading minister, this suite of rooms is typical of the earliest foreign offices. It is near a royal palace, since this is where the power in the land, in the person of the monarch, then resided. It occupies quite a small area, because the staff was not numerous, and its rooms, like the responsibilities of its officials, are distinguished by geographical area. Thus the first room, according to the cartouche over its doorway, is the 'Room of the Northern Powers' ('Salle des Puissances du Nord'), and above the door there is a view of St Petersburg seen from the sea.

It took a long time before west European chanceries generally became as well-organised as their fifteenth-century Italian counterparts (**18, 21**). But even in the sixteenth century, well-run chanceries functioning almost as foreign offices, were to be found, for instance in Spain in Ferdinand of Aragon's last years (**24**), or under Philip II whose Secretary Gonzalo Perez established the royal

45

46

archives in Simancas, or in France under Henry IV. But it was from the mid-seventeenth century that consistent and well-nigh irreversible progress in the organisational field was made, particularly in France. France's growing international obligations in the time of Richelieu, Mazarin and Louis XIV, placed an enormous and ever-growing burden on their Secretaries of State for Foreign Affairs. In order to cope, they were compelled to increase their staff, to improve their efficiency, and to put their archives into good order. Similar pressures led to similar developments in Great Britain after 1688 and within a century well-organised, though still rather small, Foreign Offices were to be found throughout western Europe. The British Foreign Office was first so called, however, only as recently as 1807.

47 A British Envoy writes to an Under Secretary, Vienna, 10th April 1702. From the Ellis Papers
Additional MS 28910, ff. 436v–437r

George Stepney wrote this letter from Vienna a short time after William III's death, when changes in the ministry were expected. He did not think his correspondent, John Ellis, an Under Secretary in the Northern Department since 1695, would be affected, however, and here he lightheartedly tells him so, comparing him, in the process, to 'the Pole-Star wch continues fix'd in all Seasons & changes'. In so doing, Stepney identifies the main value of the Under Secretaries and of the permanent staff of the Secretaries of State.

The importance of Under Secretaries, or their foreign equivalents, *Premiers Commis*, such as the Pecquets in France, or *Referendare*, such as Buol or later Bartenstein in Austria, increased considerably throughout western Europe in the early eighteenth century. In England, assistants to the Secretaries of State had appeared at the start of the seventeenth century, but they only became known as Under Secretaries in the 1670s, when their duties began to approximate to the title. For in these years the Secretaryship increasingly became a political appointment and the Secretaries, though still usually experienced diplomats, became ever more burdened with political duties and faced the likelihood of dismissal after relatively short periods in office if their faction fell from power. Thus the Under Secretaries took over many of the Secretaries' more routine duties and became the main agents, other than the ruler, for providing continuity in the execution of foreign policy. Wynne and Bridgeman, two of the Under Secretaries who had served James II's Secretaries of State, were re-appointed by William's III's Secretaries of State after 1688, and George Tilson (104) served Tory and Whig

ministries as Under Secretary of State for the thirty years following 1708. In time their experience and expertise made them the effective heads of their offices as their modern successor, the Permanent Under Secretary in the Foreign and Commonwealth Office, is of his.

Like most of the other Under Secretaries, John Ellis (1643–1738) entered the Secretary of State's office immediately after leaving university, and spent almost all his career, before being appointed Under Secretary, in various branches of what, today, would be called the civil service. As this letter demonstrates – and as has become typical of Under Secretaries – he became very friendly with the envoys with whom he had to correspond and for whose welfare he was primarily responsible. He resigned office in 1705 after the latest of a series of differences with Secretary of State Sir Charles Hedges – the C.H. referred to in the letter. Ellis is said to have been one of the many lovers of Charles II's mistress, Barbara Villiers, Duchess of Cleveland.

48 C. Whitworth, *An Account of Russia as it was in the Year 1710*. Printed at Strawberry Hill for Horace Walpole Jr, 1758. From the library of the Hon. Thomas Grenville
Department of Printed Books G.4228

The title page contains an engraved view of Horace Walpole's famous 'Gothick' pseudo-castle of Strawberry Hill near Twickenham. His coat of arms can be seen in the floral border. The engraved portrait of the author, Charles Whitworth (1675–1725), created Lord Whitworth of Galway in the Irish Peerage in 1721, was inserted in the early nineteenth century.

Whitworth came of a minor family, possessing recently acquired estates in Staffordshire. After an education at Westminster School, Trinity College, Cambridge, and possibly the Middle Temple, he became the secretary of George Stepney, then Envoy in Berlin, in 1699. He spent the following years as British Resident at the Imperial diet in Regensburg and as chargé d'affaires in Vienna during Stepney's absences. From 1704 to 1712 he was in Russia, rising from Envoy (1704–9) to Ambassador Extraordinary and Plenipotentiary (1711–12), much of 1711 being spent on special missions to Poland, Prussia, the Palatinate, and Vienna. In May 1714 his abilities won open recognition from the Tory ministry who appointed him, staunch Whig though he was, Britain's representative at the Congress of Baden in Switzerland (39). Between 1716 and 1722 he represented Britain at Berlin and the Hague, one of the most important European postings. A British plenipotentiary at the Congress of Cambrai from 1722 to the summer of 1725 (**46**), he died in London in October 1725 and was buried, close to Stepney, in Westminster Abbey.

Long before Whitworth's time, men had spent their lives serving their countries abroad. In this sense Spinelly (**25**) or Thomas Roe (**58**) as well as Whitworth could be regarded as career diplomats. However, the service itself was hardly professional. Though the grades increased from two (Ambassador and Resident) to six before 1689, there was no fixed career structure, only primitive salary scales, and no fixed pensions. Pay was often irregular and the appointment of ambassadors was primarily dependent on considerations of wealth, birth, and political and family connections. Most envoys regarded their work, as Roe professed to do, as a form of 'honourable banishment' and usually embarked on it in the hope of winning favour and profitable posts at home. 'Foreign service' as Sir Philip Meadows senior wrote in 1703 'may sometimes prove a good stirrup but never a good saddle'. After 1689, however, the service gradually became better organised and an increasing number of diplomats became professional in their outlook (**53**).

Whitworth's *Account of Russia* is modelled on the final reports or *relazioni* (**163**) made famous by Venetian diplomats. It was intended for the information of Whitworth's masters because of the general ignorance of Russia that then prevailed. Indeed the manuscript of the 'Account'

in Whitworth's Papers (Additional MS 37359, ff.225–248) contains a note that, although drawn up in 1710 'it was not given before April 1711 and then to Mr Secy St John, Duke of Shrewsbury and Lord Halifax'. Whitworth covers the geography, ethnography, economy, religion, constitution, government and recent history of Russia. He gives perceptive character sketches of Peter the Great and his ministers and goes into considerable detail in his description of Russia's economic and naval expansion under the Tsar. Horace Walpole printed the *Account of Russia* to show 'what lasting benefits ambassadors and foreign Ministers might confer on mankind beyond the temporary utility of negotiating and sending intelligence'. It became an immediate success.

49 The bill for extraordinary expenses, 12th December 1698 to 12th March 1699, submitted by James Cressett, English Envoy Extraordinary to the Elector and Dukes of Brunswick-Lüneburg
Additional MS 59892A

The basic pay of Ambassadors and Envoys, even when they received it, was not sufficient to meet all their expenses. From an early date it became accepted practice for them to submit bills for their 'extraordinary' business expenses at regular intervals to the Secretaries of State by way of the Under Secretaries.

This bill covers Cressett's expenses for stationery, postage, entertainment, representation, and information-gathering. The largest single item (£60), significantly, is for 'entertainments for publick ministers'. Cressett was then at a congress and needed to represent William III worthily. Moreover, as Talleyrand was to say, 'les bons dîners font la bonne diplomatie' ('good meals make for good diplomacy') (**41**). It should also be noted that Cressett's intelligence-gathering was not only covered by the paltry-sounding £17, 'For Postage of letters in the Courts of Lunenburg and for gazzettes and Printed papers', for the 'pensions to ye Postmasters' at Amsterdam, Bremen, and Hamburg, were almost certainly paid in return for their opening and transcribing of letters from and to envoys of other countries which passed through their hands (**123**). Many postmasters found such activities a very profitable source of income before the nineteenth century. The £24 'given at the New Year according to custom' and at least part of the £26 of 'necesary expenses' probably conceal minor bribes or 'sweeteners' to well-placed officials and ministers at the Brunswick courts. Even the £20 donation 'for Establishing the French Protestant Church at Zell' might not have been given purely as

48

a fitting gesture by the representative of Europe's leading Protestant ruler. One of the members of the French Protestant community in Celle was the wife of the Duke of Brunswick–Lüneburg–Celle. Some of the most precious intercepted material to come into English hands at this period emanated from her husband's post office. Beneath the bill, the Secretary of State for the Northern Department, James Vernon, authorises payment and at the bottom of the page is a note that the bill had been entered in the official records.

The rates of pay for envoys were originally fixed according to rank and posting in 1669 and were adjusted in 1689, the rates for 'extraordinaries' being fixed in the next year. They remained unaltered for the next century even though only ten years later, in a letter to Under Secretary Ellis of 17th March 1699 (Additional MS 28903, f.40), Cressett grumbled, on the subject of this very bill, that he could not 'without the greatest folly imaginable continue in the service at this rate . . . I hope my friendes will pardon me if I am not willing to leave a wife and children to the mercy of such Gentlemen as sit in the treasury'. Nevertheless diplomats like Stepney and Whitworth were ready to continue serving and the fixing of the rates of pay was one of the earliest and most important steps towards the professionalisation of the British diplomatic service.

49

50 List of foreign envoys in London and British envoys abroad, 1789, from *The London Calendar or Court and City Register for England, Scotland, Ireland and America for the year 1789:* **pp. 92–93**

These lists give a good impression of the development of diplomatic services throughout Europe during the eighteenth century, but particularly of the British diplomatic service a few years after the appointment of the first Secretary of State for Foreign Affairs.

The number of official grades has been further increased from the basic six of 1689 (Ambassadors, Ministers Plenipotentiary, Envoys Extraordinary, Residents, Secretaries of Embassy, Agents), the most recent addition being Secretary of Legation, which had come into being in the 1780s. The increasing importance of subordinates is shown by their mention in the lists. It was often they who did the real work, leaving aristocratic ambassadors like the Duke of Dorset to play the courtier and *grand seigneur* (and, in Dorset's case, according to popular belief, cricket). There are very few full Ambassadors for they were expensive and their status often gave rise to disputes over etiquette and precedence which much reduced their effectiveness as negotiators. It is only since 1945 that full Ambassadors or their equivalents, such as High Commissioners among members of the Commonwealth, have become the normal diplomatic representatives, and these years have witnessed a great decrease in the formalities and ceremonial attaching to Ambassadors.

There are other notable features in these lists such as the increased number of permanent British posts in Europe and of permanent missions of other countries in London. This development had been the result of Britain's growing international importance, and it in its turn compelled increasing efficiency in the Secretary of State's office. The British Envoy Extraordinary and Plenipotentiary in Russia, Charles Whitworth (1753–1825) was the great-nephew of his namesake (**48**) and pursued an even more successful career in Russia, Poland and France, being created Earl Whitworth in 1815. By 1789 several families, such as the Keiths, the Keenes, the Walpoles and the Edens, already had a tradition of diplomatic service abroad. This demonstrates that diplomacy was becoming recognised as an honourable profession in its own right. Moreover, in these years official retirement pensions were introduced for British diplomats. It should be noted how, by 1789, the residences of diplomats in London were to be found mainly near the British Court and Government in the fashionable West End of London, only a little to the east of the area where most embassies are situated today. In the seventeenth century ambassadors seem to have lived mainly around Lincoln's Inn Fields (33). This had then been a new and elegant district but by 1789 only relatively minor envoys still resided there. The Austrian and Russian Consuls lived in the City of London among their fellow-merchants.

Despite all the changes that had taken place since 1689, the British diplomatic service of 1789 was still far from 'professional'. It continued to contain many young members of aristocratic families who regarded diplomatic service abroad only as a stepping-stone to high office at home and promotion to the upper ranks remained dependent on patronage, wealth, political loyalty, and (usually) birth. Exceptions to one or more of these rules, such as the wealthy but non-aristocratic William Eden (1744–1814), then Ambassador to Spain, were beginning to appear, though as late as 1918 there was a property qualification of £400 a year for entrants to the Diplomatic Service. A genuine career structure, entrance to the service through merit, and a general acceptance that diplomacy could be a career in its own right, had to await the middle of the nineteenth century.

51 The British Embassy in Paris
Exhibited photograph: Department of the Environment

The British Embassy in Paris was built for the Duc de Charost in 1722 and served as his family's town residence for the next sixty years. For about eighteen months between 1790 and 1792 it was occupied by Count Souza, the Portuguese Ambassador, and functioned as his embassy building. In 1814 the British Government bought it from its owner since 1803, Napoleon's sister Princess Pauline Borghese (formerly Bonaparte) for 800,000 francs including the furniture. The stables, which were separately owned, were purchased for 61,500 francs. It was the first permanent British embassy building and has been lived in by successive ambassadors to France since the summer of 1814, when the Duke of Wellington took up residence there.

Until well into the nineteenth century envoys generally transacted business either at Court or in houses which they had rented or bought for the duration of their missions. Embassies as we know them today did not exist, though diplomats frequently took over homes from their predecessors thereby establishing a continuity of diplomatic representation from one building. In London this sometimes came to be commemorated in the names of the streets on which these houses lay, such as Portugal and Sardinia streets near Lincoln's Inn Fields, or Poland Street near Soho, the address of the Polish Envoy according to the *London Calendar* of 1789 (50).

The late seventeenth century saw the establishment of certain 'national' palaces, like the 'Spanish Palace' in Vienna which were apparently acquired and maintained by governments for their ambassadors in major states (166). There were, however, exceedingly few of these palaces, and it was only after 1860 that permanent Embassy buildings became common. By then only large buildings could house the staff which the ambassadors of great powers needed in order to perform all the duties expected of them.

52 Twentieth-century diplomatic uniform
Reproduced by courtesy of Sir James Bowker, GBE, KCMG

The British diplomatic uniform evolved in the years following the Battle of Waterloo and is based on the military and Court uniforms of the period. Its adoption and the adoption of similar diplomatic uniforms by most other states was symptomatic of the rising status of the career diplomat throughout Europe and his desire to be recognised as belonging to a distinct profession.

For it was in the last century, and particularly after 1850, that modern diplomatic services and foreign ministries were created in response to the increasing demands placed on governments. By the middle of the century resident British diplomats were to be found throughout the world. In 1789 (50) the only permanent British mission outside Europe had been that at Constantinople and the only non-European envoy in London was the Minister representing the United States of America – and that post was vacant in 1789. The introduction of steam ships, railways and the telegraph speeded the pace of diplomacy and facilitated its spread. It also speeded the pace of the events being reported, necessitating quicker responses. The growing pressures are illustrated in the increased number of despatches and other messages which British envoys sent to the British Foreign Office. From 12,402 in 1826 the number had risen to 101,515 in 1900 and just four years later to 125,011.

In order to cope, the size of Embassy staffs and of the Foreign Office increased vastly. Permanent Embassy buildings with proper office accommodation had to be provided for ambassadors, and the rambling complex of buildings near or in the courts of Europe which the staff of the royal Secretaries of State had gradually taken over (45, 46) were replaced by imposing office buildings in the capitals, such as the Foreign Office in Whitehall and the French and German foreign ministries in the quai d'Orsay in Paris and the Wilhelmstrasse in Berlin. At the same time the internal structure of the ministries expanded with new specialist depart-

52

international politics and statesmen. The work itself seems to have been secondary, as it had been with Robert Trevor (43) more than one-and-a-half centuries earlier.

53 F. de Callières, *De la manière de négocier avec les Souverains*, **Brussels, 1716**
Department of Printed Books 595 c.26

François de Callières (1645–1717) was active as a diplomat in the service of Louis XIV. Between his first mission to Poland in 1670 and his last to Lorraine in 1700 he served repeatedly in Poland, Savoy, and the United Provinces. During the Nine Years' War (1688–97) he was almost continuously engaged after 1694 in confidential peace negotiations with the Dutch and was consequently appointed one of the French plenipotentiaries at the Congress of Rijswijck (1696–7). For a contemporary mention of him at this time see **115**. After 1700 he worked as a secretary in the royal administration in Versailles. He occupied his free time writing books on style and was elected to the Académie Française in 1689. In his last years he wrote this book, *De la manière de négocier avec les Souverains, de l'Utilité des Négociations, du choix des Ambassadeurs et des Envoyez et des Qualitez nécessaires pour réussir dans ces Emplois* ('Of the Manner of Negotiating with Sovereigns, of the Utility of Negotiations, of the Choice of Ambassadors and Envoys and the Qualities necessary for success in these Duties'). The title summarises its contents. The frontispiece is an allegory representing peace being given to Britain, the Holy Roman Empire and the United Provinces by France and Spain (all identified by their arms) after the War of the Spanish Succession.

Callières stresses the need for honesty in negotiations ('a lie always leaves a drop of poison behind') and describes the secret of negotiations as 'the harmonisation of the interests of all the parties concerned'. The distinguishing feature of the book is the author's emphasis on diplomacy being a profession in its own right and he talks of the 'freemasonry of diplomacy'. He was the first theorist to regard diplomacy in this way. Once again, however, practice was in advance of theory. Callières was involved in the establishment of the first school to be devoted to the training of future diplomats in 1712 and he probably wrote this book with the school in mind.

The school soon closed, but this short work has been repeatedly printed and praised by later practitioner-theorists like Harold Nicolson who in the 1950s described it as 'the best manual of diplomatic method ever written'.

ments and new intermediate grades being created at ever shorter intervals, while in embassies a hierarchy of secretaries, counsellors and attachés evolved to take the place of the embassy secretary and the ambassador's private secretary and suite which had generally coped adequately enough in the eighteenth century. The quality of the staff on balance probably improved too, following the introduction of an examination system into the British Foreign Office and Diplomatic Service in 1856 and the coming of competitive exams in 1872.

Nevertheless the Foreign Office and Diplomatic Service were still the least 'professional' parts of the British civil service in 1900. Several of the most important posts were and indeed are filled by non-professionals, and as late as 1894 the young Bertrand Russell spent three months at the Paris Embassy working as an unpaid attaché because his grandmother, the widow of the Victorian Prime Minister Lord John Russell, wanted to wean him from an unsuitable girlfriend in England by introducing him to Parisian high society and

DE LA
MANIERE
DE NEGOCIER
AVEC
LES SOUVERAINS,

De l'utilité des Negociations, du choix des Ambaſſadeurs & des Envoyez, & des qualitez neceſſaires pour réüſſir dans ces emplois.

Par. M. DE CALLIERES,

Conſeiller Ordinaire du Roi en ſes Conſeils, Secretaire du Cabinet de Sa Majeſté, ci-devant Ambaſſadeur Extraordinaire & Plenipotentiaire du feu Roi, pour les Traitez de Paix conclus à Ryſwyck. Et l'un des Quarante de l' Academie Françoiſe.

BRUXEL,
Pour LA COMPAGNIE.

M DCC XVI.

7 THE SPREAD OF WESTERN-STYLE DIPLOMACY THROUGHOUT THE WORLD

The first records of diplomatic activity are to be found outside Europe (1–5) but resident diplomacy seems never to have developed there indigenously (54). The distances separating great powers, the nature of their international relations and the philosophies that lay behind them may have been at least partially responsible for this (55, 60). There had been spasmodic diplomatic contact between Europe and Asia from early times: Haroun Al-Raschid, the famous Caliph of Baghdad immortalised in the *Arabian Nights*, sent an envoy to the Court of the first Holy Roman Emperor, Charlemagne, at the start of the ninth century, while in 1290 Edward I of England sent Geoffrey de Langley to the Mongol ruler Arghun to negotiate an alliance against the Seljuks. But permanent diplomatic relations were inaugurated in 1535 when France sent an official Ambassador to Constantinople. By 1583 England had also sent a resident Ambassador to Constantinople (56) and under James I English resident envoys appeared in India (58). While the primary impetus was commercial (57, 59), political factors also played their part in Constantinople (56).

An apparent recognition of the differences between European and non-European diplomatic customs led the Europeans to make special provisions for and to adopt special forms in their dealings with non-European powers (57, 61, 62). These however concealed European attitudes of superiority and a reluctance to apply Europe's modes and rules of international conduct beyond the continent's confines (61). A similar attitude of superiority displayed towards the Europeans, allied this time with isolationism almost prevented the establishment of any diplomatic relations between the European powers and Peking before 1860 (60). By 1900, however, Western international law and customs and, as a corollary, resident diplomacy, had come to extend throughout the world (63).

54 Emperor Yekuno Amlak of Abyssinia receiving Muslim Ambassadors. From Isaiah, Daniel, and Books of the Apocrypha. Ethiopic, late eighteenth century

Department of Oriental Manuscripts and Printed Books. Oriental MS 503 ff.75v–76r

The Emperor, who reigned from 1270 to 1285, is seated at the right with the Muslim Ambassadors in attendance. At the far left is a group of slaves, with their arms respectfully crossed, standing by their camels. The Ambassadors seem only recently to have arrived. The difference in size of the Emperor, the Ambassadors and the servants reflect their relative status in the eyes of the person who commissioned the manuscript.

Civilisations and rulers outside Europe remained in diplomatic contact with each other from early times (1–4). But despite the sophistication attained (4), resident diplomacy seems to have been unknown among them.

55 Jahangir's Dream, c.1618–22. From an album in the possession of the Freer Gallery of Art, Smithsonian Institution, Washington, D.C. Reproduced as plate 21 in S. C. Welch *Imperial Mughal Painting* 1978 [not illustrated]

This painting was commissioned by the Mughal Emperor Jahangir (which translated means 'the world-seizer') who ruled from 1605 to 1627. It commemorates a dream in which he had been made happy by the Persian ruler, Shah 'Abbas Safavi, who appeared before him in a well of light. At the time the Shah was posing a serious threat to the Mughal Empire's northwestern frontier.

The artist, Abu'l Hassan, goes out of his way to flatter his master. Jahangir stands in the midst of a halo composed of the light of the sun and moon, and is portrayed as more imposing and much taller than the weak-looking Shah whom he is embracing in friendship. The powerful lion, on which Jahangir stands, reposes confidently over most of central Asia, pushing the feeble sheep bearing the Shah into the Mediterranean.

Despite Jahangir's wishful thinking and the artist's flattery, the Shah remained antagonistic and became more than a match for the Emperor. In 1622 he finally took Qandahar, the key fortress on the northwestern frontier. The Shah's portrait was probably based on portraits done from the life by the artist Bishndas who had accompanied Jahangir's ambassador, Khan 'Alam, on his special mission to Shah 'Abbas in 1613.

እባ፡ይኩና፡እም፡ሰቤሁ

ተበሳጹ፡አጋእዝት

◀54

The picture illustrates some of the reasons for the apparent failure of resident diplomacy to appear indigenously outside Europe. The distances involved were enormous and while there were many minor rulers, there were very few major ones. These could usually expand without endangering the vital interests of other equally powerful states and without needing to be on permanent watch for possible allies. Under these circumstances resident diplomacy was less practicable than in Europe and less necessary.

Under Jahangir the distances were beginning to be less important, however. Western-inspired angels supporting the halo demonstrate that European influences were becoming ever stronger in Northern India.

56 List of questions concerning the establishment of permanent Anglo-Ottoman diplomatic relations 1581–2. From the Burghley Papers

Lansdowne MS 112, f.109

The first steps towards the establishment of permanent Anglo-Ottoman diplomatic relations were taken in 1578 when the most important English merchants trading with the Levant sent two agents to Constantinople. Despite initial success and an exchange of letters between Queen and Sultan, their negotiations for a charter of privileges, called 'capitulations', for English merchants in the Ottoman Empire, failed. The French Ambassador had grown jealous and the agents' status seems to

have been too low and unofficial for them to combat French hostility effectively. Both sides remained interested in establishing diplomatic relations, however. They had a common fear of Philip II, who had recently added Portugal to his dominions, and a common interest in commerce; the Sultan apparently wanted Cornish tin for his cannon. In November 1580 a Turkish ambassador arrived in England on a special mission, and in the following September the Levant Company was established to control English commercial activity in the Middle East. Before it could operate effectively, the capitulations agreed on in June 1580, but later cancelled, had to be renegotiated. Amidst a flurry of reports on the commercial and political advantages of diplomatic relations with Constantinople, English discussion also turned to the status and duties of the envoy to be sent to the 'Grand Signor' or Sultan. This list of questions entitled 'Matters to be consydered for the honor of her Matie and of the Realme' was drawn up at that time.

It touches on the duties of the 'Messenger' or 'Nuncio' that it was then intended should be sent in advance of a full ambassador. Should he confine himself to negotiating the ambassador's privileges (question 5) and presenting the Queen's letters and possible presents (2) and leave formal audiences (4) and commercial negotiations (6) to the agent? It also implies the aims intended by establishing diplomatic relations. They were commercial: 'whether the Nuncio . . . shall make demand . . . for any grettar pryvyledge or benefyte to the Marchant*es* then was before granted', (i.e. in June 1580) (6); but also political: 'Yf Question be asked of the Nuncio touchinge the state of her Matie & of the Realme yn these warres with spayne or otherwyse: what answere shall he make theryn' (7) – for Elizabeth wished the Turkish fleet to put to sea to divert Philip II's attention from England and the Netherlands.

The main difficulties are raised in the first, third and fifth questions concerning the status of the nuncio and ambassador: specifically (3) was the ship carrying the Nuncio to be a royal ship? It was, in any case, determined that the ambassador should 'have as great allowances for hys entertaynement there as have the ambassadors of France, Polonia & other Christian prynces sythe her Matie is a prince of absolute power nor inferiour nor nedye of help of any of them' (5). The question of presents for the Sultan was particularly thorny (1) 'sythe he taketh all presents of the Christian princes to be as tributes: and for such are they regystered in hys Records, whiche beynge once begonne he looketh for the contynuance thereof as of dutye, and the greater value that the presente ys made, the greater dutye & subiection he taketh hold of therbye'. For the Ottoman Sultan-Caliph, like the Chinese Emperor, dominated a whole civilisation and was unfamiliar with a system of equal, fully sovereign states such as existed in Europe. As 'a prince of absolute power', Elizabeth would resent her representative being treated as the subject of another ruler. Yet to give no presents might be regarded by the Sultan as unnecessarily insulting.

By November 1583, the procedural and substantive problems had been solved and William Harborne, a merchant from Great Yarmouth who had previously resided in Constantinople, left England as 'the Queen's true and undoubted orator, messenger, deputie and agent' at the Sultan's court. Commonly called 'Ambassador' and paid not by the parsimonious Queen but by the Levant Company, he was the first in a line of Ambassadors that has continued to this day, although paid by the British Government since 1804.

While this document relates specifically to Anglo-Ottoman relations, it is of general relevance to the opening of permanent diplomatic relations between European powers and the non-European world. It hints at the political and commercial advantages that the Europeans hoped would thereby be gained, and the rôle that the first envoys were expected to play. Above all, though, it summarises the dilemma that often confronted European statesmen when contemplating the establishment of diplomatic relations with powers whose customs and philosophies were fundamentally different from theirs.

57 Letter of James I to an un-named oriental ruler, Westminster 20th/30th March 1609/10 (see plate no. III)

Additional Charter 56456

This letter was written a fortnight prior to the departure for the Far East of Sir Henry Middleton, a merchant, sea-captain and occasional privateer. His voyage was financed by the recently formed (1599) East India Company which played a similar rôle in the Far East to that played in the Middle East by the Levant Company (56). The letter, which is signed by the King, solicits the oriental ruler's 'frendshipp and Amitie' and his 'Royall protection for the settling of a factorie . . . with such securitie and libertie of commerce as shalbe most convenient for the advancement of the mutuall profitt and commoditie of each others subiects'. The name of the ruler is left blank on the address panel, to be filled in by Middleton when the occasion arose. Middleton was then to hand the letter over with a small present from James I. Unlike the plain, Latin letters addressed to European royalty (100), this letter is in English and is gaudily decorated.

Up to a century ago it was common practice for British generals, admirals, consuls, and explorers, such as David Livingstone, to carry documents like these, often in the form of treaties with the details left blank. They sometimes became the foundation for British commercial rights and, occasionally, even colonies. Middleton himself was less successful than many of his successors. On reaching Aden in Arabia he was imprisoned. He escaped, but his efforts to establish a factory in Surat, on the coast of western India were unsuccessful. Before he could return to England, he died in Java (1613) when his boat was set on fire by natives.

This letter illustrates the importance of commerce as an impetus to the expansion of Western diplomacy, particularly in the Far East which most seventeenth-century European leaders considered too distant to be of any political importance for Europe. The letter also indicates the special manner in which European countries handled their relations with non-European powers – and initially with Russia. They were often not the responsibility of the Minister in charge of (European) Foreign Affairs, but of national commercial or military councils, depending on the special nature of the relationship. The form of the letters used in communicating with their rulers were quite different from those employed inside Europe (154), as were the rules concerning the entertainment of their envoys in England (11).

58 Sir Thomas Roe at the Court of Jahangir, 1615 (see plate no. V)

British Museum: Department of Oriental Antiquities: 1933–6–10–01

Sir Thomas Roe, bearded, with close-cropped black hair and in European dress, stands among courtiers on the left of the picture, holding what appears to be a book. The Emperor is seated at the right. The precise subject of the miniature is uncertain. It has been described as showing Jahangir investing a courtier with a cloak, but it might represent Roe reading his introductory oration (112) during his first audience as English Ambassador to the Mughal Court.

Sir Thomas Roe (?1581–1644) was the first regularly accredited English diplomat to serve as a resident Ambassador both inside and outside Europe. Before the start of his diplomatic career in 1615 he was sent by Henry, Prince of Wales, on three voyages of discovery, in search of gold, to the West Indies and South America. Later he saw service in the Netherlands. During his three years at the Mughal Court (1615–18) he negotiated a commercial treaty which came to be regarded as having laid the foundations of the greatness of British India. He visited Persia on his homeward journey. He became English Ambassador in Constantinople in 1621 and was successful not only in his commercial dealings but also in his efforts to improve Anglo-Algerian relations and to win Bethlen Gabor, the Prince of Transylvania, for the Protestant alliance in the Thirty Years' War. He departed in 1628 and between 1629–30 mediated successfully between Gustavus Adolphus, King of Sweden, and Sigismund III, King of Poland and formerly of Sweden. After eight years in England, Roe was involved as mediator in the abortive negotiations with the Empire, France and Sweden, to bring an end to the war between them (1636–42). He finished his career as Ambassador Extraordinary to Vienna, from 1642 to 1643.

While Ambassador to Constantinople, in 1627, Roe was given the Codex Alexandrinus, one of the three earliest manuscripts of the Bible, by Cyril Lucar, Patriarch of Constantinople and previously of Alexandria, for presentation to Charles I. It is now one of the British Library's most treasured possessions.

59 Nishan-i-sherif of Ahmad I, 1604

Department of Oriental Manuscripts and Printed Books: Cotton Roll xiv. 10

The *Nishan-i-sherif* was a legally binding declaration made by an Ottoman Sultan. This one confirms the Capitulation of 1580 concluded between English

agents and ministers of Murad III (36). It had consequently been confirmed on several occasions. Surmounting the document is the *tughra* or personal sign of Ahmad I, taking the form of an elaborate monogram incorporating his name and patronymic. It is illuminated in blue and gold. The text below includes all the articles of the original agreement.

Much of the effort of resident European ambassadors in Constantinople was devoted to maintaining their national capitulations, and securing their confirmation, in *nishan-i-sherifs* from newly ascended rulers. True of representatives from states bordering the Ottoman Empire such as Austria or Poland, who were usually – perforce – very active politically, this was particularly true of ambassadors from distant lands such as England. For even when they were not paid by the merchants through trading companies, as the English were, commerce was frequently almost their country's only interest in the Ottoman Empire. Capitulations (denoting the 'chapters' or articles of the agreement), a survival from the Byzantine Empire, were the basis for the privileges of the merchants from the European states in the Empire. By 1604 the capitulations of all nations resembled that granted to the French in 1535.

This *nishan-i-sherif* and another dating from 1599 with the tughra of Sultan Muhammed III (Cotton MS Nero B. viii, ff.46–7) were taken from amongst the national records in the State Paper Office by the Jacobean politician and antiquary Sir Robert Cotton (1571–1631). His library became part of the British Museum when it was founded in the 1750s.

59

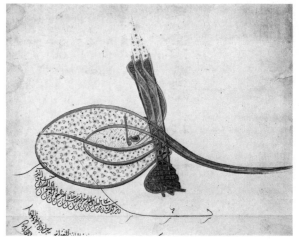

60 'The Reception of the Diplomatique and His Suite at the Court of Pekin', James Gillray. Published 14th September 1792 by H. Humphrey, 18 Old Bond Street, London

British Museum: Department of Prints and Drawings: 1868–8–8–6228

Spasmodic diplomatic contact between Europe and the Mongol rulers of China is recorded as early as the thirteenth century, but despite growing commercial links with Europe and the influence exerted by the many Jesuits who lived there in the late sixteenth and the seventeenth centuries, British diplomats first appeared at the imperial Court only in 1792. The Ambassador Extraordinary and Minister Plenipotentiary was George, Viscount Macartney (1737–1806), an ambitious and capable Irish-born colonial administrator, whose only previous diplomatic experience had been as Envoy Extraordinary at St Petersburg between 1764 and 1767. He was instructed to negotiate better trading conditions for British merchants, to secure redress for injuries done to them by the authorities, and to request the establishing of permanent diplomatic relations.

This cartoon appeared at the time of Macartney's departure from England and Gillray has done his malicious best to depict in advance the Ambassador's first audience. The Chinese Emperor reclines on a mattress on a low dais, with an ornate pagoda-like canopy above. He is waited upon by two impassive mandarins and a soldier in armour holding a sword. Smoking a long pipe, the Emperor contemptuously watches, out of his slit-like eyes, Lord Macartney, who kneels before him holding out a letter from George III signed 'GR' and counter-signed 'W.P. Sec'. (William Pitt, Secretary). The Ambassador is wearing the insignia of the Bath (164) and indicates, with his left hand, a number of presents which have been placed at the Emperor's feet. Five members of the British suite behind Macartney perform the kowtow, their heads touching the floor. Behind are others bringing presents. The Secretary to the Embassy, Sir George

60

J.G. design et fecit   *The Reception of the Diplomatique & his Suite, at the Court of Pekin,*   *Pub. Sep.* 14 *1792 by H.Humphrey, N.º 18 Old Bond Street.*

Staunton, stands full face behind the Ambassador, holding the string of a toy balloon decorated with the royal arms to which is attached a cockerel standing on a pair of breeches. Among the other gifts are a magpie in a wicker cage, a toy coach with driver, postillion, and six horses, a rocking horse, a volume of Boydell's edition of Shakespeare, a rat-trap, and bat and ball, a battledore and shuttlecock (on which is a crown), an oval miniature of George III, a toy windmill, a model of a British man-of-war, and a magic lantern.

Despite his grotesque depiction of the Chinese, much in Gillray's picture rings true. The portrait of Macartney was judged by contemporaries to be excellent, and, like most successful diplomats of the time, Macartney had been created a Knight of the Bath. The gifts satirise the presents that the Ambassador took with him as examples of British craftsmanship. They included two magnificent carriages (for summer and winter), fire arms, and mechanical toys. The miniature portrait was a standard diplomatic gift (**155**, **156**). An official letter from George III would be counter-signed, though by the Foreign Secretary and not by Pitt, who was First Lord of the Treasury. The kowtow was no exaggeration; and because Macartney and his suite performed the ceremony satisfactorily, they were well-treated, loaded with gifts and fêted by the Emperor. On his return to London in 1794 Macartney was created an Earl. In 1801 he became a Trustee of the British Museum and most of his manuscripts, including those relating to his mission to China, now form part of the collections of the British Library's Department of Manuscripts.

In one important respect, Macartney's success was more apparent than real, for the Chinese refused to allow a British or any other European diplomat to reside at their court, and continued in their refusal for the next seventy years. The British, French and other governments in their turn were reluctant to send special envoys to Peking through abhorrence for the kowtow. This the Chinese emperors insisted upon, regarding it as the symbolic acceptance by other powers of the Chinese claim to suzerainty over the world. After 1840 successive Superintendents of British Trade in China, based in Hong Kong from 1841, were given full powers to treat with China; but not until Peking had been occupied by 17,000 British and French troops and the Summer Palace had been burnt did the Chinese, by the terms of the Peking Conventions of October 1860, agree to allow foreign diplomats to reside in Peking.

61 Siamese envoys received by Louis XIV at Versailles, 14th January 1687

Additional MS 22494, f.2

Ambassadors from Oriental rulers began appearing on special missions at European courts in the earliest times, and, as communications improved, they were seen more frequently. Many were Europeans, like Robert Shirley (?1581–1628) who spent much time between 1608 and 1627 unsuccessfully attempting to persuade the leading European rulers, on the Persian Shah 'Abbas's (**55**) behalf, to ally against the Turks. Van Dyck's beautiful portraits of Shirley and his Circassian wife are to be seen in Petworth House in Sussex. On the rare occasions when the envoys were born subjects of the rulers who sent them, their appearance caused a sensation out of all proportion to the importance of their missions. Such was the case in 1686–7 when envoys from Siam (now Thailand) arrived in France to request French aid against the Dutch who were threatening to monopolise the foreign trade of their country. The visit was commemorated in pamphlets, poems, paintings, prints, tapestries, and medallions, and the envoys became objects of such curiosity to the Parisians that the King of France had to order his guards onto the streets to protect them. In the short-term, the Siamese were successful, French troops being sent to Bangkok. This provoked popular fury, however, and within a few months the Siamese King had lost his throne and the French had been expelled.

This miniature represents the first audience at Versailles. The three envoys in their national robes with high pointed hats are bowing to the King and presenting him with gifts. Louis, seated on an elaborate throne, seems to be beckoning them to approach. The design is almost identical to that of a contemporary medallion and it may have been copied from the medallion at some time after the elaborate frame had been completed, for this seems to have little connection with the subject of the picture. The Papal tiara flanked by two Habsburg Imperial crowns at the bottom are particularly curious since France was a sworn enemy of Habsburg claims and was on none-too-friendly terms with the Papacy. Moreover, during the course of the Siamese envoys' mission, Louis is recorded as having been particularly tolerant about their religion, saying that God expressed himself in different, equally valid, ways, like the differing greens of the leaves on a tree. The winged staffs with snakes entwined around them, the caducei of Mercury, messenger of the gods, are however traditional symbols of diplomacy and peace; the open books represent treaties (**131**, **132**, **133**) and among the items spilling from the horns of prosperity and plenty appear to be the chains of orders of chivalry and portrait miniatures, which were standard diplomatic rewards. Traces of the picture's former oval mount can be seen.

The depiction of the Siamese envoys in the relatively humiliating position of bowing to Louis XIV at their first audience, rather than as standing to deliver their introductory orations is significant. Despite Louis's tolerant words about their religion, assumptions of superiority underlay most of his and other Europeans' dealings with the non-European world. This was to have important repercussions for the world-wide development of resident diplomacy (**57**, **60**).

61

62 Four Sachems of the Iroquois Confederation take their leave of Queen Anne's Privy Council, early May 1710

Blenheim (Sunderland) Papers C I 26

For four weeks in April and May 1710, England played host to a Red Indian 'Emperor' and three 'Kings' who came, as ambassadors of the Iroquois Confederation, to pay their respects to their 'Great Queen' Anne, to urge the English ministry to join them in energetic action against the French in Canada and to send Protestant missionaries to them. This was most flattering and generally welcome to the English. A great fuss was made of the 'Kings' or Sachems (more properly chieftains), who stayed at the 'Two Cushions and Crowns' tavern, near Covent Garden, owned by the father of the composer Thomas Arne. The Queen formally received them and paid all their expenses as was customary with envoys from beyond western Europe (**11**), even though the Sachems were her self-confessed subjects. They were shown the sights of London, including Montagu House, later to become the first British Museum, which occupied part of the site of the present building, were taken

to the theatre to see *Macbeth* and departed from Plymouth laden with gifts similar to those that were to be sent to China with Lord Macartney in 1792. Behind them they left many of their artifacts, some of which, acquired by the British Museum's effective founder, Sir Hans Sloane, are now displayed in the Department of Ethnography's Museum of Mankind.

In this letter the Sachems take leave of the English Privy Council, promising to observe 'what is expected from their offering their belts of Wampam' (precious, specially treated dark purple or white shells, which normally acted as money, embroidered in meaningful patterns on strips of deerskin. They were used by the Iroquois tribes as formal records of transactions). The Sachems 'Henrique', the Christianised form of Te Yee Neen Ho Ga Prow, 'John' (Oh Nee Yeath Ton No Prow), 'Brant' (Sa Ga Yean Qua Prah Ton), and 'Etewn Caume' or Elow Oh Kaom (usually Christianised into 'Nicholas'), sign the letter using their totem, or clan, marks of the wolf, the bear, and the tortoise. The letter itself was written by one of the colonists accompanying the Sachems and was to be delivered by 'Queder' or Colonel Peter (hence 'Queder') Schuyler, a good friend of the Iroquois Confederation and a former acting Governor of New York.

The part played by the American colonists in the 'Kings'' visit was enormous, and they were the

62

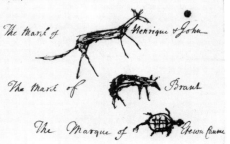

57

moving force behind it. They regarded it as a means of putting pressure for renewed action against the French in Canada on the generally unenthusiastic English ministry and of ensuring the loyalty of the Iroquois Confederation which had begun to see the advantages of playing a balancing rôle between the English and French. The Sachems, were, in fact, rather unimportant tribesmen except for 'Henrique', the so-called 'Emperor' and a great leader of the Mohawks. He was to die fighting for the British at the Battle of Lake George in 1755.

This letter comes from the papers of Charles Spencer, 3rd Earl of Sunderland (1675–1722) who was Secretary of State for the Southern Department in the first months of 1710.

Although resident European diplomats were to be found in Moscow and a few Asian courts by the early seventeenth century, it was only long afterwards that non-European resident envoys appeared in the West. In part this was due to the conscious isolationism of certain Eastern powers like China (60) or Japan. Others did not have the necessary administrative machinery or felt that the scant political and commercial rewards were out of proportion to the preliminary expense and difficulties. Even European powers like England would almost certainly not have maintained resident ambassadors in Constantinople before 1700 had other bodies, like the Levant Company, not met the expense (56).

63 Credentials of Vasili Timofeyeovich Posnikov, Russian Envoy Extraordinary to James II of England and VII of Scotland, 16th February 1687. From the Middleton Papers

Additional MS 41842, ff.171–172

These credentials, drawn up in the names of Tsars Ivan V and Peter I, are totally different in appearance from those normally employed by west European rulers (17, 100). The international status of Russia, or Muscovy as it was usually called before 1700, was to be changed under Peter. He moved his capital from Moscow to the Baltic city of St Petersburg (now Leningrad) which he founded, and in the course of his long war against Sweden, Russian armies penetrated into the heart of Germany. It became impossible for west European nations to act in an openly superior fashion towards Russia or to regard it as anything but part of Europe. The Treaty of Nystad (1721) confirmed Russia's position as a European power. In the following years it became customary for Russian envoys to reside at the principal European courts. Since 1733, Russian diplomatic representation in Great Britain has been permanent except in time of war. Although several English ambassadors resided in Moscow during the seventeenth century, being partially paid by the Muscovy Company, it was only after 1740 that British representation in Russia became continuous.

The first non-European power to be allowed to establish permanent diplomatic representation in western Europe, other than the United States and the South American republics, which were essentially European states beyond the Atlantic, was the Ottoman Empire which was formally admitted to the family of European nations under the terms of the Treaty of Paris of 1856 (44). China followed, under the Peking Conventions of 1860 (60), and by 1900 this right had been extended to all the non-European nations which had managed to avoid colonisation. Since then European diplomatic forms, privileges and rules have prevailed throughout the world.

The background to Posnikov's mission is described elsewhere (11).

II THE PRACTITIONERS

1. RECRUITMENT

In the period with which this survey is concerned, diplomats came from many different backgrounds but among the groups most heavily represented were churchmen (**64, 65**), lawyers (**70, 73**), merchants (**73**), writers (**72**), administrators (**71**) and soldiers (**68, 69**), whose work was most closely related to that of diplomats. Artists (**75, 76, 89**) were at times chosen because of their easy entrée to the rich and powerful, while several antiquaries (**74, 83, 84**) found diplomatic work a profitable side-line. Diplomats stemmed in large part from the aristocracy (**66, 67**) or the landed gentry (**64, 71, 72**), but able men of lesser birth were also able to make their way, if rarely to full ambassadorial rank (**70, 75, 76**). While envoys have been predominantly male, women played an active part long before they were able to do so in other fields (**77**). Until the eighteenth century diplomats were frequently not born subjects of the ruler or state they were serving (**73**). In the eighteenth and nineteenth century a high proportion of British diplomats were of Scottish or Irish origin (**74**). Most full ambassadors were wealthy and middle-aged, but there were exceptions (**64, 72, 74**).

64 Jean de Dinteville, and Georges de Selve ('The Ambassadors'). By Hans Holbein the Younger

Photograph by courtesy of the Trustees of The National Gallery, London

This famous canvas was commissioned to commemorate the visit in April 1533 of Georges de Selve, Bishop of Lavaux (1508/9–41) (right) to his friend Jean de Dinteville, Seigneur de Polisy and Bailly de Troyes (1504–55) (left), who was then in London negotiating a truce between England and Scotland on behalf of the King of France. The diplomatic background of both men accounts for the painting's traditional name.

The room is littered with objects. Though each has symbolic significance, like the distorted skull at the front traditionally serving as a reminder of the shortness of life, the items indicate the variety of the ambassadors' interests. Among the objects on the top of the stand against which de Dinteville and de Selve lean are a globe of the heavens, a portable cylindrical sundial, seeming to show the date of 11th April, and another polyhedral sundial. On the lower shelf there is a lute with a broken string, an open hymnal, with music to Luther's version of *Veni Creator Spiritus* and the Ten Commandments, a half-open book of arithmetic and a globe onto which Holbein has painted geographical features including the name of de Dinteville's home, Polisy, where this picture was to be seen until 1653. Half-hidden by the curtain at the top left-hand corner is a crucifix. Diplomatic theorists through the ages have always stressed the ambassador's need for versatility and would, no doubt, have applauded this display of it.

De Dinteville with the medal of the French Order of St Michael round his neck and his splendid clothes contrasts markedly with de Selve in his sombre, clerical attire. Yet it was de Selve who had the more distinguished diplomatic career, serving as French ambassador to the Emperor, Venice, and the Holy See, whereas de Dinteville served only in England, and without much success.

It was quite common before the Reformation for clerics to be diplomats. Ministers of a church to which all Europeans belonged, men of peace in a society which believed an ambassador's prime duty to be to maintain or bring about peace, experts in Canon Law which helped bind Christendom together and frequently high officers of state in their own countries, clerics like de Rosier (**12**) seemed in medieval eyes to be ideally qualified to act as ambassadors. It was only after the Reformation that this changed. Clerical envoys, like Dr Man (**28**), were more likely to cause wars than to promote peace because of their ardour for their particular creed. Later, as a result of increasing secularisation, fewer major national offices were held by clerics.

Callières was opposed to the appointment of priests as ambassadors on grounds of utility. They were not as acceptable as laymen in the many heretical or infidel courts where great powers wished to be represented in the eighteenth century, and Catholic prelates could not serve in Rome because of their divided loyalties. After 1700 clerics like John Robinson, Bishop of London and earlier of Bristol (**39, 40**), continued occasionally to be appointed as ambassadors but, by then, their clerical status played no part in their selection. Robinson (1650–1723), originally chaplain to successive British envoys in Stockholm from 1678 onwards, owed his diplomatic, ecclesiastical, and political promotions to his ability and industry and to the favour with which he was regarded by Charles XII of Sweden and by British ministries of differing political complexions.

64

65 Book of Hours written and illuminated in France and dated 1525

Additional MS 18854, ff.26v–27r

This prayerbook was commissioned in 1525 by Jean de Dinteville's uncle, François de Dinteville, Bishop of Auxerre from 1514 to 1530. Jean was probably familiar with this manuscript. He was close to his uncle in the 1520s, and his own scholarly and artistic tastes are well attested, not least by Holbein.

The decoration of the prayerbook is influenced by contemporary woodcuts and engravings and relies very much on clear and simple lines and primitive colours for its effect. The inscription noting the commissioning of the book, gold-lettered and in Latin, can be seen on the left-hand page. The elaborate frame opposite contains a depiction of the Annunciation. The arms underneath were added later and are those of René Hector, Abbot of St Jacques de Provins, in 1575, a later owner of the book. In the early nineteenth century it formed part of the library of William Beckford, the author of *Vathek*, at Fonthill Abbey.

François de Dinteville was sent as French ambassador to Rome at about the time that he commissioned this prayerbook, which conforms to the usage of Rome.

66 Thomas, second Earl of Arundel and Surrey (1586–1646), writes to his chaplain and agent William Petty. Nuremberg 17th/27th May, 1636

Additional MS 15970, f.26

In 1636 Charles I selected Thomas Howard, Earl of Arundel and Surrey (1586–1646) as his Ambassador for a special mission to Emperor Ferdinand II to urge the restoration to his German lands of the King's nephew Charles Louis, titular Elector Palatine. He was the son of the unfortunate Frederick, the 'Winter King' of Bohemia (1619–20), whose election as King had sparked off the Thirty Years' War.

Until well into the present century aristocrats were frequently used as ambassadors for the most prestigious missions. The selection of such well-born

and important figures implied particular respect for the rulers to whom they were sent. Such ambassadors could also be expected to play the rôle of courtier skilfully, with suitable attendant magnificence – and to meet the ensuing expenses, at least initially, from their own pockets. Most theorists before Callières agreed that these advantages far outweighed the ambassador's possible lack of expertise, which was in any case not necessary for most special missions, where ceremonial predominated.

Arundel came of one of the oldest English aristocratic families. Earl Marshal, he would also have been Duke of Norfolk, the premier non-royal English duke, but for an act of attainder passed against his grandfather. He was familiar with Catholic courts, having been a Catholic himself until 1615 when he conformed to Anglicanism. Since then he had been in frequent contact with Catholic rulers. He was probably the foremost English connoisseur of his time and a 'good' marriage had enabled him to purchase works of art and precious books throughout Europe. His appointment had a further advantage for the King, however. Charles had never got on well with Arundel and the mission gave him a chance to 'banish' him from court in an honourable way for a short period. Failure of the mission might also provide grounds for the Earl's permanent disgrace. Arundel himself was willing to go, for he was a personal friend of the Elector Palatine's family and he looked forward to further increasing his collections in the course of his mission. When he left London in April 1636 he was accompanied by an enormous and magnificently attired suite which included 'little honest Dr Hervey' (1578–1657), discoverer of the circulation of the blood.

The mission turned out to be frustrating and politically unsuccessful, the Emperor, whom Arundel met in Linz, refusing to allow the Elector to return to his lands on honourable terms. Initially the mission seemed likely to be a cultural failure too. On arriving in Nuremberg, Arundel gave vent to his gloom in this letter to his agent in Italy. He had found Germany 'a most myserable Countrye & nothinge by ye way to be bought of any moments, heere in this towne beinge not one Scrach of Alb: Duers (sic) paintinge in oyle to be sold, thought it were his Countrye, nor of Holbien (sic) nor any other great m^r'. The disappointment was all the more galling because he had heard that 'within thesee (sic) 3 or 4 yeeres great store of good things have bin carryed out at easy rates'.

However, in the end all was not lost. In the letter Arundel mentions he had 'one Hollarte wth me whoe drawes & eches Printes in strong water quickely & with a pretty spiritte'. 'Hollarte', whom the Earl brought back to England with him, was the Bohemian Wenceslas Hollar (1607–77), one of the most skilful and prolific engravers ever to work in this country. A few days after writing this letter, Arundel also managed to acquire a large part of the library of Dürer's friend, the renaissance humanist Willibald Pirckheimer (1470–1530), which included many precious classical manuscripts. This library and many of Arundel's other manuscripts now form part of the collections of the Department of Manuscripts.

This letter makes it clear where Arundel's main interest lay – his mission is hardly mentioned. It was the likely lack of diplomatic interest or expertise that led Callières, tactfully, to condemn the practice of selecting ambassadors on the basis of birth alone. He quoted the supposed saying of a Grand Duke of Tuscany apropos of such an ambassador, who had been sent to his court: 'We have fools in Florence, but we do not export them'. Usually rulers obviated the potential harm, however, by appointing lower-born experts as secretaries to accompany the ambassador and to undertake such negotiations as occurred. This was already the practice in medieval France and renaissance Italy and it had become general throughout Europe by the early eighteenth century.

67 Thomas Howard, second Earl of Arundel and Surrey. Engraved by Wenceslas Hollar from a portrait by Van Dyck, 1639

British Museum: Department of Prints and Drawings: p.1351

Arundel is seen in armour with the 'Lesser George', a pendant jewel, hanging from a ribbon around his neck. The 'Lesser George' was worn by Knights of the Garter as part of their everyday apparel.

Hollar's engraving gives a much better impression than the more famous portrait by Rubens in the National Gallery of the Earl's aristocratic haughtiness and reserve on which his contemporaries frequently commented.

68 Full Powers appointing Marlborough Britain's Ambassador at the Hague, Hampton Court, 27th June 1701

Blenheim Papers H. 9.

In this document, which is in the form of Royal Letters Patent, William III formally appoints John Churchill, Earl of Marlborough, his Ambassador Extraordinary, Commissary, Procurator, and Plenipotentiary ('Legatum Extraordinarium, Commissarium, Procuratorem et Plenipotentiarium' (line 8)) – usually abbreviated to Ambassador

ILLUSTRISSIMUS & EXCELLENTISSIMUS DOMINUS, THOMAS HOWARDUS,
Howardorum primus, Comes Arundeliæ et Surriæ primus Comes & Comes Marescallus Angliæ;
Baro Howard, Mowbray, Segrave, Brewes de Gower, Fitz-Alan, Clun, Oswaldestre Maltravers & Graystock
Iusticiarius omnium Forestarum Regis vltra Trentam: locum tenens Regis in Provincijs de Norfolcia
Sussexia Surria, Northumbria, Cumberlandia, & Westmerlandia, Nobilissimi Ordinis Garterij Eques: Sereniss
simi potentissimiq, Principis, Caroli, Magnæ Britaniæ Franciæ & Hiberniæ Regis, Fidei defensoris &c. in Ang
lia, Scotia, et Hibernia a secretioribus Concilijs, & ejusdem Regis Supremus & Generalis Militiæ Dux &c.

◄67

Extraordinary and Plenipotentiary – for negotiations at the Hague between the British and Dutch on the one side and the French and Spanish on the other. These were aimed at preserving peace in Europe despite the increase in international tension that had followed the bequest of Spain and its empire to the French King's grandson Philip, Duke of Anjou, by the dying Carlos II of Spain in the preceding year. William gives Marlborough 'full . . . power' ('omnem . . . Potestatem' line 9) to negotiate and, in his name, to conclude and sign any resulting agreement which William further promises to accept and ratify. The King's Latin signature can be seen at the foot of the document ('Gulielmus R.') The Full Powers are validated by the Great Seal of which a fragment remains. It shows the King in profile, on horseback, dressed as a Roman soldier and clasping a sword. The cord and tassels joining the seal to the document were originally red and gold. The document has the standard appearance and form of full powers drawn up in the Secretary of State's Office between about 1600 and 1850 (see **124** for the earlier more elaborate and Gothic-looking full powers drawn up by the officials of the Lord Chancellor's Department or Chancery).

The negotiations which Marlborough was to undertake by virtue of this document were embarked on out of deference to the belief of the age (**38**) that the possibilities for a peaceful settlement of disputes had to be exhausted before any war could justly be embarked upon. From before their start, these negotiations were not expected by the participants to be successful. Soon after Marlborough's arrival in the Netherlands they broke down and Marlborough never had to exchange these Full Powers (**125**). This is why they have remained with his papers and not in the Dutch, French, or Spanish national archives ever since. Little more than two months after the issue of these Full Powers, the Second Treaty of the Grand Alliance between Great Britain, the Dutch and the Emperor against the Bourbons of France and Spain was signed by Marlborough on William III's behalf by virtue of instructions issued at about the same time as these Full Powers. The War of the Spanish Succession then spread throughout Western Europe.

Marlborough (1650–1722) was first employed on a diplomatic mission in April 1678 when he was sent to the Prince of Orange (later William III) by Charles II. In 1685 he formally notified the French court of James II's accession and between 1702 and 1711 he was simultaneously engaged in diplomatic negotiations and waging war, normally in the Netherlands. In 1707, however, he went on an outstandingly successful special mission to the camp of Charles XII of Sweden at Altranstädt in Saxony.

Soldiers were frequently employed on diplomatic missions from the fifteenth century (**23**) to the nineteenth century (**51**). Marlborough continually employed his generals on official and semi-official missions as did his colleague in arms, Prince Eugène of Savoy (1663–1736), the Habsburgs' foremost soldier. The French kings, too, constantly used their marshals in diplomacy – generally with great success. Nevertheless Callières did not approve of this practice on the grounds that soldiers were not men of peace.

69 Medallic portrait of John Churchill, first Duke of Marlborough, 1704

British Museum: Department of Coins and Medals f1. + D. 496

Marlborough is depicted in his better-known rôle as warrior on this German medallion commemorating the Battle of Blenheim. It was executed in Nuremberg by Georg Hautsch, one of the most prolific South German medallists of the time. The inscription reads 10H. D. MARLEBURG. ANG. EXER. CAPIT. GENER. (John, Duke of Marlborough, Captain General of the English Army). Marlborough had been created a duke in 1702.

69

70 Portrait of Sir Thomas More, 1644

Additional MS 34812, f.16r

This unfamiliar portrait of Sir Thomas More (1478–1535), apparently wearing the collar of a royal counsellor, forms part of a seventeenth-century genealogical table of the Roper family into which More's favourite daughter, Margaret, married in 1521.

The inscription in the cartouche beneath is riddled with inaccuracies, and no doubt intentionally excludes all mention of More's opposition in his last years to Henry VIII's claims to supremacy over the English church and his own eventual execution. It does however mention correctly that 'he was . . . sent Embassador into ffrance, after into fflanders + performing all so well y^t he was much admired'. For it is not generally known that Thomas More was extremely active as a diplomat and must be the most distinguished English lawyer to have served as an ambassador. He was commissioned to undertake negotiations with foreign powers by Henry VIII at least a dozen times between 1515 and 1529, though he had his first experience of diplomacy as the representative of the Mercers' Company of London, in its negotiations with the Pensionary of Antwerp, as early as 1509. As an English commissioner and a loyal executor of Cardinal Wolsey's foreign policies, he negotiated with envoys of France, Charles V, and the German Hansa. He was present at the most magnificent diplomatic occasion of the sixteenth century, the meeting of Henry VIII and Francis I of France, at the Field of the Cloth of Gold in 1520, and among the treaties he negotiated and signed were those of Westminster of 1518 and 1527, both with France, both of them great, though transient, triumphs.

Undoubtedly More's legal training contributed to the development of that persuasiveness and skill in negotiation which was remarked on by those who negotiated with him. For despite his special effectiveness and eventual prominence, he was but one of the many lawyers, like de Puebla (24) or Grotius (37) who have been engaged in diplomacy. The explanation is probably partly historical and partly temperamental. Initially lawyers, like the procurators in Rome (20) and the protonotaries and notaries who drafted and attested treaties (130), did many of the jobs later done by accredited diplomats. Not surprisingly, therefore, in the sixteenth century, when diplomatic practice was in flux, lawyers seemed the obvious choice to undertake, with credentials, work that had long been done, at least in part, by lawyers. Even after the old usages had been forgotten and career diplomats had begun to appear, the knowledge of legal codes and precedents, and the experience of negotiation and of written and oral advocacy which fitted a lawyer for his profession also provided him with many of the qualities that theorists have required of would-be diplomats – and a penchant for diplomacy often accompanied a penchant for law.

By the early eighteenth century, however, Callières was dismissing professional lawyers (as opposed to gentlemen with some training in law) as too narrow, rigid, and pedantic for a profession like diplomacy where flexibility was at a premium, and modern writers on diplomacy, such as Sir Harold Nicolson, have tended to agree with this.

See 125 for a letter signed by Sir Thomas More during the course of one of his diplomatic missions.

70

71

71 A contemporary caricature of Diego Sarmiento de Acuña, Count of Gondomar, from Thomas Middleton, *A Game at Chess*, London (1625?). Frontispiece

Department of Printed Books c.34, d.38

Diego Sarmiento de Acuña, Count of Gondomar (1567–1626) served as Philip III of Spain's ambassador to James I in 1613–18 and again between 1620 and 1622. He became one of the best known but most hated envoys of the time. Throughout his mission he strove to prevent Great Britain from intervening on the Protestant side in European conflicts. He succeeded largely because he was able to win the friendship of James – the two men had several shared interests, particularly in literature, but Gondomar was also a skilled courtier. After 1618 he increased his influence with the King by holding out the chimera of a glittering dynastic match, between the Prince of Wales and a Spanish princess which he insisted would be endangered if James offended Philip in any way. All the while Gondomar managed to keep the Spanish court well informed of all that was happening in England, not least because many prominent English leaders, including the King and Queen themselves, were in receipt of pensions from him. As a representative of the Spanish monarch he was also outstanding. His insistence on being treated at all times as the envoy of the leading Christian king helped to conceal the rapid decline in Spanish power that was taking place, and at one crucial point in 1618 he succeeded in driving his frustrated rival, the French Ambassador, out of England (**146**). Gondomar's career, in Garrett Mattingly's opinion, 'illustrates the potential of the resident ambassador at its highest'.

It did, however, render him an object of the greatest suspicion and fear to Protestant Englishmen outside the court. The Gunpowder Plot of 1605 was still a recent memory and they regarded the proposed 'Spanish Marriage' as a Spanish plot to achieve peacefully Guy Fawkes's objects of subverting the Kingdom and restoring Catholicism. Gondomar was credited with fiendish aims and methods. His spies were believed to be everywhere and he was thought to be planning a Spanish invasion of England. This reputation lingered on after his departure and was utilised by Thomas Middleton in his strange patriotic satire on Spanish diplomacy, *A Game at Chess*, which was first performed, at Shakespeare's former theatre, *The Globe*, in 1624. Gondomar, in the guise of the 'Black Knight' in this frontispiece to an early edition of the play, is seen conspiratorially handing a letter from the Pope to the 'Fatte Bishop' *alias* Marco Antonio de Dominis (1566–1624), a Catholic renegade and former Archbishop of Spalatro (now Split in Yugoslavia). In 1622 Dominis had returned to Catholicism and left England with Gondomar's assistance. Their conspiracy is however being foiled by the 'White Knight', or George Villiers, Duke of Buckingham, the royal favourite who was then – briefly – in good odour with the public following the final failure of the Spanish Marriage project in 1623 and his own consequent publicly expressed hostility to Spain. In the picture above, 'The Black House' (Spain) is seen playing chess with 'The White House' (England). The significance of two men in a tub in the lower engraving is unclear. Gondomar's features are accurately portrayed. The frontispiece illustrates well the strong suspicion of Spain and of Catholics which lingered on after the sixteenth century and could only have been further inflamed when, shortly after the first performances, *A Game at Chess* was banned by the authorities.

Gondomar came of a prosperous but non-aristocratic family of administrators. He himself was only created Count of Gondomar, after the name of his birth-place, in 1617, and before coming to England he had made his name as a courtier, soldier and administrator. It was from this class and from people with this type of background that most seventeenth- and eighteenth-century career diplomats were recruited.

72 Despatch from Philip Sidney to the Earl of Leicester, Heidelberg, 3rd May 1577

Cotton MS Galba, B.xi ff.330–331

In early 1577 the poet and soldier Philip Sidney (1534–86) was sent by Elizabeth I on a special mission of condolence and congratulation to the young Emperor Rudolf II, whose father had recently died, in Prague.

In this autograph despatch he describes his audiences with the new Emperor, his mother and his brothers and sister, the recently widowed Queen of France. He then answers 'suche perticularities as I receaved in my instructions as of the 1 Emperours disposicion and his brethren 2 By whose Advice he is directed 3 When it is lykely he shall marry 4 What princes in Germany are most effected to him 5 In w^t state he is left for revenews 6 w^t good agreement there is betwixte him and his brethren 7 and what partage they have in these thinges'.

These were typical of the questions that rulers expected their special envoys to answer. Sidney gives interesting descriptions of the 'extremely Spaniolated' Imperial brothers. Rudolf II (**98**) was 'holy by his inclination givne to the warres. Few of wordes, sullein of disposition, very secret and resolute. Nothing the manner his father had in

72

Shakespeare's play *The Tempest* appeared in the year following Rudolf's death. In 1577, however, this was far in the future. Sidney returned to England in June having visited Heidelberg to congratulate the new Elector Palatine, Louis, on his accession in the Queen's name, and Dordrecht where he met William The Silent, Prince of Orange and leader of the Dutch revolt against Spain. It was generally felt Sidney had acquitted himself well, and Francis Walsingham wrote to Philip's father that 'there hath not been any gentlemen . . . these many years that hath gone through so honourable a charge with as great commendations as he'.

Philip Sidney undoubtedly owed his appointment as Elizabeth's envoy to the influence of his uncle, the Earl of Leicester, the Queen's favourite of long standing. But diplomacy has been distinguished by the number of poets and other literary figures who have been recruited to its ranks, including Chartier, the secretary of Charles VII of France in the fifteenth century, Andrew Marvell, Chateaubriand (143) and in our own day Lawrence Durrell and the Greek writer George Seferis. Indeed it is men of letters whom Callières recommends as pre-eminently suitable for the diplomatic life. But then as a member of the *Académie Française* his bias is hardly surprising.

73 J. Russell: *Propositio ad Karolum ducem Burgundiae* **(printed by Caxton probably in 1477). Formerly in the library of the Earls of Leicester at Holkham**
Department of Printed Books: 1A 55011 (De Ricci 90:2)

Early in 1470 Dr John Russell, Garter King of Arms, was sent to Ghent as one of the special English ambassadors, to invest Charles the Bold, Duke of Burgundy, the husband of Edward IV's sister Margaret, with the Order of the Garter. The investiture took place amidst magnificent pageantry on 4th February. While handing over the insignia, which included a golden Garter made by the London goldsmith John Broome, Russell delivered this laudatory oration. It was printed by William Caxton, probably in Westminster early in 1477.

Caxton as well as Russell served as a diplomat. Russell was a doctor in civil law and a churchman who eventually rose to be Lord Chancellor (1483) and Bishop of Rochester (1476–80) and Lincoln (1480–94). He was thus a natural candidate for selection as an ambassador. In 1470 he was sent on this mission of ceremony because he was the appropriate herald, but his later missions to Scotland (1474 and 1486) and Brittany in 1486 (23) had political significance.

Caxton owed his selection as an English envoy for several commercial negotiations between England

winning men in his behavior but yet constant in keeping them. And such a one as thoughe he promise not much outwardly hath as the latines say *Aliquid in Recessu*.' Matthias and Maximilian (10), two of his younger brothers, were 'franke of themselves to the lyking of this Countrey people especially Maximilian who seemes in deede to promise some great worthyness'. Much of this description was to prove inaccurate, but nothing was so wide of the mark as his answer to the sixth and seventh points. 'The brethren', Sidney writes, 'do agree very well . . . (they) will be contented with Pensions'. Ultimately the younger brothers turned against the Emperor in Prague who, like Prospero in *The Tempest*, had increasingly withdrawn from the world and closeted himself in his castle with his art treasures, and his court of alchemists, astrologers and astronomers like Kepler and Tycho Brahe. Maximilian took the Tirol and Matthias seized Hungary and eventually Austria and Bohemia. Rudolf was on the verge of losing his Imperial crown itself when he died in 1612. The bitterness of the conflict gave rise to a famous German drama, *Brüderzwist im Hause Habsburg*, by Grillparzer.

and Burgundy and the Hansa Merchants in the 1460s to his experience as a merchant and his position as Governor of the English Nation in Bruges – roughly the equivalent of the earliest Venetian Bailos in Constantinople (13). In the Middle Ages it was by no means unusual for merchants to be involved as envoys in commercial negotiations, because of their detailed knowledge, and merchants and bankers often acted as unofficial resident envoys before 1500 (see numbers 21 and 132). Even as late as the seventeenth century the English Levant Company occasionally succeeded in getting merchants appointed as English ambassadors in Constantinople. But by then merchants were generally regarded as too humble to fill such exalted positions, and they were relegated to the consular service. This often played a vital rôle particularly outside Europe and in wartime, but until very recently it was kept quite separate from and treated as distinctly inferior to the 'mainstream' diplomatic services of European states.

Latin orations were rarely copied or printed for circulation in England, but the custom was widespread in Italy. Indeed the influence of renaissance Italy is to be seen not only in the text of this oration but also in the description of Russell as orator ('oratoris'), the contemporary Italian term for envoy which had been unknown to du Rosier (12), as well as ambassador ('ambassiatoris').

74 Private letter of Sir William Hamilton to the British Foreign Secretary, Lord Grenville, Caserta, 6th January 1796. From the Dropmore (Grenville) Papers

Additional MS, 59031, ff.190–191

Sir William Hamilton (1730–1803), famous as the complaisant husband of Nelson's mistress, Lady Hamilton, and as a leading participant in the early excavations at Herculaneum and Pompeii, served as Britain's Envoy Extraordinary and (1767) Plenipotentiary in Naples and Sicily between 1764 and 1800. It was for these services that he was created a Knight of the Bath in 1772, the year his first collection of Greek vases was purchased for the British Museum.

This letter was written after Hamilton had suffered 'several attacks of a bilious complaint some of which have been attended with danger'. Fearing that would-be successors, who had tried to bribe him to retire, had turned to the Foreign Secretary 'as with my consent', he begs Grenville 'to pay not the least attention to them as I shall . . . whenever I feel that age and infirmities begin to render me incapable of serving His Majesty at this Court as I cou'd wish . . . give the first notice thereof to your Lordship'. But

that 'thank God is by no means the case at the moment'. Four years later, however, Hamilton's continued bad health led to his resignation.

An echo of the increasingly 'professional' ethos of the time is contained in the reason given by Hamilton – who was always short of money – for his refusal of the 'considerable annuity' that had been privately offered him in addition to a possible royal pension: 'this kind of jobbing I have ever looked upon as highly indecent and injurious to His Majesty'.

As an antiquarian and collector, Hamilton was typical of several diplomats and consuls, such as his contemporaries Sir Horace Mann (1701–86), Horace Walpole's correspondent and Britain's representative in Florence for forty-eight years after 1738 and Joseph Smith (1682–1770), Britain's consul in Venice (1740–60), from whom George III acquired many books that form an important part of the British Library's King's Library and many paintings which are still in the royal collection. In the next century, Charles, Lord Stuart de Rothesay (1779–1845), an ardent bibliophile, in the course of a long career served as British representative in Portugal (1810–14 and 1825), the Netherlands (1815), France (1815–24, 1824 and 1828–30), and Russia (1841–4). A Book of Hours written by Bartolemeo Sanvito and illuminated by Giulio Clovio, which was once in his possession, is now British Library Additional MS 20297. Few other occupations could enable connoisseurs to be paid to reside in countries they loved and give them privileges and a standing which facilitated their collecting. Their governments usually benefited too from having as envoys men who were thoroughly acquainted with the courts where they resided and were often on very friendly terms with men of importance.

As a Scot Hamilton was also typical of many eighteenth-century British diplomats. For after the Union of England and Scotland in 1707 diplomatic posts were a means by which Scotsmen could be given office and eventual reward, and the Scots as a whole conciliated, without unduly offending English susceptibilities – out of sight, out of mind. As a result, in 1770, Scotsmen represented George III in Vienna (Stormont, 105), Prussia (Mitchell, 113), Russia (Cathcart, 137), Poland (Keith, 105, 106), Naples (Hamilton), and Brussels (Gordon). It was for similar reasons that Anglo-Irish and Scottish diplomats were to be found in the less prestigious missions outside Europe in the nineteenth century.

75 A political letter written by Rubens, Antwerp, 29th June 1628

Additional MS 33964, ff.224–225

The painter Peter Paul Rubens (1577–1640) was repeatedly employed on diplomatic missions: by the Duke of Mantua in 1603 and, in the 1620s and early 1630s, by the Infanta-Archduchess Isabella, Regent of the Spanish Netherlands and later by her nephew Philip IV of Spain. Rubens made a good envoy. He had a natural interest in international affairs, he became a skilled courtier and his artistic ability gave him easy access to the kings, princes, and statesmen of the day.

This autograph letter in Italian and Latin demonstrates Rubens's grasp of international affairs. It was written to an un-named correspondent, probably in Paris at a time when French royalist forces were besieging La Rochelle in the hope of reducing that defiant Protestant town, which with English support had been acting almost as a state within a state, to obedience to Louis XIII and Cardinal Richelieu. Spain and France were then in uneasy alliance but for three years Rubens had been striving in vain to reconcile Spain and Great Britain.

Rubens says he already considers La Rochelle completely lost ('perduta senza remedio') let the English do what they might – and he hears that Charles I and the Duke of Buckingham have been in Portsmouth supervising preparations for the despatch of a fleet. He notes that the English anger at the Spaniards has considerably cooled, perhaps because there is much talk of a war with France, and because of the advantages England gains from the Spanish trade. He had found the Earl of Carlisle ('il Conte Carlil') [James Hay, Earl of Carlisle c.1580–1637, a leading English diplomat with whom Rubens had had secret discussions in the previous month] as usual, more pro-French than pro-Spanish ('piu francese di Spagniolo'), but extremely angry with Richelieu ('picchato sopra modo contra illos aut illum potius qui nunc penes vos rerum potitur'). Changing the subject Rubens mentions a new canal being constructed from Antwerp which would keep the Dutch, who were at war with Spain, at a distance. Ruminating on the incredible profits made by trading companies, like the Levant Company (56) he prophesies that they will eventually make themselves masters of the other hemisphere. Apropos of this Rubens adds that a great land, not to say a new world ('novum orbem'), has been discovered beyond the tropics, towards the South ('ultra Tropicum versus Austrum'). It will be an epoch-making event, but as yet there are no details as to how it was discovered or the nature of the land.

Many of Rubens's prophesies were fulfilled. The English fleet that set sail from Portsmouth in September, following Buckingham's assassination in August, was unable to save La Rochelle, which surrendered in October. The Earl of Carlisle's letters reveal that at this time he was furious at Richelieu and by November he was urging an alliance with Spain against France. The Dutch never succeeded in taking Antwerp after 1628, but their trading companies, and those of England did come to dominate the East Indies (now Indonesia) and India respectively. And Australia did exist even if its official date of discovery was delayed.

One year after this letter was written, Rubens was engaged in negotiations in London, on the Spanish King's behalf, for the restoration of diplomatic relations and the exchange of ambassadors between England and Spain. His mission was successful and he commemorated it in his great painting 'Peace and War' which is now in the National Gallery. He left London with a knighthood in March 1630. The peace treaty between England and Spain was signed in London eight months later.

75

76 Miniature of Charles I as Prince of Wales by Balthazar Gerbier, 1616

Victoria and Albert Museum: P.47–1935

Balthazar Gerbier (?1591–1667), the artist of this miniature portrait of the sixteen-year-old Prince of Wales, was a friend of his fellow artist and Netherlander, Rubens. In 1629, during his mission to London, the great artist stayed at his home in Bethnal Green. As a gesture of gratitude and friendship Rubens painted a portrait of Gerbier and his family and – making use of the children closest to hand – Gerbier's little sons and daughters appear as cherubs in Rubens's painting 'Peace and War'.

Gerbier, an artist, architect, courtier, propagandist, projector, and diplomat, was born in the Netherlands of French Protestant stock. His skill as a draughtsman and military architect brought him to the notice of the Dutch leader, Prince Maurice of Orange-Nassau, who recommended him to the Dutch Ambassador in London, Noel de Caron. In 1616 he came over to England with the Ambassador, but soon found himself employment with the royal favourite George Villiers, later to be created Duke of Buckingham. Gerbier served Buckingham in a number of ways. He purchased works of art for him and, when necessary, provided them himself. He also helped to design some of Buckingham's houses, including York House near Charing Cross, of which he was appointed Keeper. He gradually won the Duke's confidence to the extent that he accompanied the Duke and the Prince of Wales to Madrid in 1623 and painted a miniature of the Infanta, whom Charles was courting, for transmission to James I. By this time Gerbier was undertaking confidential diplomatic missions on Buckingham's behalf, and he first came into close diplomatic contact with Rubens in Paris in 1625. At the time Rubens was executing a series of paintings commissioned by the French King's mother, Marie de' Medici, while Buckingham was in Paris to act as Charles's proxy at his marriage to Princess Henrietta Maria of France. Rubens spoke to the Duke of the advantages of a peace with Spain and two years later, in response to further feelers, Buckingham sent Gerbier to conduct secret negotiations with Rubens while the two men were ostensibly engaged on a tour of Dutch towns in search of works of art. Nothing came of the negotiations, but the artists remained close friends.

After Buckingham's assassination, Gerbier passed into the service of Charles I who knighted him in 1628. From 1631 to 1641 he acted as the King's official diplomatic agent in Brussels. He was none too faithful and was known to have betrayed certain official secrets to the Infanta-Archduchess Isabella, but without immediate detriment to his career. For

in 1641 he was appointed Master of Ceremonies to Charles I. The remaining years of his life were, however, difficult. Justifiably mistrusted by Royalists and Parliamentarians alike because of his unreliability and equivocal conduct, he was forced to rely on his skills as an architect in England and abroad in order to survive. Yet he seems to have remained hopeful of a change and from the 1640s until his death in England in 1667, a steady flow of self-justificatory pamphlets and grandiose colonial and financial schemes aimed at English, French, and Dutch audiences emanated from his pen.

It should be noted that Gerbier's foreign origins did not prevent him from serving as a fully accredited British diplomat between 1631 and 1641. Indeed, despite growing popular resentment, foreigners continued to act as British representatives abroad until well into the eighteenth century – and sometimes they occupied important posts such as Paris or Vienna. In Russia the practice of employing foreigners survived into the 1820s when the Greek-born Count Capo d'Istria served as Tsar Alexander I's Foreign Minister and occasional special ambassador. For until the rise of nationalism at the turn of the eighteenth and nineteenth centuries an ambassador's place of origin was considered of minor relevance to his selection if his master was convinced of his personal loyalty and native ability.

76

77 Catherine of Aragon as Spanish Ambassador in England writes to her father Ferdinand of Aragon, Greenwich, 17th July 1507

Egerton MS. 616, ff. 32–33

Many women played an active rôle in diplomacy long before the legal emancipation of their sex in Europe this century. While female rulers, influential queens-consort, dowagers and mistresses (121, 150) spring to mind in this connection, there were a few ladies who served as properly accredited ambassadors. One of the most notable was Catherine of Aragon during her time as widow of Arthur, Prince of Wales.

Arthur's death in 1504 robbed her of the settled and prosperous future she had been expecting. Her father Ferdinand of Aragon and Henry VII soon reached a vague understanding that she should marry Arthur's younger brother Henry, but neither king was ready to allow the marriage to take place without considerable haggling over the size of the dowry and at least a show of looking for alternative brides and bridegrooms. The negotiations were further complicated by the widowerhood of the two kings and the widowhood and unstable temperament of Catherine's sister, Juana, the lawful Queen of Castile, in 1506, which left a kingdom looking for a master. Ferdinand was remarried by 1505, but continued looking for a husband for Juana, and Henry for a wife for himself, who would serve their dynastic interests. As their attention switched from England to Castile, Catherine, a mere pawn in the negotiations, was neglected by both rulers. By 1507 her marriage to Henry was no nearer and she had been reduced to penury. Ignorant of the true state of the negotiations, she naively blamed Ferdinand's resident ambassador Dr de Puebla (24) for her pitiable condition. After accusing him of indifference, idleness, dishonesty, venality, incapacity, and treachery in repeated letters to her father, she finally asked Ferdinand to send a special ambassador to England. Ferdinand replied by sending his daughter formal credentials as his ambassador, a special cipher for her correspondence, background information containing his reasons for delaying the payment of her dowry, and official instructions to convey these to King Henry and make what use she could of him!

In this autograph despatch, Catherine informs Ferdinand that she has handed her credentials and cipher to Henry, who was well satisfied with both. The King, she writes, is busily preparing to send an ambassador to Spain to negotiate his marriage to Juana but she has heard that the French King is trying to arrange a match between Juana and his nephew (and Ferdinand's new brother-in-law), Gaston de Foix. She asks her father, therefore, to use all his diligence to ensure that the marriage of Juana and Henry VII takes place. Catherine signs the letter as Princess of Wales.

Catherine's diplomacy was to prove unsuccessful and it was only Henry VIII's chivalry on his father's death that led to their marriage in 1509. Yet her period as an ambassador did open her eyes to the ways of the world and taught her how to negotiate. Her knowledge of both proved to be assets when she acted as her husband's deputy during his absences in France in the following years, and, much later, during the years of the divorce.

One of the notable female diplomats of the next century was Charles I's youngest daughter Henrietta Anne, Duchess of Orleans (1644–70) who, as Louis XIV's representative, negotiated the secret Anglo-French Treaty of Dover with her brother, Charles II, in May 1670. Though the twentieth century has seen a gradual increase in the number of female diplomats, the upper echelons of the diplomatic world remain overwhelmingly male.

2. 'THE PROFESSIONALS'

In the course of the nineteenth century the first true professional practitioners of diplomacy are found. Metternich (**78, 80**), Talleyrand (**79, 80**), and Palmerston (**81, 82**) are among the best known, but Palmerston had no experience as an envoy and Talleyrand relatively little. They all had a very human side to their characters.

78

78 Sketch by Metternich and the Marquis de Caraman, Verona, November 1822. From the Lieven Papers
Additional MS 47274, f.10

This sketch of a man and a dog in front of two trees was drawn in a bored moment during the Congress of Verona by the French and Austrian plenipotentiaries the Marquis (later created Duc) de Caraman (1762–1839) and Prince Metternich who transmitted it to the Russian Ambassador in London, Prince Lieven (1774–1857).

As Austria's Foreign Minister, Clemens Wenzel Nepomuk Lothar, Count and later Prince von Metternich-Winneburg (1773–1859) directed the foreign policy of Austria and its allies and thus effectively controlled the destiny of most of central and southern Europe from the fall of Napoleon until the revolutions of 1848 which swept him from power. Before becoming Foreign Minister in 1809, he attended an academy for diplomats in Strasbourg and served as Austrian envoy in Dresden (1801), Berlin (1803) and Paris (1805). In the following years he represented the Court of Vienna at most of the major international gatherings.

Metternich had wide interests outside the fields of politics and diplomacy and was a skilled amateur artist whose works are represented in several European collections of prints and drawings.

79 Engraving of Talleyrand as an old man, with a reproduction of his signature
Additional MS 40690, f.56

Charles Maurice de Talleyrand-Périgord (1754–1838) is perhaps one of the best-known diplomats in history, though he spent only a short period as an envoy. He was born into an aristocratic family and trained for the church, becoming Bishop of Autun in 1788. In the following years, however, he sided with the revolutionaries and rejected his background and career. He was first employed on a diplomatic mission in 1792 when he was sent to London in an unsuccessful attempt to conciliate the British government. The Terror drove him into exile in England and the United States but in 1797, a year after his return to France, he was made Foreign Secretary by the Directory. Despite occasional differences and periods in disgrace, he played a major part in consolidating the power of Napoleon Bonaparte. After 1805 he was largely responsible for breaking up the British-led European-wide coalition against France and for creating the Napoleonic 'new order' in Europe. For these services Napoleon created him Prince of Benevento, a town in Southern Italy. In the following years the differences between the two men grew, culminating in Talleyrand's opposition to the French invasion of Russia in 1811 which proved disastrous to Napoleon. In 1814 he deserted Napoleon and the Allies foisted their valuable new recruit on the Bourbon Court-in-exile as Foreign Minister. Louis XVIII rid himself of Talleyrand's services as soon as was decently possible after the Restoration, but not before Talleyrand had enabled France to have a say in the creation of the post-Napoleonic European settlement at the Congress of Vienna (41). After the revolution of 1830, which brought the liberal-minded Louis-Philippe, Duc d'Orléans, to the French throne in place of his distant cousin the legitimate but ultra-conservative King Charles X, Talleyrand served as France's Ambassador in London until his retirement in 1834.

This engraving gives a splendid impression of the old survivor, whose skill was acknowledged by even his worst enemies. It also contains more than a hint of the cynic, the gambler, and the lecher. Talleyrand's presumed illegitimate son and grandson the Comte de Flahault (1785–1870) and the Duc de Morny (1811–65) inherited a fair share of their sire's ability and served Louis-Philippe and Napoleon III in Vienna, London, and St Petersburg.

79

80 Letter from Metternich to Talleyrand, Mannheim, 26th June 1815. From the Morrison Collection of autograph letters and historical documents
Additional MS 39757. ff.37–8

This letter was written just after Metternich had heard the news of the second and final abdication of the Emperor Napoleon I following his defeat at Waterloo.

Despite the Allies' military success and the realisation of their main objective ('le grand but de la guerre paroît atteint'), the Austrian Foreign Minister confides to his French colleague ('mon cher Prince') that he is worried about the future. *He* was convinced that a man proclaimed French King by foreigners in France would never reign peacefully ('J'ai si fort la conviction que le Roi proclamé en France par les étrangers ne regnera jamais tranquilement') unless by a policy of moderation and conciliation ('sage conduite . . . conde-scendences justement exprimées') he won over the French ('gagne les esprits') so that the majority willingly submitted to his rule ('la majorité . . . *prononce le voeu d'être gouverné par lui*'). Yet, Metternich hints, he fears an extreme royalist reaction ('la force de quelques préjugés'). Knowing from their many previous conversations that Talleyrand shared these views, and stressing his

own wish for peace and the withdrawal of Allied troops from France ('Nous devons tous rentrer chez nous, & cette coalition est la dernière), Metternich begs the French Minister to do what he could to help the common cause ('la cause commune') and to keep him informed of all he does. For himself, Metternich promises to do his best to steer the ship of state well over seas that were becoming rougher as cross-winds appeared.

This autograph letter shows that Metternich was not the unthinking reactionary of popular imagination, and gives a good impression of the persuasive charm and – at least early – perspicacity on which contemporaries remarked. Talleyrand and the French King Louis XVIII shared his conviction that moderation was necessary following the Bourbon Restoration but they were unable to curb the royalist 'White Terror' that, as Metternich had predicted, broke out in France a short while after this letter had been written.

81 Juvenile notebook of Lord Palmerston containing rough sketches of boxers
Additional MS 59853. ff.25v–26r

Henry John Temple, third Viscount Palmerston (1784–1865), came of an Anglo-Irish family whose members had been active as diplomats since the seventeenth century (103, 168). He first became involved in foreign affairs as a Lord of the Admiralty in the Duke of Portland's ministry in 1808, the same year in which he spoke in Parliament in defence of diplomatic secrecy. He served as Secretary at War continuously from 1808 to 1828 under successive Prime Ministers. As Foreign Secretary (1830–4;

1835–41; 1846–51) and Prime Minister (1855–8; 1859–65) he came almost to personify Britain abroad, but he never represented Britain diplomatically at any point in his career.

An early indication of his famous pugnacity can be seen in these doodles which he scribbled into his mathematics book, opposite notes on logarithms, while at Harrow School in about 1800.

82 'Now for it! A set-to between Pam, the Downing Street Pet, and the Russian Spider'. Cartoon by Leech, February 1855. By permission of the Proprietors of 'Punch'

'Punch' 17th February 1855

This cartoon shows Palmerston as he appeared to many of his British contemporaries. It was published shortly after he had become Prime Minister for the first time, his predecessor, the Earl of Aberdeen, having resigned when confronted with Parliament's demand for a full enquiry into the inefficiency and apparent indolence which had marred his ministry's conduct of the Crimean War since its outbreak in the previous year.

Palmerston was expected to prosecute the war more energetically. Leech portrays him as a prize fighter, with Mr Punch as his second. His features are depicted quite realistically, unlike those of his opponent, Tsar Nicholas I of Russia, who resembles Humpty-Dumpty and has every reason to look worried since he is obviously no match. Prussia had caused considerable irritation in London through its stubborn policy of neutrality and so its monarch King Frederick William IV is naturally, if unfairly, portrayed as the Tsar's none-too-sober second. To make the cartoon's message quite clear the British lion, sitting above the other spectators with its arms crossed, looks confidently towards 'Pam', as Palmerston was popularly known. By the middle of the next year the Tsar had indeed died and the Crimean War had come to a satisfactory conclusion for Britain (44).

Yet, splendid though Palmerston appeared, and fitting though his pugnacity was to a country at the very height of its power, he can hardly be placed in the same class as a diplomat as Metternich, Talleyrand, or even Castlereagh. For as Callières stressed, the duty of a diplomat and the prime test of his success was the harmonisation of conflicting interests.

NOW FOR IT!

A Set-to between "Pam, the Downing Street Pet," and "The Russian Spider."

February 17, 1855.]

[Punch. No. 710.

3. ON THE FRINGES

Strange characters have lurked on the fringes of diplomacy, particularly in more recent times. For regular foreign ministers and officially accredited diplomats have tended to lack the flexibility to undertake the intrigue and the spying that are sometimes necessary but which have come to be regarded as dishonourable. The field has therefore, perforce, been left open for shadowy, ambiguous, or amoral characters who could, if necessary, be easily disavowed, such as Philip von Stosch *alias* 'John Walton' (**83**, **84**), the Chevalier, *alias* the Chevalière d'Eon (**85**, **86**) or – today – 'James Bond'.

83

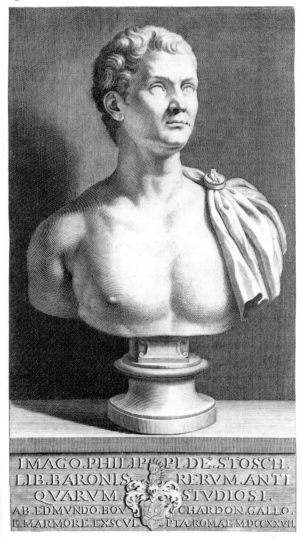

IMAGO.PHILIPPI.DE.STOSCH. LIB.BARONIS. RERVM.ANTI QVARVM. STVDIOSI. AB.EDMVNDO.BOV CHARDON.GALLO. E.MARMORE.EXSCVL PTA.ROMAE.MDCCXXVII.

83 Portrait of Baron Philip von Stosch, *c.*1727. **Formerly pasted into P. von Stosch,** *Gemmae Antiquae Caelatae* **(Amsterdam, 1724)**
Department of Printed Books: 682 k.9

Baron Philip von Stosch (1691–1757) was one of the many fascinating characters on the fringes of eighteenth-century European diplomacy. A German Protestant by birth and by inclination an antiquary and connoisseur, he aspired to be a scholar. He spent his earlier years travelling around Europe, making the acquaintance of leading scholars and several of the more prominent statesmen of his day. After 1721 he settled in Rome where he worked as a collector and dealer specialising in ancient coins and engraved gems. He soon became very friendly with the cardinals and aristocracy who resided in the city. In 1724 a large volume of fine engravings of ancient engraved gems from European collections was published in Amsterdam under the title *Gemmae Antiquae Caelatae* (Ancient Engraved Gems). It was dedicated to the Emperor Charles VI who, in return, presented the Baron with his portrait and a gold chain. The book established Stosch as an expert in that field. In 1731, after years of growing tension, culminating in an attack on his coach, he was expelled from Rome by the Papal authorities. The rest of his life was spent in Florence.

This engraving of a bust by Bouchardon dating from 1727 was drawn in Rome by Johann Justinian Preisler (or Preissler) and engraved in Nuremberg by Georg Martin Preisler, who executed many of the engravings in the *Gemmae Antiquae Caelatae*.

This is, no doubt, the way in which the Baron wished to be regarded by his contemporaries. There was, however, a very different side to the picture. Stosch was an intriguer, and, in the judgement of many, a spendthrift bisexual atheist, blasphemer, liar, and thief, who was not above swallowing gems as a means of gaining illegal possession of them. In addition to this and his eccentric life style, he was for over thirty years a British spy under the name of 'John Walton'.

84 Letter of 'John Walton' to the Duke of Newcastle, British Secretary of State for the Southern Department, Rome, 22nd September 1725
Public Record Office: S.P. 85/15 ff.438–439

Stosch kept several British ministries informed of the activities of James Edward Stuart, the 'Old Pretender', son of James II and Stuart claimant to the British thrones from 1701 until his death in 1766. For after the failure of the uprising of 1715, the Old Pretender had been compelled to reside in Rome with which Britain had had no official diplomatic links since 1688. Stosch was an excellent choice as an undercover agent. He was well connected, his antiquarian interests provided a convincing 'front', at least initially, and he had some diplomatic experience, having been employed on diplomatic missions by the Dutch, the Saxons, and possibly the Austrian Habsburgs. In late 1721 he was instructed to reside in Rome and to report to the Secretaries of State on the doings of the Stuarts, their adherents, and any English travellers. In return he was to receive £400 – which was soon increased to £520 – a year. It was a very reasonable and even generous sum for those days.

This letter is representative of those he sent from Rome. It contains news of the movements of the Pretender's supporters, of the rumoured pregnancy of his wife (their second son Henry, the last royal Stuart, who died in 1807, was born the next year), of the education of their older son Charles ('Bonnie Prince Charlie') and of an interview with Philip V of Spain's former minister, Cardinal Giulio Alberoni. Most of the letters report happenings in the Papal Court. At the close Stosch turns to his own affairs. Melodramatically proclaiming 'mon argent est fini' ('I have no more money') and that he has not enough to survive on, let alone to pay his 'emissaires', his best channels for procuring news of the activities of the King's enemies, he demands to be paid or recalled. The British, he complains, had taken advantage of his political beliefs ('per-suasions') at a very uncertain period, to drag him from his library against his will and send him to Rome where for more than four years, at the risk of his life, he has performed the functions of a disgraced sentry ('sentinelle perdue') rather than a diplomatic minister. But now he has been reduced to such straits that he has not got enough money either to live in Rome or to leave it.

These grumbles are to be found in most spies' letters before 1900, but at least in 1725 Stosch was still giving relatively good value for money in terms of the 'hard' news he transmitted to London. After his expulsion from Rome this ceased to be the case. Despite the network of spies whom he claimed to have in his employ his weekly letters from Florence rapidly degenerated into a dull journal of the Pretender's activities culled increasingly from the public gazettes. He was still spasmodically paid for his 'services' even after 1745 when the activities of the Jacobites ceased to be of great concern to British ministers. Yet, on his death in 1757, his collections had to be dispersed to meet the mountainous debts he left behind him. Part of his collection of sulphur casts of antique gems is now in the Scottish National Portrait Gallery in Edinburgh.

85 Engraving of the 'Chevalière d'Eon' executed, possibly from a portrait miniature, by J. Condé, London, c.1790

Additional MS 34277, f.1

The engraving shows the Chevalier d'Eon dressed as a woman and wearing the Cross of the Order of St Louis. It had been bestowed on d'Eon in 1763 when he brought from London the British ratification of the Treaty of Paris which ended the Seven Years War. The engraving was inserted into one of his schoolbooks, dating from 1745, in the course of the nineteenth century.

Charles-Geneviève-Louis-Auguste-André-Timothé Eon de Beaumont (1728–1810) was one of the strangest characters ever to appear on the diplomatic stage. The son of a noble but impoverished French provincial administrator, and a lawyer by training, his good looks, skill as a fencer and brilliance as a wit and writer came early to the notice of the French court at Versailles. In 1755 Louis XV, without consulting his ministers, sent him on a secret mission to Russia to deliver offers of alliance to the Tsarina Elizabeth, who since her accession in 1741 had been implacably hostile to France. D'Eon's mission was successful, and it was agreed to restore diplomatic relations, but, reputedly, d'Eon only gained the Tsarina's confidence after he had disguised himself as a woman and taken the name Mademoiselle Lia de

85

Beaumont. In 1757 he returned to Russia, a Secretary of Embassy, and over the next two years played an important part in negotiating a formal Franco-Prussian alliance. For these services he was made a Captain of Dragoons and given a pension by the French King. He distinguished himself as a soldier in the Seven Years War and in 1762 went to London as Secretary of Embassy, first to the Duc de Nivernais and then to the Comte de Guerchy. All the while he continued to be employed as Louis XV's personal agent. This led to difficulties, when de Guerchy demanded custody of the embassy's accounts and secret archives which, with Louis XV's tacit support, d'Eon refused to surrender. The ensuing controversy was conducted in public through pamphlets and the law courts. Victory was finally d'Eon's, but from 1767 he ceased to be Secretary of Embassy, though remaining in England as Louis XV's secret agent. In 1774, however, the King died and his successor demanded d'Eon's papers.

It was now that d'Eon openly adopted female attire. The reason for this is unclear. When rumours about his supposedly female sex had begun circulating a few years earlier, he had indignantly denied them. In 1774 or 1775, however, he might have regarded the adoption of woman's dress as a means of courting publicity and putting pressure on the French King to meet the price he demanded for his papers. For, as was often the case in the course of his career, d'Eon was in desperate need of money and he feared bankruptcy and anonymity following Louis XV's death.

In the short term he was successful and by the terms of an agreement negotiated by the playwright Beaumarchais, d'Eon received a large sum of money for his papers from the King. It was, however, stipulated that in return d'Eon should officially renounce his male status and permanently adopt female attire. D'Eon's last years were particularly hard. Deprived of his royal pension following the French Revolution, he was forced to earn his living as a touring female fencer and fencing teacher. After being seriously wounded in 1796, he had to depend on charity and even then spent five months in a debtors' gaol in 1804. His true sex was finally established only after his death. He is buried in the grounds surrounding Old St Pancras Church, near King's Cross Station in London.

D'Eon was the model for Chérubin in Beaumarchais's play *The Marriage of Figaro* which formed the basis for the famous Mozart opera.

Many rulers and statesmen in addition to Louis XV have pursued foreign policies distinct from and often contradictory to the 'official' policy of their foreign ministries. The agents recruited have tended to be far more disreputable and less able than d'Eon.

His career does indeed illustrate the dilemmas and difficulties frequently caused by such agents' divided loyalties.

86 Letter of the 'Chevalière d'Eon' to the Comte de Maurepas, Versailles, 8th February 1779
Egerton MS 1049, ff.21–23

D'Eon soon tired of female dress, and in 1778 he applied to the Comte de Maurepas, the French Prime Minister, for permission to serve with the French forces in the War of American Independence. His request was refused, but he was led to believe that a further application would be favourably considered after he had spent another year as a woman with a respectable family near Versailles.

In this letter he renews his request, asking to serve

86

in the French fleet under Comte d'Orvilliers, since French troops were not then engaged in a land war. Referring to himself throughout in the French female form, he writes that his 'noviciate' has passed, but that it is impossible for him to take professional 'vows' as a woman on the grounds of expense. Despite his royal pension, his debts in France and England, where he still has his apartments and library, are crushing. After providing for his mother and his sister's family there is not enough left even to make habitable the family château in Burgundy and so he needs the additional income to be gained from active service. Moreover, the enforced lack of exercise was proving disastrous to someone who had always been active – it is ruining his physique, depressing his spirits and, in short, will kill him ('le repos me tue totalement'). His position is making him a butt for public malice and rightly so. While he could, if ordered, wear skirts in peacetime, this is impossible in wartime. Recalling his long years of courageous military and political service on behalf of Louis XV, he begs to be allowed to continue serving his King and Country, and says he is ready to promise in writing to behave himself in the future. For, as he sadly concludes, the stupidest of all rôles is that of a maid at court when he could again be acting as a lion in the army. ('Le plus sot des rôles à jouer est celui de Pucelle à la Cour tandis que je puis jouer encore celui de Lion à l'Armée'.)

Maurepas, according to an annotation, probably in his hand, spoke to the Foreign Minister, Vergennes, about d'Eon's request, but to no effect. Worse was to follow. Later that year the Chevalier was unjustly accused of being a British spy and was imprisoned in the Old Castle of Dijon. He was released after a month, only to be banished for a further six years to his family's château at Tonnerre in Burgundy.

4. DIPLOMATS IN OTHER FIELDS
Diplomats have on the whole been a highly versatile group of people and have produced an impressive number of theorists (87), historians (88, 91), playwrights (92), poets (93) and even a few artists (89).

87 Letter of Abraham de Wicquefort to Constantijn Huygens, Paris, 9th December 1651
Egerton MS 2195 f.5

This letter was written following the unexpected death of the young William II, Prince of Orange, in 1650, when the Orange-Nassau family were trying to ensure the smooth succession to the Principality of Orange, a French fief, of his posthumous son William Henry, the future William III of England. The negotiations in Paris were complicated by a dispute over the guardianship of the young Prince between his mother Mary, the English Princess Royal, who was supported by France, and his grandmother Amalia, widow of Prince Frederick Henry (d.1647), and his uncle Frederick-William, Elector of Brandenburg, the husband of William II's eldest sister.

Wicquefort, then the resident in Paris of the Dutch Republic and of Brandenburg, soon found himself involved. In this letter to Princess Amalia's adviser, the famous Dutch poet, painter, statesman, and diplomat Constantijn Huygens (**158**) he reports the opinion of the French official in charge of the case that it would be best to let matters rest for the moment and revive them at a later, more propitious date. Amalia and the Princess Royal's recent show of good manners towards one another had not been sufficient to erase the bad impression created by their mutual distrust. Wicquefort suggests that some 'recognition' ('recognoissance') be given to his agent in the affair, and asks Huygens to support his own interests at court.

Many of the most important theorists of diplomacy had diplomatic experience (**12**, **26**, **37**, **53**), but to none was this of greater significance for his writings than to Abraham de Wicquefort (1606–82). The obvious abilities of Wicquefort, who came of a good Dutch regent family, led him to be employed as a diplomatic agent by the Dutch Republic, and Brandenburg, Poland, Cardinal Mazarin of France, and the Duke of Brunswick-Lüneburg-Celle. However, although energetic, industrious, perspicacious and intelligent, he lacked money and prudence. The result was disastrous. In 1659 he had been imprisoned in the Bastille, in spite of his diplomatic status, for passing official secrets to a foreign power. Yet in 1676, when resident of Brunswick-Lüneburg-Celle in the Dutch Republic and Secretary to the Estates of Holland, he had abused his privileged position to do the same once again. This time, despite his vociferous claims to diplomatic immunity, he was sentenced to imprisonment for life, the Dutch authorities arguing that no national, employed in his homeland by a foreign power, could enjoy diplomatic protection.

From his prison cell Wicquefort continued the battle, under the pseudonym L.M.P. ('Le Ministre Prisonnier'), in his *Mémoires touchant les Ambassadeurs et les Ministres Publics* (published in Cologne, 1676–9). The book immediately made its mark as did its successor *L'Ambassadeur et Ses Fonctions* (published in 1681) which he wrote following his escape from prison in 1679 in Celle. As might be expected the two works grant the ambassador and his suite far greater privileges in the execution of their duties than previous writers had conceded. Not surprisingly, too, they also emphasise Wicquefort's belief, born of experience, that, in the words of his English translator 'an Ambassador is not better formed in the College than in the Shop'. And with those sentiments most theorist-practitioners other than Callières, the founder in 1712 of the French school for diplomats, seem to have agreed.

88 P. de Comines *Croniques du Roy Charles huytiesme de Ce nō. . . coⁿtenāt la verité des faictz et gestes dignes de memoire dudict seigneur.* **Enguillebert de Marnef, Paris, 1528**
Department of Printed Books: 1319, i.13

The 'Chronicles of the reign of Charles VIII . . . containing the truth of the events and actions worthy of the memory of the said lord' form the second part of the *Memoires* of Philippe de Comines (**22**). He wrote the first part, which deals with the years 1464–83 and 1489–91, at the behest of Angelo Catone, Bishop of Vienne. The second part, covering the French expedition to Naples (1494–5) with a few pages on the death of Charles VIII and accession of Louis XII in 1498, was begun in 1495 and finished in October 1498. Comines was a participant in many of the events he describes and knew most of the protagonists. Yet unlike most other fifteenth-century chronicles, the *Memoires* are remarkable for their detachment, their analytical treatment of the events described, and the virtual absence of moral judgements. This has led its author to be compared to his Italian contemporary Machiavelli.

Many retired diplomats have become historians of their times, if only to earn money and to justify their own actions to posterity.

89 Medallic portrait of the diplomat and artist Michael Mercator executed by himself, 1539
British Museum: Department of Coins and Medals: M. 6793

This silver medallion shows Michael Mercator in profile. He is wearing a cap and a fur cloak and bears a chain around his neck. The legend reads: A REGE ANGLORUM PRIMI MILITIS CREATI EX VENLO EFFIGIES (Portrait of the first Knight from Venloo created by the King of the English). The reverse contains the engraved inscription: MICHAEL. MERCATOR. ÆTATIS SVÆ XLVIII. GRATIA. DEO ET REGI. M.D.XXXIX (Michael Mercator at the age of 48. Thanks be to God and the King. 1539).

Michael Mercator (1490/1–1544) came of one of the leading families in the town of Venloo in the Netherlands, which then formed part of the Duchy of Guelders. From 1527 to 1541 he was active as a musical instrument maker and as a diplomat in the service of Henry VIII and Floris of Egmont, Count of Buren and Lord of Ysselstein. He went on several secret diplomatic missions and was well rewarded for them, particularly in early 1539 when Henry VIII granted him an augmentation to his arms, consisting of a part of the English royal arms, and knighted him. This medallion commemorates the occasion. Mercator seems to have used 'Laus (Praise

...) or 'Gratia (Thanks ...) Deo et Regi' as his personal motto.

The credentials drawn up for him by the Count of Buren on 15th October 1538, and addressed to Henry VIII's Secretary, Thomas Cromwell, (British Library Cotton MS Galba.B. x. 86) speak glowingly of Mercator's abilities as an artist and a maker of musical instruments, and the British Museum possesses a handsome uniface portrait plaque of Henry VIII that was probably executed by him in 1528 (*Medallic Illustrations of the History of Great Britain and Ireland* vol. I p. 31 no. 18). Mercator died in Venloo to which he had retired in 1541.

Several diplomats have been skilled artists (**75, 76, 78**).

90 S. von Herberstein, *Moscoviter Wunderbare Historien ... Erstlich ... zu Latein beschriben: Jetz zu malen aber ... durch H. Pantaleon ... verteütschet und in truck verfertiget* (**'Wonderful Stories of the Muscovites first written in Latin but now translated into German and prepared for the press by H. Pantaleon'**) *N. Brillinger und M. Russinger, Basel, 1563*
Department of Printed Books: 9455. h.3

Sigmund von Herberstein's book *Rerum Moscoviticarum Commentarii* ('Notes upon Muscovy') was first published in Vienna in 1549. It was an immediate success and by 1589 it had undergone eighteen different editions and had been translated into Italian, English and German. The German edition that found most favour was not Herberstein's own rather sober translation of 1557 (*Moscovia der Haupstat in Reissen* – 'Muscovy the Chief State in Russia'), but this translation by the Basle historian and doctor, Heinrich Pantaleon.

The book satisfied popular curiosity about Russia which had been growing since the Grand Duchy of Muscovy had shaken off its vassalage to the Tatars in the late fourteenth century. In contrast to its brief and rather fanciful predecessors, written by former envoys or travellers who had had little contact with Russians outside the court and who did not understand Russian, Herberstein's account was based on discussions with Russians of all classes, on his study of original Russian sources and also his own personal experience of Muscovy gained in the course of his missions to Grand Duke Vasili III in 1517 and 1518, and 1526 to 1527. *Moscovia* is also far more wide-ranging than any previous work, covering the geography, history, religion, social structure, customs, constitution, and economy, not only of Muscovy but also of its neighbours such as the Tatars, the Lithuanians and the other Baltic peoples, and the whole of Scandinavia. Furthermore

89

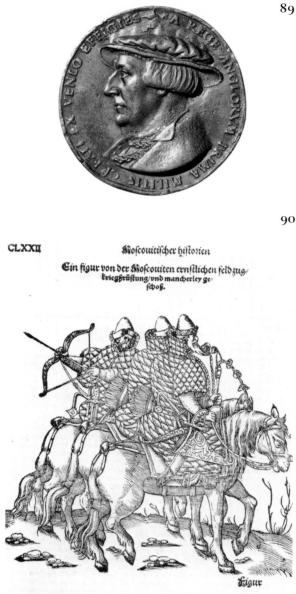

90

it is well illustrated, with realistic maps, views and pictures by Augustin Hirschvogel, Hans Sebald Lautensack, and others. The pictures include engravings of mounted Muscovite noblemen and archers in quilted clothing and with side arms, saddlery, and bridles showing strong Tatar influence, and there is one illustration of Russians travelling by horse-sledge and ski-ing – surely one of the earliest depictions of skiers. A recent study, by Bertold Picard, concluded that Herberstein's *Moscovia* 'fashioned European posterity's image of Russia for several centuries'.

Herberstein (1486–1566) became familiar with the Slavonic languages in the Wippach district (now Vipava in Yugoslavia) where he was born. He was given a good humanistic education and attended

Vienna University before studying law. After a period of military service, for which he was knighted, he entered the service of the Emperor Maximilian and then of his younger grandson, Charles V's brother, the Archduke Infante Ferdinand, later to become King of Hungary and Bohemia and eventually Holy Roman Emperor. Between 1515 and 1533 he went on no less than fifty-four special diplomatic missions, above all to Hungary, Bohemia, Poland, and Muscovy, where his knowledge of Slavonic languages was of particular value. Herberstein went on most of the later missions unwillingly since – as was long to be the case – he did not regard himself as a professional diplomat but as a Councillor ('Kammerrat') responsible for the administration of the finances of the province of Lower Austria in which Vienna was situated. Indeed he continued in this post for nine years after his last diplomatic mission.

He is nevertheless an early example of the many diplomats who made use of their experiences to write scholarly books when approaching or actually in retirement.

91

91 Portrait of Sigmund, Freiherr von Herberstein, in Turkish dress, 1559. From: *Gratiae posteritati Sigismundus Liber Baro in Herberstain . . . actiones, suas a puero ad annum usque aetatis suae septuagesimum quartum, brevi commentariolo notatas reliquit* (**'Brief annotated commentary on the actions of Herberstein from boyhood until his seventy-fourth year'**) *R. Hofhalter: Vienna*, 1560. **From the Grenville Library**
Department of Printed Books: G. 7215

This portrait of Herberstein in old age is taken from an extra-illustrated copy of his short autobiography completed in 1558. It shows him wearing the splendid Turkish robes presented by the Sultan whom he visited at his headquarters near Budapest, as one of King Ferdinand's special envoys, in 1541. The painting on the right is the original from which the engraving on the left was taken. The name of the artist is unknown.

In addition to *Rerum Moscoviticarum Commentarii*, and its German translation, Herberstein wrote two autobiographies and a history of his family.

92 Letter of Sir George Etherege to the Earl of Middleton, Regensburg, 31st January/10th February 1686/7. From the Middleton Papers
Additional MS 41836, ff.232–3

Sir George Etherege (?1635–92) was a Restoration rake and playwright, best known for his play, *The Man of Mode; or Sir Fopling Flutter*, of 1676. Insofar as he had any profession it was that of diplomat. Between 1668 and 1671 he served as secretary to Charles II's Ambassador in Constantinople, Sir Daniel Harvey, and in 1685 he was sent as James II's Resident to Regensburg, the seat of the German Imperial Diet (Parliament). His mission was probably a ploy to enable him to escape from his gambling debts and it seems that very little was expected of him – except perhaps that he use his leisure to write another play.

Nevertheless he apparently went out with the zeal of a reformed character, determined to prove himself worthy of his employ. His enthusiasm speedily waned. Little occurred worth reporting in his twice- or thrice-weekly despatches to the Secretary of State and he was soon completely bored. Moreover the excessive formality of the envoys of the German states made him feel his inferiority as a mere Resident – one of the lowest diplomatic grades – and his rumbustious character had difficulty in finding an outlet. As he put it in a private verse letter to Middleton, a former boon-companion in London, 'From hunting whores and haunting Play/And minding nothing else all Day/And all the Night too, committed 'an Indiscretion at play' (gambling), laying the blame for such stories on 'idle(r)s' – probably meaning his puritanical secretary, Hugo Hughes.

Etherege's situation improved gradually. He finally found himself a suitable mistress ('Meeting with one, by chance, Kind-hearted/Who no Preliminaries started/I enter'd beyond Expectation/Into a Close Negotiation . . . I was pleas'd with what she gave'). He began to take such pleasure in writing good despatches that he even made enquiries about serving James II in Berlin. By June 1688, when he paid for three days of lavish celebrations to commemorate the birth of a son – later to be known as the 'Old Pretender' – to the King, he had even won the respect of the German envoys. Soon after January 1689, however, he left Regensburg to follow his master into exile in France, where he died, apparently impoverished, three years later.

He wrote no more plays.

93 St-John Perse (Alexis Léger) *Anabasis* Translated by T.S. Eliot (London 1930)
Department of Printed Books

Marie René Auguste Alexis Saint-Léger Léger (1887–1975) was born on the West Indian island of St Léger des Feuilles near Guadeloupe. After an adventurous youth spent travelling in the Far East, he joined the French Ministry of Foreign Affairs in 1904. Secretary-General of the Ministry in 1933, he struggled in vain later in the decade to stiffen the resistance of the Prime Minister, Daladier, and the Foreign Minister, Bonnet, his political masters, to the aggressive policies of Hitler and Mussolini. Dismissed in 1940, he fled to the United States where he became an adviser to Roosevelt on French affairs. The Vichy Government deprived him of his French citizenship, which was restored in 1945.

Under the pen-name of Saint-John Perse, Léger was one of the leading poets of his generation. His best known work is probably *Anabase*, which appeared in 1924 and was translated into German by Hugo von Hofmannsthal and into English by T.S. Eliot. Eliot, who regarded the poem as 'a piece of writing of the same importance as the later work of Mr James Joyce', described it as 'a series of images of migration, of conquest of vast spaces in Asiatic wastes, of destruction and foundation of cities and civilisations of any races or epochs of the ancient East'.

Although Léger's writings were burned by the Vichy Government, he was awarded the Nobel Prize for Literature in 1960.

For other diplomat-poets, see **72**.

92

you will say' in London, he had been reduced in Regensburg to 'converse with Fools and write dull Letters/To go to Bed twixt Eight and Nine/And sleep away my precious Time/In such a sneaking idle Place/Where Vice and Folly hide their Face . . . For Pleasure here has the same Fate/which does attend Affairs of State/The Plague of Ceremony infects/Even in love the softer sex/Who . . . Rather than lose the least Respect . . . (send) to know before/At what a Clock she'll play the whore . . . This seems to me a scurvy Fashion/Which have been bred in a free Nation'.

In this official letter to Middleton, written after a year in Regensburg, he confesses that 'All the news I have to send you by this post is that there is none'. He recounts how he has been defending James II's good name against Dutch slanders and reports a letter from a friend in Vienna containing news of growing German and Habsburg opposition to exorbitant French demands. Towards the close he shows signs that at least some of his efforts at self-reform were succeeding. He proudly reports that 'tho' I have but little money left I owe nothing in the Empire' and he indignantly denies having

III THE MISSION

1. SELECTION AND APPOINTMENT

The process of recruiting ambassadors has generally been informal until the final stages. The prevailing considerations were for centuries the candidate's acceptability to those sending and receiving him and his ability to meet the cost of representing his master worthily. This meant that good birth, political acceptability and wealth were at a premium, with diplomatic experience being of less importance (94). The latter could generally be supplied by the secretary. Because many diplomatic postings were of minor political importance, seemingly eccentric factors have been involved. Not infrequently there was a desire to send into a form of honourable exile a well-known national figure who was unpopular with the ruler or ruling group, be it the madcap Earl of Peterborough in the reigns of Queen Anne and George I, or Alexander Dubcek who was sent as Ambassador to Turkey shortly after losing his position as First Secretary of the Czechoslovak Communist Party in 1969. For the same reason, the choice of an ambassador has at times been made not by the head of state or government but by the secretary of state or even – as in Sunderland's case (94), where the intention was to flatter potentially valuable allies – by someone outside the government. The selection of a candidate, however, was likely to prove only the start of a process which could last for months. Ambassadorships were rarely accepted with alacrity. There was considerable preliminary bargaining, and many a candidate refused to accept appointment (95) unless given firm assurances of eventual reward, be it high political office or a profitable sinecure at home. William Stanhope always regarded his diplomatic career as a path to a peerage (see W. Stanhope to L. Schaub, Madrid 29th July 1721, Additional MS 4204 ff.55–6) and in 1729 he refused to return to Madrid as Ambassador until he was created a baron, as Lord Harrington. His obstinacy was exceptional. His aspirations were not.

94 Letter of Charles Montagu, Lord Halifax, to Sarah, Duchess of Marlborough, 15th May 1707 (O.S.)

Blenheim Papers (Papers of Sarah, Duchess of Marlborough) E.36

For much of the War of the Spanish Succession, large numbers of German troops were tied down in Hungary, attempting to suppress a widespread revolt led by Magyar nobles and gentry against their kings, the Austrian Habsburg Emperors. In order to free these forces for action against the Bourbons, the British leaders mediated between the Habsburgs and their rebellious Hungarian subjects. The early efforts of Queen Anne's envoy in Vienna, George Stepney (47, 167) were unavailing, his partiality for the rebels, many of them Protestant, succeeding only in alienating most of the Viennese ministers. By December 1704 Godolphin, the Lord Treasurer, and Marlborough (68, 69) had decided that a special envoy would have to be sent. Godolphin wished to appoint a leading Whig, since his ministry was becoming increasingly dependent on Whig support in Parliament and such a move would be a conciliatory gesture towards them. However, the likely expense and difficulty of the mission and the absence of suitable rewards in terms of titles or the prospect of high office deterred all the candidates originally approached. On 11th May 1705, news of the death of Emperor Leopold I reached London and Godolphin decided that the mediation should be combined with a special mission of condolence to the new Emperor, Joseph I. This made it considerably more attractive. It would be shorter, less expensive and more prestigious, and the possible failure of the mediation could be disguised. The post was filled within a few days.

This letter tells how on the 13th May Godolphin visited Lord Halifax, one of the Whig leaders, and 'spoke to me of sending some Man of Quality to Vienna, in such a manner as if He would have Us [i.e. the Whig leaders] propose somebody to be employ'd in that [mission of] compliment. I was not prepared to offer one and that discourse fell. I have since thought that if there was a disposition to make Ld Sunderland, secretary [of state], the employing Him on such an Embassy for three or four months might properly introduce him into the method of busnesse. The Queen would be better acquainted with Him and He would *soften by degrees*' (Charles, third Earl of Sunderland (1675–1722) was notorious for his tactlessness and extreme Whig views which, to the Queen's horror, had earlier verged on atheism and republicanism). 'If the Emperor ever makes peace with the Hungarians it will be done at his first entrance on the Government and it would give great Reputation to the English Minister that was then employed. The mourning would make his Equipage lesse expensive, the Relation He has to your Grace [Sunderland was her son-in-law] would make the [Emperor's] Present [for Sunderland] more valuable and extraordinary allowances on such occasions have been generally made . . . Your Grace can best determine whether such a short excursion would bring him quicker into the Secretary's office and I would form my judgement by that. The ramble would not be unpleasant . . . and the commission would be profitable if the prize was certain.'

Within ten days of this meeting, Queen Anne had agreed to appoint Sunderland on the terms outlined by Halifax. At the close of 1706, a year after his return from Vienna, the Earl was appointed Secretary of State for the Southern Department.

This letter gives a good impression of the way in which many ambassadors were recruited in Europe during the eighteenth and nineteenth centuries, of the principal factors – birth ('quality'), political and family connections and wealth – involved in their selection and of the considerations and inducements that led candidates to accept appointment.

95 Andrea Piccolomini to the Priori of Siena, Pienza, 26th November 1481

Additional MS 16163 f.15

Andrea Nanni-Todeschini-Piccolomini belonged to one of the leading families of Siena, and was the nephew of Pope Pius II. He was therefore an obvious choice to represent the Republic at other courts. In this letter from his family's home near Siena, he thanks those who have done him the honour of selecting him as ambassador to the King of Naples. Necessity, however, reluctantly forces him to disobey. For certain undisclosed obstacles ('impedimenti') have been placed in his way by the party of the Cardinal – Archbishop of Siena (Andrea's brother, Francesco) and they prevent him from leaving Pienza under any pretext. He asks the Priori to choose a new ambassador by whom, he is sure, they will be better served.

The post of ambassador was rarely accepted with alacrity. Apart from the cost, and the irregular payment, the separation from one's near and dear and the discomfort to be expected en route to or from one's destination, an embassy also involved absence from court, and thus from chances of promotion. As Ralph Winwood, then James I's ambassador in the Hague, asked in a letter to a colleague in 1606, 'who would live exiled from his country in a place of continual care and toil without present profit or hope of future preferment?' As early as 1271, the Venetians threatened with a heavy fine any citizen refusing to undertake an embassy, and Florentine ordinances of 1421 stipulated that any ambassador who was not 'prompt and obedient' in leaving for his post could be deprived of his civic rights. But even those statutes do not seem to have deterred malingerers.

2. PREPARATION AND DEPARTURE

Before the last century, several months often passed between an envoy's selection and his departure. Count Conrad von Starhemberg, the Emperor Charles VI's Envoy Extraordinary and Minister Plenipotentiary to George I, was ordered at the beginning of 1721 to leave for London, but only finally left at the end of August 1722. This was exceptional, but even the most eager diplomatic representative could not leave at once. The appointment of his staff and household, which was often large (108) took time, particularly if his choice of secretary had to be ratified by the monarch or the secretary of state (104). There was often much haggling over salary and expenses and the allotment of ceremonial plate for the ambassadorial table (102). The would-be ambassador was expected to learn as much as he could of the political and social background of the court for which he was intended. He therefore had to read through all the recent correspondence from there and to contact the relevant envoy at his own court and any compatriots who had worked or had close connections with the country. Moreover he normally got into correspondence with the man he was to replace, so as to learn still more and to prepare for his own arrival (105). In the meanwhile his instructions (97, 98), additional instructions, and secret instructions (99), were being prepared and he often had the chance to have them clarified or altered before they were put into their final form. When suite, equipment and documents were ready the ambassador normally had a formal leave-taking audience with his master (107) where he 'kissed hands' on receiving his official letter of appointment (96); and was also presented with his credentials (100), other introductory letters, his passport (101), instructions, and papers such as his cipher table (103) and, when appropriate, full powers (123). The consequent departure could be a personal wrench (106).

The ambassador's journey was often lengthy and could involve subsidiary missions to courts en route (97).

Increased administrative efficiency (see Part I Section 6) and improved communications have since 1800 shortened the period between an envoy's selection and his departure, but the essential procedures remain the same.

96 Ambassador's letter of appointment signed by James I, 2nd July 1619. From the Aston Papers
Additional MS 36444 f.1

James I officially informs Sir Walter Aston, a Gentleman of the Privy Chamber, of his 'intention . . . so soone as those businesses which have hitherto been treated in Spaine . . . shall . . . be settled to send you thither as *our* Amb*assadour* to reside in that Court'. He orders him to '*p*repare and dispose of *y*ourself, and *y*our businesse accordingly. And for that we are resolved shortly to send the Lord Digbie into Spayne againe as *our* Amb*assadour* Extra-ordinarie wee think it fitt, that you accompanie him thither, both for that wee shall give him charge so to communicate *our* businesse unto you as may the better enable you for your future service as likewise for that when wee shall see it fitt wee shall send you thither *our* L*ett*ers of Credence with such farther instructions as shalbe necessarie for you.'

Formal letters of appointment signed by the monarch were the final stage in the process of selecting ambassadors. They were usually plain in appearance, being officially intended for the ambassador's eyes alone. The form and wording were standardised, and essentially consisted of formal greetings to the recipient, some expression of his worthiness for his new employment, mention of his destination and, briefly, of the purpose of his mission, and orders to prepare himself for departure. The ruler's signature authenticated the

96

appointment of which the recipient had already been informally told and to which he had agreed. This letter is somewhat unusual in not being countersigned by a Secretary of State (**153**).

Sir Walter Aston (1584–1639) left for Spain in 1620 and remained in Madrid until 1625. His relations with John, Lord Digby, later created Earl of Bristol, were uneasy, but the friendship that developed between himself and the Prince of Wales, who came to Madrid to woo the Infanta Maria, in 1623 (**71**), more than compensated for this. In 1627, the Prince, now Charles I, created him Baron Aston of Forfar, and he served as ambassador in Spain again between 1635 and 1638. The expense of these embassies considerably reduced the fortune of £10,000 which he had inherited from his father, one of the richest men in Elizabethan England.

97 The Earl of Sunderland's instructions as Envoy Extraordinary and Plenipotentiary to Vienna, Windsor, 17th June 1705

Blenheim (Sunderland) Papers. S.2. (formerly C 1 2)

These instructions, sealed and thus authenticated and authorised with an impression of one of the ruler's signets bearing the royal arms, written in English and signed by the monarch at the start and initialled by him or her at the finish, are typical of post-medieval English diplomatic instructions. Previous instructions had taken the rather unwieldly form of a long list of items written on a roll of parchment, often consisting of several strips with the royal seal attached by cords or parchment thongs to the foot. Even then, though, they were in the vernacular, for they were theoretically private documents meant for the ambassador alone. By the fifteenth century, however, it was common for the rulers to whom the ambassador was sent to demand to see the instructions, so they took on a neat official appearance while simultaneously becoming less important in themselves. For potentially embarrassing items – often containing the real purpose of the mission – were excluded and relegated to totally informal secret instructions.

This document contains detailed instructions concerning the 'public' part of Sunderland's mission. While travelling through the Netherlands on his way to Vienna, he is to urge the Dutch leaders and the Portuguese Ambassador in the Hague to agree that one general should be placed in overall command of the allied forces in Portugal. He is also to visit the Duke of Marlborough 'to concert with him the necessary measures for the better Execution of Your Commission'. In Vienna, having delivered to the new Emperor the Queen's messages of condolence and of congratulation on his accession,

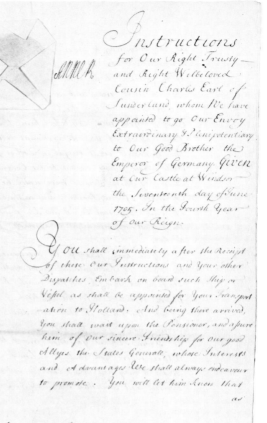

97

he is to try to mediate between him and the Hungarians and to get both sides to accept Anglo-Dutch guarantees of any agreements reached between them. Finally he is to press the Austrians to send military help to the Duke of Savoy, whose lands were being overrun by the French and to send troops as a diversion to the Rhine. The instructions include the precise arguments Sunderland was to use at all stages in the negotiations.

The instructions also include more formal sections, not particular to Sunderland's mission, which are to be found in most European post-medieval diplomatic instructions. They give a good idea of the ambassador's duties other than negotiation. Thus Sunderland is to 'protect any of our subjects that may have occasion of reasonable Favour or Justice in any Case . . . of such consequence as to deserve the Interposition of Our Name'. He is to 'correspond [constantly] with Our Ambassadors and Ministers in Forreign Courts for your mutuall Information and Assistance in your respective Negociations'. He should also 'carefully maintain a good correspondence with the Ministers of other Princes and States residing in that Court and penetrate . . . into the private Designs of their

Masters . . . And what you can discover of this kind as well as the Inclinations of the Ministers of the Court of Vienna, you shall give Us a constant and particular account by one of Our Principall Secretarys of State'. He is then told how to act in the company of ambassadors, so as to avoid disputes over precedence. 'At Your return We shall expect a compleat Narrative of what has happened . . . with a particular Account of all Matters and Affairs relating to that Government and the Ministers employed in it'.

Finally Sunderland is told he will 'observe such further Instructions and Directions as You shall receive from Us or one of Our Principall Secretarys of State'. For initial instructions were almost invariably supplemented by others. The present instructions had been prepared even before Sunderland's selection, and he was given additional, more up-to-date, instructions before he left, for instance naming the Earl of Galway as the general whom the British wished to see as Commander-in-Chief in Portugal. During the course of his mission, Sunderland received further instructions in the form of official letters from the Secretary of State for the North, who was responsible for Vienna.

98 Instructions of Emperor Rudolf II for Johann Khevenhüller, Freiherr von Landskron und Wernberg, his Ambassador to Philip II of Spain, Prague, 8th February 1593

Egerton MS 2679, ff.17–24

While the basic nature and essence of diplomatic instructions were the same throughout Europe, their form varied from court to court, depending on the differing traditions of the chanceries involved. In contrast to British instructions, these are in Latin, as befitted the Holy Roman Emperor who ruled, or claimed to rule, over most of the peoples of central Europe. The Emperor's signature and his fine armorial seal, with traces of the paper that used to cover it, are at the end and not beginning of the document, which is countersigned by the Emperor's Secretary and the Imperial Vice-Chancellor. The cord consists of intertwined black and gold threads, the traditional colours of the Holy Roman Emperors and later Austrian Emperors.

The instructions deal mainly with Turkish and Italian affairs. Rudolf wished for Spanish assistance against the Turks, who then occupied most of his kingdom of Hungary and were thus threatening to

Vallis Tari negotium quod attinet cum olim Parmae et Placentiae Dux Octavius restitutionem illius loci hoc obtentu negauerit, quod Pontificis Maximi ius aut bonitatem sibi usurpantis interdictum intercederet, eius vero filius deinde Princeps Alexander obstaculis per nos apud Pontificem remotis, sese excusauerit, quod a Ser.tis ipsius prohibetur, petet Orator noster serio, ut Ser.tas ipsius restitutionem illam non tantum non impediat aut remoretur, sed apud modernum Ducem Principem Rainutium auctoritate potius sua efficiat, ut locus ille Vallis Tari qui omni iure nobis et Sacro Imperio subest in nostram quamprimum restituatur potestatem.

Restat denique nostro nomine in Italicis cum ipsius Ser.te agendum, Cum contingere nonnunquam soleat, ut nostri et Sacri Imperij Vasalli ad Ser.tis ipsius protectionem confugiant, atque ab ipsa presidium nobis insciis et inconsultis expetant, ne id cuiquam Vasallorum nostrorum, qualiscunque sit in posterum absque nostro assensu concedatur.

24

Quidquid autem Orator noster in his omnibus effecerit aut obtinuerit, quidue ipse expedire iudicauerit, primo quoque tempore nobis accurate perscribet.

Quibus sedulo ac prouide, fideliterque ac prudenter, uti hactenus nostra curare consueuit, praestandis Orator noster, erga quem benignissimae voluntatis affectum gerimus, gratiam nostram caesaream magis magisque promerebitur. Datum in Arce nostra regia Pragae, die octaua mensis Februarij Anno Domini Millesimo, quingentesimo, nonagesimo tertio, Regnorum nostrorum, Romani decimo octauo, Hungarici vigesimo primo et Bohemici itidem decimo octauo.

Jacobus C. à Seufftenau

Ad Mandatum Sacrae Caes.ae Maiestatis proprium

Jo. Barvitius

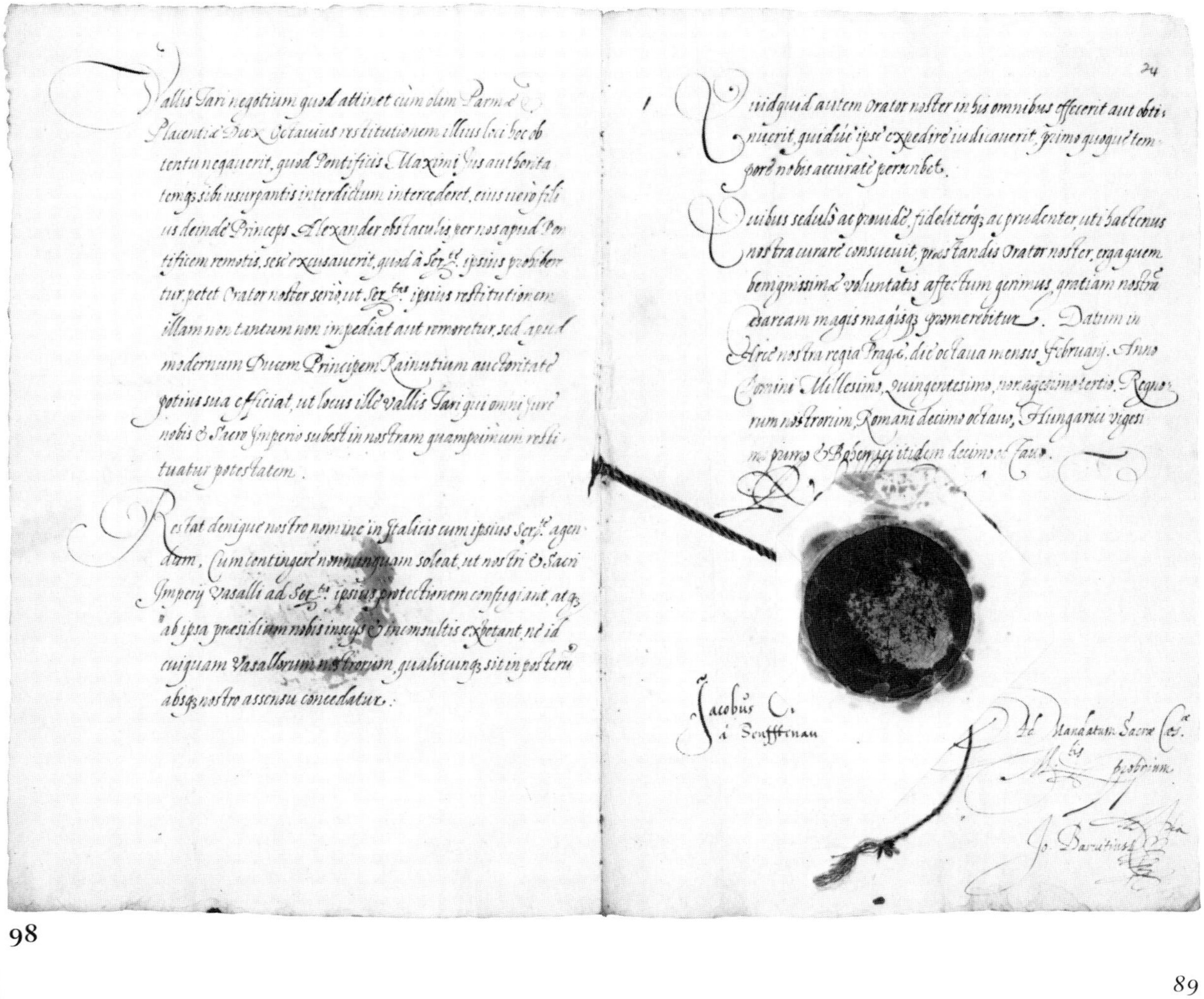

98

take Vienna which lay a day's ride away from their lines. Being the suzerain lord of most of northern Italy, as Holy Roman Emperor, Rudolf also wanted Khevenhüller to champion the Empire's Italian interests in Madrid. For Philip II, nominally Rudolf's deputy in Italy as Imperial Vicar General, dominated the whole peninsula as Duke of Milan, King of Naples, and lord of several fortresses along the Tuscan coast.

The most remarkable diplomatic instructions were those of France and Venice. They were often extremely lengthy documents which made full use of previous ambassadors' reports and of the skills of the specialists employed in their administrations. In addition to instructions for their envoys, they also contained detailed analyses of the recent histories, policies, and leading personalities of the courts for which the envoys were intended. They are often literary as well as political masterpieces.

99 The Earl of Sunderland's secret instructions, Camp at Meldert c.2nd August 1705

Blenheim (Sunderland) Papers D II 5

The Duke of Marlborough dictated these secret instructions to Sunderland while the two men were together at the Allied camp in Flanders. Evidently they were scribbled down in great haste, for Sunderland switches from the first person to the second person when referring to himself. The reason for the secrecy is clear, for the instructions relate primarily to military and political affairs of the greatest importance which could not be exposed to public scrutiny as the formal instructions were only too likely to be. Indeed the Earl is ordered to confide the contents of these instructions only to the new Emperor and to Count Wratislaw, Marlborough's closest collaborator among the Habsburg ministers then in Vienna.

Sunderland's first objective was to get Prince Louis of Baden removed from his command on the Rhine and replaced by Prince Eugene of Savoy who was popular with British and Dutch alike. For relations between Prince Louis, the German Commander-in-Chief, and Marlborough were bad. Louis' inactivity had been such that he was suspected of being in treasonable correspondence with the French. Since 'the allies will never trust their troops with him', Sunderland is to urge that 'he be dropt or remov'd in the gentlest manner . . . [or] . . . be offer'd to command either in Hungary, Italy or anywhere but the Rhin'. In the interim he 'should be Press'd to begin the siege of Saar Louis as soon as Possible'. Marlborough is certain this will be an easy affair, and tells Sunderland to inform Wratislaw of his own plan to take 'Geneppe and the sources of the

99

rivers here'. Furthermore he hints that – contrary to what Sunderland's public instructions said – the main action henceforth would be in the North, with Eugene and himself collaborating as they had done in the Blenheim campaign of the previous year.

Sunderland's second duty is to persuade the Austrians to write to the Dutch to get them to invite Marlborough 'to go to Vienna at the end of ye Campagne for a few days to concert measures for the next . . . ye reason of this is, y^t by the states [of the Dutch Republic] desiring of this, Ld. M. [Marlborough] may be enabled to tye them down to comply with what shall be agreed.' For, Marlborough remarked, 'Holland is weary allmost of the war, at least a great Party [is]'.

Thirdly Sunderland was to try to reconcile Wratislaw and Stepney, the English Queen's resident envoy in Vienna, who had become estranged because of Stepney's support for the Hungarian rebels. Sunderland was to 'desire Stepney to be cooler' while telling Wratislaw that Stepney 'shall be remov'd to Holland' as soon as a replacement could be provided.

Lastly Sunderland was 'to live in friendship and Confidence' with the Hanoverian minister in Vienna, and 'ioyne with him in everything for his Master's interest'. For Marlborough was already reckoning with the Elector of Hanover's accession to the British throne as George I.

100 The Earl of Sunderland's credentials for the Hungarian Estates, Windsor, 17th June 1705

Blenheim (Sunderland) Papers S2 (formerly C 1 2)

Credentials or a letter of credence take the form of a letter from the ruler or rulers of one state to the ruler or rulers of another, introducing his or their envoy, briefly explaining the purpose of his mission and asking the recipients to believe or 'credit' (from the Latin word 'credere' which means 'to believe') what the envoy says on his or their behalf. The letter thus provides formal evidence of the bearer's diplomatic character and its delivery to the recipient by the envoy in the course of his first ceremonial audience marks the official start of a diplomatic mission.

Within western Europe the letters were generally simple in appearance, though conforming to the style of each national chancery. They were generally written in Latin or French, which from about 1700 began to replace Latin as the diplomatic language. Nevertheless the vernacular is occasionally to be found before 1700, particularly in renaissance Italy (17), in late medieval England and France, and in the France of Louis XIV. Outside Europe the vernacular was almost invariably used and credentials were often extremely ornate (57, 63). Usually an ambassador presented other letters of introduction, following his first audience, to individual members of the ruler's family or court. While generally identical to credentials in appearance, they rarely included the creditive formula, substituting for it the request that the recipient assist the envoy in the execution of his duties.

The present credentials were never delivered, since no occasion for this arose before Sunderland's efforts to embark on formal mediation ended in failure in November 1705. In form they are typical of post-medieval English credentials and other official royal letters. The Queen, the Hungarians, and Sunderland are given their official titles. Noting the heroic rôle the Hungarians had long played in defending the Christian faith against the Turks and the miseries brought by war, Queen Anne exhorts the Hungarian 'Princes, Lords and Commons' ('Principes, Proceres, Ordines') to settle their differences. She is ready to help in ending the war and for that reason has sent Sunderland as her Envoy Extraordinary and Plenipotentiary ('Ablegatum Nostrum Extraordinarium et Plenipotentiarum'). She asks the Estates to show complete trust in him in all that he says in her name ('Rogamus Vos plenam ei adhibere fidem in omnibus, quae Nostro Nomine dixerit'). The letter is signed by the Queen and counter-signed by Robert Harley, the Secretary of State responsible for diplomatic relations with Vienna. The back of a papered royal signet seal bearing an impression of

100

the royal arms can be seen on the right-hand page. While, judging from its position, it would normally have sealed the letter, formal letters of this kind seem generally to have been kept open until just before presentation, and then only lightly sealed. Its prime function therefore must have been to provide further authentication for these credentials.

Envoys to congresses were not furnished with credentials since they were not accredited to any court or ruler.

101 Queen Anne's passport for the Earl of Sunderland as her Envoy Extraordinary and Minister Plenipotentiary to the Court of Vienna, Windsor, 17th June 1705

Blenheim (Sunderland) Papers S2 (formerly C 1 2)

This parchment document takes the form of letters patent. Queen Anne requests her foreign allies and their representatives to provide assistance and free and unimpeded passage through their lands to her Envoy Extraordinary and Plenipotentiary to the German Emperor, Charles, Earl of Sunderland and Baron Wormleighton, and his suite. The passport is signed by the Queen, countersigned by Robert Harley, her Secretary of State for the North, and sealed with an impression of the royal arms from one of her signet seals. The two blue sixpenny stamps showing a Tudor rose surrounded by the Garter and surmounted by a crown, confirm payment of the necessary stamp duty (tax).

Passports were essential for envoys since they formally established their special status when they were travelling through the lands of third parties. In 1541, the French envoys to the Sultan and the

Venetian Republic, Rincon, a Spaniard, and Fregoso, a Genoese, tried to reach their destinations more quickly by smuggling themselves through the Milanese, which was ruled by their master's rival, the Emperor Charles V. While en route they were murdered at the orders of the Governor of Milan, whose action was justified by the Emperor on the grounds that the two men had not presented their passports to his officials before entering his territories.

For an example of a medieval diplomatic passport see **8**.

102

102 Warrant for plate for Sir Thomas Chaloner, Elizabeth I's Ambassador to Philip II of Spain, St James's, 30th September 1561

Additional MS 5756, f.251

Before ambassadors left for their posts abroad, they were provided with magnificent silver, silver-gilt or even gold vessels and plate to enable them to represent their masters worthily. At the end of their appointments, the plate was supposed to be returned but until well into the nineteenth century, it rarely was. When not pawned or dispersed during the mission by irregularly-paid envoys, as a means of meeting their expenses, it was retained by them and their families as pledges against the payment of their salaries and 'extraordinary' expenses. Thus it was that several noble families laid the foundations for their magnificent collections of gold and silver.

In this warrant with the signature of Elizabeth I (possibly a stamp) and one of her papered signet seals, John Astley, the Master and Treasurer of the Queen's Jewels and Plate, is ordered to deliver to Sir Thomas Chaloner (1521–65), Elizabeth's newly appointed ambassador to the court of Spain 'for his better furniture in that charge . . . one Bassyn and Ewer guilt, one paire of guilt pottes, one payre of guilt fflagans, sixe guilt Boulles with two covers, one guilt layer (laver), two guilt Saltes with a cover, twentie and sixe Trenchers parcell guilt and white, twelve platters white, thirtie and fower [four] disshes white and fower cawcers [saucers] white.' All of this was 'to be redelyvered unto you . . . or the whole value thereof at his retorne'. At the foot of the warrant an officer has noted the precise weight of the plate and vessels and this has been inserted into the text of the warrant.

Four days later the plate was delivered and, in an indented receipt (Additional MS 5756, f.252), Chaloner bound himself, his heirs, executors, and administrators to redeliver the plate 'at sutch tyme as he shall retorne or leave her highness service . . . or ells thole [the whole] value of the same plate and vessell to be . . . leveyed of his goodes and landes within this Realme'. Despite the threats, and later efforts of the Master and Treasurer of the Queen's Jewels and Plate, Chaloner and his heirs never seem to have returned these ambassadorial furnishings.

With the coming of permanent embassy buildings and the regularisation of the payment of salaries to diplomats in the course of the nineteenth century, the embassies themselves were provided with plate and furnishings on a permanent basis, like any other government-owned building, and the ambassadors were expected to make do on their salaries alone.

For some early eighteenth-century diplomatic plate, see **140**.

103 Sir William Temple's cipher table, 1675, from the Temple Papers

Additional MS 9800, ff.134–5

Cipher tables were an essential part of the envoy's equipment and by the seventeenth century the tables usually came in the form of large printed sheets containing lists of words, names, letters, and parts of words arranged systematically, opposite which numbers or occasionally signs could be written. There was also plenty of room to add extra words, and meaningless numbers which were intended to confuse. Envoys were frequently given several ciphers with the same objective; the French

103

Ambassador to England in 1713 was furnished with six. Nevertheless the cost of an effective code or cipher was extremely high and most diplomatic ciphers were accordingly old or simple, and could be broken by experts without much difficulty. This normally did not matter, however, since simple codes were generally intended only to deter casual 'snoopers' who lacked the time or opportunity to study the letters in detail, while the messenger was resting or changing horses.

This is one of the cipher tables given to Sir William Temple (1628–99), the outstanding British diplomat of the 1660s and 1670s, when he was sent as a mediator on Charles II's behalf, to the Congress of Nijmegen (1675). The handwritten additions contain the names of the people, places, and subjects which were expected to be discussed there. A previous attempt to bring peace between France, the Spanish and Austrian Habsburgs, and the Dutch at 865 (Cologne) under 1009 (Swedish) mediation in 1673 and 1674 had failed and now 927 (Temple) at 897 (Nijmegen) was to mediate between 1171 (plenipotentiaries) of 787 (France) and 964 (its enemies), hoping to secure at least 742 (a

suspension) of hostilities, for generals and admirals such as 952 (Condé), 1187 (Turenne), 1094 (de Ruyter) and 1101 (Tromp) were still engaged in 770 (battle) most of which was taking place in the Netherlands and around 1160 (Messina) which was in [from another code] 97-39-74-409 (rebellion) against 921 (Spain). 986-409 (Negotiations) were expected to centre round the fate of towns like 1037 (Charleroy), 1032 (Antwerp) and 779 (Dunkirk). 927 (Temple) was expected to be in particularly close contact with 830, 991 (the Dutch *Stadholder*, the prince of Orange) and his 1117, 1124 in 897 (Ambassador, Beverningk, in Nijmegen) (**129**). The leading French and Austrian leaders were 950 (Colbert), 1070 (Louvois), 882 (Hocher) and 1069 (Lamberg) and the final peace treaty which would emerge after several 1170 (projects or drafts) would be based on 934 and 1169 (the Treaties of Westphalia (1648) and the Pyrenees (1659)). An accompanying sheet states that numbers ending in 3 or 8 were to be meaningless or null and that certain numbers had two meanings.

104 Letter of George Tilson to the Earl of Nottingham, Secretary of State for the South, c. January 1703. From the Hatton-Finch Papers

Additional MS 29589, f.499

Until the nineteenth century the ambassador was responsible for employing and paying all of his staff except for Secretary of Embassy. Since the early seventeenth century the latter had been formally appointed, accredited and paid by the monarch acting through the Secretaries of State. Nevertheless in practice the Secretaries of State normally accepted the Ambassador's nominee. The post of Secretary of Embassy was sought after by able young men of moderate birth and income as it offered the prospect of eventual promotion in the royal service. This was the way in which both Charles Whitworth (**48**) and George Stepney (**47, 167**) commenced their careers.

In this letter George Tilson, Clerk in Lord Nottingham's office, informs him of his wish to go to Berlin as Secretary to Lord Raby (**39, 40**), Queen Anne's newly appointed Envoy Extraordinary and Plenipotentiary to King Frederick I, 'for my improvement by travell and foreign conversation'. 'I thought it my duty not to make any steps in that matter without your Lo:^ps particular approbation and leave', he writes '[and] I assure myself that your Lo:^p··· will not look on this as a piece of levity or unsettledness but rather as proceeding from an earnest desire of improving my small stock of knowledge and thereby making myself more fit for your Lo:^ps Service'. On his return from Berlin Tilson was created Under Secretary, a post he held with great distinction until his death in 1738.

For part of Lord Raby's ambassadorial plate of 1705 and 1706 see **140**.

105 Letter from Viscount Stormont to Sir Robert Murray Keith, Vienna, 2nd September 1772. From the Hardwicke (Keith) Papers
Additional MS 35503, ff.246–7

In the summer of 1772, Sir Robert Murray Keith (1730–95) returned to London in triumph. While serving as British Envoy in Copenhagen he had been responsible for saving George III's sister Sophia Matilda, Queen of Denmark, from life imprisonment by her husband following the discovery of her affair with the Danish first minister, Count Struensee. A grateful master had immediately created Keith a Knight of the Bath and a few months later he was appointed to one of the plum diplomatic posts, as Envoy Extraordinary and Plenipotentiary in Vienna, where his father, Robert Keith (*d.* 1774), had served thirty years earlier. Before his departure he contacted the man whom he was to replace in Vienna, David, seventh Viscount Stormont (later second Earl of Mansfield) (1727–96) who had been appointed Ambassador to France.

In this letter Stormont gives Keith some advice about his move to Vienna. He himself had enjoyed his time in the Austrian capital and 'as to you, Dear Sir, you have already several Cordial friends in this country (some of them hereditary ones) and will soon make more and in all probability when the Day comes, You will leave Vienna with as much regret as I do. With Respect to Politicks . . . I shall with the utmost Pleasure and Satisfaction communicate to you the little I know but You come just at the opening of a New Scene [this refers to the First Partition of Poland between Russia, Prussia, and Austria which had taken place a few months earlier], with which all that passed before has little or Nothing to do. As soon as I know . . . the Road Yr. Principal Baggage is to take I will apply for the usual General Passport'. He advises Keith to take advantage of the 'Première Entrée' – the diplomat's right to import what he liked, free from excise, during his first few months (six, in Vienna) at a post – and particularly in his 'first Provision of foreign wines the Duty upon which is very exorbitant. There is one Point where foreign Ministers some times meet with Difficulties . . . (the Austrian authorities) sometimes make Difficulties about passing Books which they think exceptionable' – this was a 'sore . . . Place' with the Empress Maria Theresa herself: 'the Books that are . . . particularly disagreeable to Her are light french Romances, such

as *Candide* for Instance, as to Books of History, Politicks etc. tho' they are in the list of prohibited Books, no Difficulty is made.' Turning to accommodation, Stormont apologises that 'when I came into this House which I hired ready furnished I disposed of all my furniture so that I have little or nothing of that sort of any value and as my Cellar is near Empty There are few articles that could be of much service to you', but he mentions servants' beds, kitchen utensils, some china, 'several carriages and a set of Horses which tho' not first Rate will I imagine suit you very well'. Finally he asks Keith, before he sets out, to 'send to Lord Mansfield's [Stormont's uncle] to know if there are any Letters or Parcels for me'.

The letter gives a good idea of what the ambassador needed to know before his departure and of the non-political problems he was likely to face on arrival at his post.

106 'Henriette' bids farewell to Sir Robert Murray Keith, British Envoy Extraordinary and Plenipotentiary to the Court of Vienna, London, 20th October 1772. From the Hardwicke (Keith) Papers
Additional MS 35504, f.107

Sir Robert Murray Keith (**105**) seems to have had a way with women. While he was travelling through Germany on his way to Vienna in 1772 as Envoy Extraordinary and Plenipotentiary, his brother Basil wrote, on 23rd October (Additional MS 35504, ff.111, 112), that 'The Haggs and their Jerrys are still mourning your departure . . . I am glad to inform you that Harriet is much better [but] I found her in a sad way'.

The confirmation comes in this (tear-?) stained letter from Henriette – who cannot be identified more closely: 'Vous s'avés aimer et par Consequent vous pouvés juger de mon etat present mon amour pour vous est Sans affectation et vous en étes convaincu oh toi mon pere, mon protecteur, et mon tout prend pitié de ton henriette, ne l'abandonne pas, elle est perdue Sans toi. Souviens toi l'ami de mon Ame que tu m'as adopté pour ta fille je t'apartiens, je n'ai d'espoir qu'en toi, en toi sont fondées toutes mes esperances, je ne puis etre heureuse sans toi . . . adieu toi que j'aime je vais me coucher. Si j'étois avec toi je me porterois bien, ecris moi bien souvent je te prie . . .' (You know how to love and so you can judge my present state. My love for you is without affectation and you know it very well indeed. Oh my father, my protector and my all, take pity on your Henriette, don't abandon her, she is lost without you. Remember, my soul-mate, that you adopted me as your daughter. I belong to you.

All my hopes are founded on you. I can't be happy without you . . . Farewell my love, I'm going to bed. If I were with you I would be well. Write to me really often, I beg you.)

The letter's seal bears the impression of a burning heart.

Henriette's fate is unknown, but Keith remained in Vienna for the next twenty years. Parting could be a wrench.

106

107 The English ambassadors taking leave of their master. From the Legend of St Ursula. Vittore Carpaccio (c. 1455–1522) (see plate no. VIII)
By courtesy of the Accademia Gallery Venice (photograph *Scala*)

Carpaccio painted this picture in 1495, as is recorded in the little inscription on the bottom step of the dais, facing the spectator, and he depicts the ceremonial of late-fifteenth-century Italy. The scene is set in the great marble hall of an Italian renaissance-style urban palace. The King, surrounded by councillors, is seated on a throne on the dais and is holding the ambassadors' credentials. The first ambassador kneels before him and is about to receive them. He seems to be carrying a red-covered scroll in his left hand, possibly containing his instructions. The second ambassador at the foot of the dais is bowing and raising his hat, as though about to kneel also. In the background a young scribe is writing away busily, apparently describing the ceremony at the dictation of the young aristocrat standing next to him – possibly the Secretary of Embassy who was expected to keep a full record of the mission. Little shields painted with heraldic arms are suspended from the large candelabra of the ceiling and generally there is considerable bustle, as would accompany any departure. Through the open doorway the spectator catches a glimpse of a crowded courtyard and beyond it, through an archway, the streets of the town.

For the same scene depicted by one of Carpaccio's Flemish contemporaries see 9.

108 Safe-Conduct for the Earl of Sunderland, Camp at Corbeck sur Dylle, Netherlands, 3rd August 1705
Blenheim (Sunderland) Papers S2 (formerly C 1 2)

On his journey to Vienna, Lord Sunderland passed through enemy lines. In the eighteenth century such proceedings were quite normal and he had no difficulty in receiving this safe-conduct from Maximilian Emanuel, the Elector of Bavaria who had lost his German lands following the Battle of Blenheim and was then acting as Bourbon Governor of the Southern Netherlands. The pass authorises Sunderland to proceed unhindered from the Allied lines to Frankfurt-am-Main, so long as he does not go close to the lines of the French and Spanish or the fortresses held by them. The arms surmounting the document and on the wafer seal are those of Philip V of Spain as can be seen from the lilies of France on the centre shield. They are surrounded by the collars of the Burgundian Order of the Golden Fleece and the French Order of the Holy Spirit. The safe-conduct is signed by Maximilian Emanuel and countersigned by his secretary, von Reichard. Sunderland's suite was rather small, since he was travelling in war time on a short mission of condolence. Nevertheless, the safe-conduct lists eight gentlemen who probably acted as aides, twenty servants, four of them on horseback, three 'Berlin' carriages with six horses each, two smaller coaches drawn by four horses each and an escort of twenty horsemen or dragoons provided by the Elector for protection against robbers. It was not uncommon for embassies to number well over a hundred people and to include a full aristocratic household with orchestra. In 1669, Henry Howard, later (1677) sixth Duke of Norfolk, took over 200 people with him on his special embassy to Morocco, and a Portuguese diplomat appointed ambassador to the Congress of Cambrai had a house floated down the River Scheldt to the town for himself and his suite. Not surprisingly, envoys often took a long time to reach their destinations. While it took Sunderland little more than three weeks to reach Vienna from London in 1705, it took Louis XIV's Ambassador to Denmark and his large household and staff two and a half months of constant travelling to cover the distance between Paris and Copenhagen in 1709.

MAXIMILIEN EMANUEL

Par la grace de Dieu, Duc de la Haute & Baſſe Baviere,
& du Haut Palatinat, Comte Palatin du Rhin, Grand Eſchan-
ſon du S. Empire & Electeur, Landgrave de Leichtenbergh,
Vicaire General des Pays-Bas, &c.

 Tous Lieutenans, Gouverneurs, Chefs, Capitaines, Officiers & Gens de guerre, tant de cheval que de pied; enſemble à tous Juſticiers, Officiers & Sujets du Roi, qui ce regardera, & ces preſentes ſeront monſtrées, Salut. Nous vous mandons, & commandons par cettes au nom de Sa Majeſté, de laiſſer librement & ſeurement aller & paſſer *Monſ: le Comte de Sunderland allant de l'armée des Alliez à Franckfort, auec huit Gentilshommes de ſa ſuite, vingt Domeſtiques, dont quatre ſont à Cheval, trois Berlines à ſix chevaux, deux Chariots à quatre chevaux, et une Escorte de vingt Cavaliers, ou Dragons contre les voleurs, à condition de n'approcher plus prez de deux lieues les lignes Places fortes, et armées de deux Couronnes.*

/ / / /

ſans *luy* faire ou donner, ni ſouffrir être fait ou donné aucun trouble, ou empêchement au contraire, ains plûtôt toute ayde, faveur & aſſiſtance requiſe; à durer le preſent Paſſeport *e de quatre Mois. Fait au Camp de Corbeck ſur Dylle le troiſième* *t de l'an mille ſept cent et cincq.*

M E manuel

De Reichart

THE ROMAN CATHOLIC CHAPEL,
(LINCOLNS INN FIELDS.)

London Pub. 1st April 1808 at R. Ackermann's Repository of Arts 101 Strand.

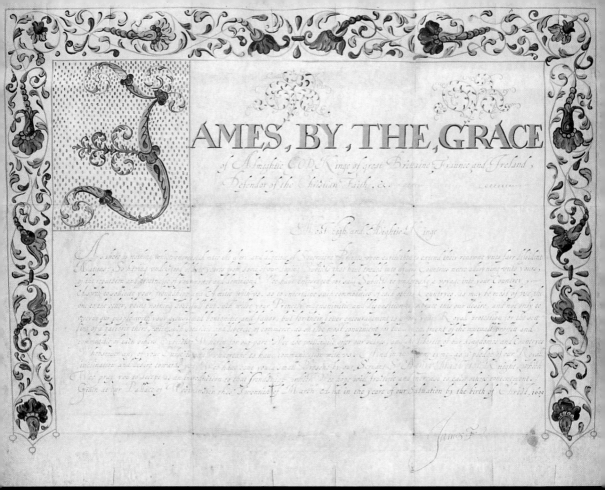

JAMES, BY, THE, GRACE

of Almightie GOD, Kinge of great Brittaine, Fraunce, and Ireland, Defendor of the Christian Faith, &c.

Most High and Mightie Kinge

As there is nothing which more indeereth the glory and dignitie of Soveraigne Princes upon earth then to extend their renowne unto farr distant Nations: So having understood of late years how some of our lovinge Subiects that have traded into divers Countries neere adioyninge unto yours, by the request and great encouragement of some of them, wee have endevoured our said Subiects to undertake a voyage into your Countries hoping to atchieve your friendshipp and amitie with us, as to entertaine such commodities of such nations Countryes, as may be most of use, the one to the other, being nothing dovbtfull but such unto your Princely magnanimitie and disposition to embrace into our desire, and not only to receive our people with your accustomed benignitie and favor, but further, better encouragement to give our Royal protection for the setting on of a happie trade, with such conveniencie and libertie of commerce as the most convenient to the mutual benefit and comoditie of each other. And thus, wisheinge for our parte, Wee doe willinglie offer our ayde, and Libertie of our kingdomes and Countryes whensoever any of your Subiects shall be desirous to have communication with us. And in token, evene, as a pledge of our Royal inclination and desire towards you, Wee have sent you these Presents by our Servant, S[ir] Walter Mathew and Knight, possible We pray you to accept as an introduction to that frendshipp, which Wee hope will flourish and increase to our mutual contentment. Given at our Pallace of Westminster this Twentie of March, &c. &c in the yeare of our Salvation by the birth of Christ, 1600.

James R.

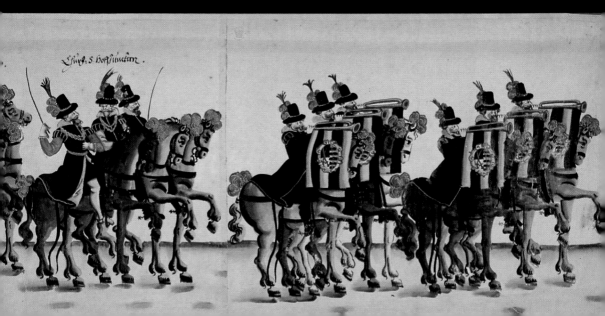

Ksiąg. S. Horstiunciam.

VI (133

IX (122)   X (164)

JACOBUS DEI GRATIA MAGNÆ

de Sa dite Majesté, et les Deputez des
dits Seigneurs Estats Generaux ont signé
la presente, et y ont fait apposer le Cacres de
Leurs armes, à la Haye L'onzième de ⸺
Novembre L'an Mil sept cent et un.

Marlborough

Winde

F. Blekade

A. Heinsius

W. de Nassau

De Weede

L.L. Hazen

B.V.V. Velde

Wichers

3. ARRIVAL AND PRESENTATION AT COURT

The ceremonial surrounding an ambassador's arrival originated in the court of the Byzantine emperors and was extremely elaborate. At the frontiers of the country he would be greeted by important noblemen representing their master or (in the case of a republic) masters. They would escort him to a place of reception a short distance outside the city where the court or government resided. A large procession of several coaches, with troops, servants, pages in the ambassador's livery, and musicians would then form. The ambassador would make his way to a palace or mansion reserved for ambassadors through crowded streets, with churchbells ringing, cannons thundering and perhaps fountains running with wine. Riding in a carriage drawn by the six horses reserved for royalty or their representatives, the ambassador would receive military salutes and would probably be formally welcomed to the town by the civic authorities.

A few days later, after discussions with the official in charge of receiving ambassadors (a Byzantine creation which made his modern reappearance in seventeenth-century France), leading ministers and possibly the monarch himself, the ambassador had his first audience. After another procession and amidst surroundings of even greater magnificence, he formally delivered his letters of credence (111) and formal greetings from his master(s) (112). Afterwards the ambassador of a European state was normally given a few days' hospitality. If he was not west European, this would extend throughout his stay. In this period he would be visited by the envoys of other countries or, if he was a mere envoy himself, he would go to visit the ambassadors resident at the court. Afterwards he would move to his residence, rented or purchased, and place his master's arms over its principal entrance.

These ceremonies were punishingly expensive for ambassador and hosts alike and could be marred by unseemly disputes over precedence which were known to have cost lives (146). By mutual consent the ceremonies were gradually dispensed with, and became reserved only for those eminent ambassadors who demanded them, as the Earl of Manchester did while in Venice in 1707 (110). By the eighteenth century envoys were simply received at court, without previous processions or consequent hospitality, to present their credentials; and this is all that survives in the United Kingdom today where the newly arrived ambassador is taken to Buckingham Palace in a small demure black horse-drawn coach to be formally introduced to the Queen and to present his letters of credence to her.

109 The coach used by Roger Palmer, Earl of Castlemaine, as James II's Ambassador to Pope Innocent XI, January 1687. Drawn by A. Cornelii and G.B. Lenardi, engraved by A. van Westerhout. **John Michael Wright**, *Ragguaglio della Solenne Comparsa fatta in Roma gli Otto di Gennaio MDCLXXXVII dall' Illustrissimo . . . Signor Conte di Castlemaine, Ambasciadore Straordinario di . . . Giacomo Secondo Ré d'Inghilterra . . . alla Santa Sede Apostolica in andare publicamente all'Udienza della Santità di . . . Papa Innocenzo Undecimo* (Rome 1687) Plate 6

Department of Printed Books: 603. i. 19

In 1687 the Earl of Castlemaine (1634–1705), the unhappy husband of Charles II's notorious mistress, Barbara Villiers (Duchess of Cleveland in her own right), was sent to Rome as Ambassador Extraordinary on a mission of compliment by James II. Castlemaine was a worthy, dignified man, who had previously served as Ambassador in Constantinople. Above all, however, he was a pious Catholic like the King and was willing and able to lavish money on his mission. Wright, Castlemaine's Secretary, commemorated the embassy in print and commissioned a series of drawings and engravings of the Ambassador's plate and of his coach from local artists and the Flemish engraver van Westerhout.

This magnificent baroque carved and gilded coach illustrates how throughout the elaborate ceremonial the Ambassador was seen to be acting as his master. The doors contain James II's monogram and the cherubs support his royal crown and not Castlemaine's coronet. A similar coach, the 'Goldener Wagen', made for the ceremonial entry into Paris of Prince Joseph Wenceslas of Liechtenstein (1696–1772), as the Emperor Charles VI's Ambassador (1738), is still in the possession of the Liechtenstein family. The ceremonial surrounding ambassadors was modelled on that which surrounded their masters (10).

109

110

110 The British Ambassador's entry into the Doge's Palace, Venice, 22nd September 1707. By Luca Carlevaris (1663–1730) (see plate no. VII)
By courtesy of the City of Birmingham Museums and Art Gallery

In 1707, in the process of diplomatic missions to several European courts, Charles Montagu, Earl and later (1719) Duke of Manchester, (1662–1722) was sent to the Republic of Venice as Queen Anne's Ambassador Extraordinary. A wealthy Whig magnate, who had already spent some time in Venice, most recently as William III's Ambassador in 1697 to 1698, he was instructed to press the Republic to enter the War of the Spanish Succession on the side of the Allies. From the first, he set out to overawe the Venetians through his magnificence as representative of one of Europe's most powerful rulers.

This picture, commissioned by him from the leading Venetian topographical artist of the day, shows the Earl on his way to his formal audience with the Doge. The Earl, simply dressed in blue and carrying a black tricorn hat, is seen being greeted by a red-robed Venetian dignitary as he steps from a gondola. The larger black gondolas bear his arms and carried his suite. Cannons on the man-of-war at the side of the painting are booming and a procession of Venetian patricians, dressed predominantly in red, stretches from the edge of the canal to the doors of the Doge's Palace. In the background one has a beautiful view of eighteenth-century Venice.

This painting was almost the only benefit that accrued from Manchester's mission. His stay was marred by disputes with the authorities over his ambassadorial privileges; and the Venetians stubbornly refuse to be awed by him or to alter their policy of neutrality, tilted in favour of the Bourbons. So successful was the painting in conveying the splendour of a diplomatic mission, however, that, twenty years later, Carlevaris painted virtually an identical picture for the then Imperial Ambassador to Venice.

The painting remained in the possession of the Dukes of Manchester at Kimbolton Castle until 1949.

111 The arrival of Ambassadors at the Court of the King of Brittany. From a series of paintings illustrating the legend of St Ursula, painted by Vittore Carpaccio (c. 1455–1525) between 1490 and 1495 (see plate no. XI)
By courtesy of the Accademia Gallery, Venice (Photograph: Scala)

The picture shows the arrival at the court of Brittany of pagan ambassadors who have come to request the hand of the King's daughter, Ursula, for their master's son Etherius. To illustrate this legendary scene, Carpaccio has depicted a diplomatic ceremony in the Venice of his day. The ship which brought the ambassadors and their suites is seen in the background while in the foreground the first and most important ambassador hands a letter, which would be his letter of credence, to the King. Behind him kneels the other ambassador followed by their suite. The King is surrounded by several courtiers and councillors, wearing their collars and robes of office. Beyond the walls of the palace there is an idealised Venetian scene. A gondolier plies his trade, and Venetians chat and walk dogs on the Piazza.

The central scene would have been familiar to courtiers throughout Europe both then and later (60). Even nowadays the ceremonial is similar, though there is likely to be music, and the ambassador would not kneel.

For other diplomatic pictures illustrating the legend of St Ursula, see **9, 107**.

112 Aeneas Sylvius Piccolomini at the court of James I of Scotland, 1435. Fresco in the Piccolomini Library, Siena Cathedral, by Bernardino di Betto Vagio, known as Pinturicchio (1454–1513)
By courtesy of the Opera del Duomo, Siena

This picture shows the stage in the formal audience, following the delivery of the credentials, when the ambassador declaimed a formal oration explaining the purpose of his mission while transmitting greetings from his master. Such orations were highly valued in renaissance Italy and were frequently published (73). Tests of the ambassador's learning and eloquence, they could also play their part in influencing important groups inside and later outside court. Normally the ruler replied to the oration in similar style. By the eighteenth century formal orations were delivered only by particularly eminent ambassadors like the Earl of Manchester, whose speech was immediately printed and circulated throughout Europe. Envoys simply exchanged words of greeting with the ruler to whom they were sent, while meticulously noting any special sign of favour done him. Thus in 1742 Robert Keith, senior, noted with pride in his letter to the Secretary of State that Maria Theresa, the Queen of Hungary and future Empress, had granted him her last public audience before going into confinement.

Pinturicchio painted the frescoes in the Piccolomini Library in Siena Cathedral at the behest of Cardinal Francesco Nanni-Todeschini-Piccolomini, who wished to commemorate the life of his uncle Aeneas Sylvius Piccolomini (1405–64), the humanist scholar who was elected Pope, as Pius II, in 1458.

At an earlier period Pius II had been active as a diplomat. While in the service of Cardinal Albergati at the Congress of Arras he undertook an adventurous secret mission to Scotland which he recorded in his memoirs. The artist has allowed himself considerable licence in his depiction both of Scotland and the mission. The turbaned figures to the left of the throne refer to Piccolomini's later preoccupation, as Pope, with a crusade against the Turks.

4. DUTIES

INFORMATION

The gathering and transmission of information is one of the diplomat's principal duties and was the main function of the earliest residents. Information can be gathered in a variety of ways: directly from the ruler himself (113) or, more usually, his ministers; from other ambassadors at the court; from consuls elsewhere in the country or empire (particularly, before the nineteenth century in the cases of Spain and empires outside Europe) or from ambassadors elsewhere (114), with whom ambassadors are generally expected to correspond (97). Attendance at court is also useful (115), since it gives the chance for informal discussions and enables the diplomat to pick up news. Talleyrand was not the first to remark that an ambassador's task would become impossible if more people knew how to hold their tongues. Information thus gained can be supplemented by bribing well-placed informants, minor officials and even, occasionally, ministers (117). Instructions, extracts or printed versions of important despatches sent from home (116), newspapers, newsletters (115), and printed gazettes subscribed to from foreign and domestic sources (see 49), keep an envoy abreast of events elsewhere; and the news obtained can be bartered against other infor- mation. If relations between two countries are bad, spies and malcontents have to be relied on (118). This is very much a last resort, however, since these reports are often trivial and very unreliable.

The ambassador normally transmits his information to his country's foreign minister (119) though he might keep in contact with other leading figures (120), including the ruler himself. For these might be the true directors of foreign policy, or be responsible for a more important 'unofficial' foreign policy. The Secretary of Embassy was expected to keep his masters informed of apparently less important matters (121), in much the same way that modern attachés, appointed by different ministries and 'attached' to the embassy, report to their departments on developments in specific fields, like defence or trade.

Until the last century, ambassadors normally had to utilise the local postal services or couriers for their mail, putting the confidential sections of letters into increasingly complex ciphers (120) and codes (121) and occasionally using 'invisible' ink (118). Although cheaper than other methods, these letters tended to be intercepted by post- masters who copied the more interesting ones for other courts and their own masters (123, 49).

More urgent and confidential messages were sent by one's national courier, such as the British King's or Queen's Messengers (122), but even these letters could be intercepted. In this period a wise envoy sent duplicates or triplicates of his despatches by different routes to ensure their arrival. Since 1850, the telegraph, telephone and aeroplane have enabled diplomats to keep in continuous contact with their masters and have increased their workload by forcing the pace of world events. But there is still a place for more reflective or confidential reports carried by messenger or – most safely of all, because inconspicuously – by trustworthy private individuals.

113 Letter from Frederick II of Prussia to Andrew Mitchell, Potsdam, 17th August 1756. From the Mitchell Papers

Additional MS 6843, f.11

This letter was written at a time when the Empress Maria Theresa, still aggrieved at Frederick the Great's seizure of her province of Silesia sixteen years earlier, was trying to weave a European-wide diplomatic net, which was to include France and Russia, against Prussia. In this note to the British envoy in Berlin, Andrew Mitchell, Frederick refutes 'des imputations des plus ridicules' (most ridiculous imputations) which, he says, have been circulated about him by the Austrian resident in Hamburg in order to blacken his name in Russia and everywhere else. In an autograph postscript in misspelt French he mentions an enclosure from which Mitchell will see all of his enemies' 'Mechans projits' (wicked designs). 'Vous veréz l'Indispensable Necessité ou je suis de Les prevenir, et que pour denouér ce Noeux Gordien il n'y a d'autre remède que de le Coupér avec l'Epee' (You will see my indispensible need to thwart them and that the only way to untie this Gordian knot is to cut it with the sword). Twelve days later he unleashed the Seven Years War by invading the territory of Austria's ally, Saxony.

The relationship between Frederick (1712–86) and Mitchell (1708–71), who served as British representative in Berlin from 1756 until his death, was close. The two men had shared interests and, at least for the first few years, Mitchell was the principal agent of Frederick's most powerful ally. As a result, the King confided many of his thoughts and intentions to him, and even allowed the Scotsman to accompany him on his campaigns. Few envoys have succeeded in living on terms of such intimacy with the rulers to whom they were accredited, though Gondomar (71), for instance, did. But envoys would normally expect to be kept informed by the ministers if not by the monarch himself of the views and intentions – if only ostensible – of the courts at which they resided.

114 Private letter from Lord Lyons, British Ambassador in France, to Sir Augustus Paget, British Envoy Extraordinary in Italy, Paris, 2nd September 1870. From the Paget Papers

Additional MS 51231

This letter was written by the British Ambassador in Paris to his counterpart at the Italian court during the Franco-Prussian war of 1870 and only a few days after Napoleon III, the Papacy's most powerful defender, had withdrawn his troops from Rome. Lyons writes that it is certain that Russia and Austria are really becoming better friends in the hope that their united front may prevent Prussia from imposing harsh terms on France. The Italian Ambassador in Paris has spoken to him 'at great length' of joint Austro-Italian action to the same end, though Vimercati, 'a scamp of whom you know I suppose as much as I do', had suggested that Italy offer France a hundred thousand men: 'of course an occupation of Rome is a necessary accompaniment of either plan'. Lyons himself suspects that the Italian government is 'feeling very much tempted to get up an insurrection or a semblance of insurrection at Rome in order to have a pretext for marching in to "protect" the Pope'. Turning to military affairs, he reports that 'the French hopes rise and fall from hour to hour'.

Two days after this letter was written, Napoleon III surrendered to the Prussians at Sedan and the 'Second Empire' came to an end. On 20th September Italian troops effectively completed the unification of Italy by fighting their way into Rome.

Ambassadors were expected to correspond regularly and their letters gave the opportunity to corroborate rumours and to transmit information of particular relevance to the recipient which might not have got into letters from the Foreign Minister. They also helped to bind together the diplomatic corps.

113

115 Newsletter from Paris, 28th February 1697/8, from the Ellis Papers

Additional MS 28921, ff.222–3

This newsletter records the movements of the exiled James II and his Queen ('it was remarked they were very melancholy, they have I think no great reasons to ye Contrary') and the appointment of 'Monsr de Callière' (**53**) as Secrétaire du Cabinet following the Congress of Rijswijck. It is mainly concerned with the activities at the French court in Versailles of William III's newly arrived Ambassador, the Earl of Portland. He had been 'very kindly received' by Louis XIV, his son the Dauphin ('Monseigneur'), and by his brother the Duke of Orleans ('Monsieur') at the King's Levée (the ceremony of getting out of bed) and at dinner and on that very morning he was going 'to hunt the wolf with Monseigneur'.

Trivial though these activities sound, they were not without their importance. The state of relations between countries could be judged by the way their envoys were treated and a considerable stir was caused when Louis XIV permitted Portland the extraordinary privilege of holding his candle during one of his levées. The stir was justified; so close had Anglo-French relations become that secret negotiations were going on between them to redraw the map of Europe in order to avoid war on the death of Carlos II of Spain (**39, 68**). Presence at court also enabled the ambassador to pick up gossip and to carry on informal discussions with ministers – particularly at the dinner table when, after a few glasses of wine, an astute envoy might persuade his host to indulge in a few confidences.

Newsletters seem generally to have been the responsibility of unaccredited members of the ambassador's suite. Circulated to envoys at other courts and to the Under Secretary and the Chief Clerk at home, they provided the raw material for the 'public' information contained in early newspapers such as the *London Gazette*, compiled by an official in the Secretary of State's office, where extracts were often reproduced verbatim. Newsletters could also be procured regularly from foreign non-diplomatic sources.

116 A page of confidential *print*, July 1879. From the Layard Papers

Additional MS 39153, f.79

The introduction of confidential *print* in the nineteenth century marked an enormous expansion of the old practice of circulating extracts or copies of important diplomatic despatches with the Secretary's of State's instructions. Confidential *print* consists of copies of letters, telegrams, instructions, and all manner of diplomatic documents sent to or from missions throughout the world, selected and printed at the Foreign Office which has had its own printing press since 1829. It plays an essential rôle in keeping British diplomatic representatives informed of official British reactions to events as they occur. This page contains three despatches sent in one day from Turkey by the then British Ambassador, Sir (Austen) Henry Layard (1817–94), the discoverer of Nineveh, who had embarked on a diplomatic career in middle age. In the first and longest despatch to Lord Salisbury, the Foreign Secretary, he gives a detailed description of the successful audience of the newly elected Prince of Bulgaria, Prince Alexander of Battenberg (1857–9), with his suzerain lord, the Sultan. By the time this was written, Salisbury would already have known that the meeting went well from a telegram that Layard had sent off at 10.30 pm on the previous night. Despite its auspicious beginnings, the reign of Prince Alexander, the uncle of Lord Mountbatten of Burma, was to end, in 1886, with his being kidnapped from his palace in Sofia by Russian agents and his consequent abdication. It would, indeed, in his own words, 'have been better for his own peace and happiness had he continued in his previous position (as a Russian soldier) which was in every way agreeable and suitable to him'.

117 Letter from the Portuguese Ambassador in England, Joao Pereira Dantas, to Lady Cecil, 23rd May 1562

Cotton MS Nero B. i, f.84

In this letter to the wife of Queen Elizabeth I's famous minister, the Ambassador says that as he himself is shortly to leave England, the affairs of his sovereign need a patron and protector. He thinks that to nobody could they be better entrusted than to Sir William Cecil. Should the latter accept, he would receive a pension of 2000 gold pieces a year; moreover, the first payment would be before Dantas's departure, so that it would be available as a dowry for the Cecils' daughter. The Ambassador prefers to make this detailed proposition to Lady Cecil rather than to Sir William, 'because you are less occupied'. Even Callières (**53**) found little to condemn in the ambassador's practice of offering bribes to ministers. Rather, he argued, ministers were to be condemned for accepting them – for ambassadors were only doing their duty of trying to further negotiations. Rulers and, officially, their ministers frowned on the practice, yet it flourished at the courts of Vienna, Madrid and Stockholm in the seventeenth and eighteenth centuries; and James I of England, his Queen and many of his ministers were in receipt of Spanish pensions. Reluctance to accept bribes could be circumvented in a variety of ways. The monarch might be told and persuaded to accept the situation. Presents could be made to the minister's family under a variety of pretexts. Necklaces could be given to his wife, for instance, and British envoys in Stockholm in the 1720s offered education at Eton to leading ministers' sons. If the minister jibbed even at this, the prospect of payment after completion of the desired service could be held out. In general it can be said however that on the whole bribes served little purpose, since ministers were rarely if ever influenced by them.

It was far cheaper, easier, and far more worthwhile to bribe well-placed minor officials like clerks in the foreign ministry, members of another envoy's household or postmasters (49) to provide copies of any interesting letters or documents that passed through their hands. Good salaries, regularly paid, have tended to decrease the attraction and extent of bribery, but the practice of paying 'slush money' or hiring spies in important ministries is far from dead.

118 Letter in 'invisible' ink sent from Paris during the Revolution, 29th July 1795. From the de la Puisaye Papers
Additional MS 8056, ff.184–5

This letter is ostensibly a receipt for a consignment of rice sent by a merchant in Paris, called Marsollier, to Gregorio Letoni, a merchant in Bellinzona in Italian Switzerland. The sender's Revolutionary credentials seem impeccable. He dates the letter by the Revolutionary Calendar (primedi, 11 thermidor, an 111e), though condescending to add, underneath it, the 'old style' (V(ieux) S(tyle)), and he addresses Letoni as 'Citoyen', concluding the letter with the standard Revolutionary greeting 'Salut & Fraternité' (Greeting and Brotherhood).

These words, however, probably served to warn the recipient that things were not as they seemed. For beneath the ostensible message, there is a lengthy letter written apparently in lemon juice which would have been invisible to the naked eye until after the letter had been placed over a flame. The letter is from royalists in Paris and gives an account, partly in code, of their activities and of the general situation in Paris where many royalists were being guillotined following the failure of a British-backed landing of emigrés in Brittany ten days earlier. This letter was sent from Bellinzona to Comte Joseph de la Puisaye who forwarded a copy to the French royalist agent, d'Antraigues, in Verona. He then sent on the news contained in the letter to Francis Drake, the British Minister Plenipotentiary

118

in Genoa; who informed the British Foreign Secretary, Lord Grenville.

The employment of malcontents or dissidents as spies was very much a last resort. The information they provided was usually trivial and extremely distorted; and the news conveyed often proved to be based only on highly-coloured gossip. Since the dissidents frequently wanted to use outside powers for their own ends, they reported only what the recipients wished to hear. As Philip II of Spain experienced in the sixteenth century and foreign supporters of the exiled Stuarts two centuries later, the results could be disastrous for themselves.

'Invisible' ink was rarely employed for the transmission of secret information. Even if the recipient noticed it, the writing was often so faint, even after having been placed over a flame, as to be virtually illegible, as in this instance.

119 Draft despatch of Sir Richard Browne, Charles I's resident in Paris, to Secretary of State Nicholas, Paris, 25th November/5th December 1642
Additional MS 12184, ff.130–1

Resident diplomats are expected to report regularly on developments in the country where they reside and on the negotiations of its government. They normally do so in despatches to their minister of foreign affairs. Until the last century two or three despatches a week enclosing copies of letters, memorials, reports, and other relevant documents usually sufficed. These were supplemented, at periods of about six weeks, by 'relations' which could be over 200 pages long, giving detailed analyses of the situation at court, of the leading personalities and factions; and of the country's military and economic situation. For over a century ambassadors have been in continuous contact with their masters by railway, telegraph, and more recently by telephone. Since formal despatches can be placed before a potentially hostile parliament or cabinet at demand, or may have to be shown to other ambassadors by the recipient, ambassadors have always reported or speculated on the most sensitive matters authoritatively, but without the danger of publicity, in private letters (**41**).

Most despatches by British diplomats are in the custody of the Public Record Office, but the British Library has many originals and private letters, particularly those addressed to Secretaries of State like Middleton or Carteret who took their official papers with them into retirement. Ambassadors' papers are also rich in drafts and copies of their despatches, which are frequently autograph and more revealing with their deletions, annotations, and last-minute additions, than the neat versions.

This draft despatch was written by Sir Richard Browne (1605–83), the father-in-law of the diarist John Evelyn and the resident in Paris from 1641 to 1660 of Charles I and the exiled Charles II. It describes the last days and death of Cardinal Richelieu, the appointment of Cardinal Mazarin as his successor and the action of the sickly Louis XIII, who was to die a few months later, in summoning the Parlement of Paris. Browne mentions the rumoured causes of the Cardinal's death, medical and psychological ('the cardinal's high spirit could not brooke that [the king's favourite, Cinq Mars] a Gascon, a Soldat de Fortune, a Capⁿ of mousquetors should be counterpois'd wth his eminent merits'), he delivers his own epitaph on Richelieu: 'certain it is that as this Cardinal hath rais'd ye Crowne of France to a great hight, so if he had liv'd but some yeeres longer he would have given a mortall wound to ye Spaniard to whom in this one Heroes death, nature hath now vouchsafed a Trophy of farre more value and importance then the great victory lately gayn'd over the house of Austria by the valour and fortune of the Sueds. He is heere generally lamented by all good patriots who have in a manner lost the Genius of the State and the most glorious subject the Christian world hath seene these many ages.'

120 Letter from Elizabeth I's Ambassador in France, Sir Nicholas Throckmorton, to Lord Robert Dudley, Amboise, 22nd May 1560
Additional MS 32091, f.180

In addition to his correspondence with the Secretary of State, an ambassador usually wrote to the monarch or influential figures at court who directed his country's foreign policy or, indeed, a 'secret' foreign policy at variance with the 'official' policy (**85**).

In this letter to Queen Elizabeth's favourite Robert Dudley, later created Earl of Leicester, Nicholas Throckmorton (1515–71), who had recently arrived in France, recommends the skill of one Portinari, a military engineer and comments, partly in cipher, on the state of France. The Wars of Religion were brewing (**30**) and he confirms, as he has previously written, that the French '*have som othe(r) to do at home* and . . . shall be *unable to attempt thys yere ani* grete matter *agenst England or Scotland*'. He therefore urges that England should take a firm line in its negotiations. For if '*you abate your sayles or Corage* . . . [France] will be *violent, heavy and obstinate* . . . therefore in a matter of suche consequence harvest *ys not to be made yn may unles* you have . . . a lasting pease and a unfayned suertie'.

Cipher (the substitution of letters or forms for letters or words) – often mixed with code (the substitution of a number for a word or name) – was much used in the sixteenth century (**25**) to deter casual snoopers when a confidential letter was en route to its destination.

121 Thomas Crawfurd, British Secretary of Embassy in Paris, reports to the Secretary of State, Lord Carteret, Paris, 30th May 1721. From the Carteret Papers
Additonal MS 22521, ff.116–7

The Secretary of Embassy was expected to keep the Secretary of State informed of matters which might have escaped the Ambassador's notice.

In this letter Thomas Crawfurd writes, partly in cipher, of a subject dear to his contemporaries' hearts: the love life of the profligate Duc d'Orléans (1674–1723), Regent for the infant Louis XV of France: 'It is of very great importance as I am told and makes very great persons concern themselves in it'. The Regent, jealous of the love affair of his long-standing mistress, Madame de Parabère with the Chevalier de Berengan, had taken a new mistress, Madame d'Auvergne, '*a handsome Lady . . . the wife of an Officer in the Foot Guards*'. According to a friend who was 'the Depositaire of all *his thoughts and trades in Love*', the Regent had been prevailed on to banish Madame de Parabère from court 'and

Monday is appointed'. Crawfurd concedes however that 'the whole affair may change betwixt [now] and then' for Orléans and Madame de Parabère had often quarrelled and been reconciled in the past. And so it soon proved in this case. But which ever way this episode might have turned out it would probably not have mattered much since Orléans, contrary to what his contemporaries believed, never seems to have allowed his mistresses or notoriously dissolute 'roué' friends to influence his generally wise conduct of French affairs.

At the close of the letter Crawfurd complains 'it is so tedious to write in Cyphers that the post does not allow me to give . . . a full account of this matter . . . but by the first Courier I shall give . . . more particulars'. This underlines the point that cipher and code (the two terms were usually confused in practice) were generally not used in the most important letters before the nineteenth century. Indeed so 'tedious' was it to compose a letter in cipher, that diplomats who were not as conscientious as Crawfurd became negligent and their letters were often easily intelligible despite their use of code or cipher.

122 Queen's Messenger's Badge of 1854/1855 (see plate no. IX)

British Museum: Department of Medieval and Later Antiquities: Montagu Guest 1550

The Messenger's badge was originally worn on the breast, and the ribbon was only introduced in the nineteenth century. This silver-gilt badge has a blue ribbon of watered silk and contains the Garter legend on a background of blue enamel set with the royal arms under crystal. The Messenger's traditional symbol, a silver greyhound, is suspended underneath. On the reverse the badge is inscribed *W Hampton Q.M. War Department*. King's (or Queen's) Messengers are responsible for conveying British ambassadors' instructions and despatches. Traditionally they have enjoyed freedom of passage and priority over regular mails in the execution of their duties. Until 1772, however, they were few in number, with none under the direct control of the Secretaries of State – even afterwards there were initially only sixteen. As a result envoys normally had to make do with their local post offices or express services ('estaffettes') (49). In the nineteenth

120

121

century messengers were used more frequently, but although swift and more secure than the ordinary post, they were readily recognisable and tended to attract attention to themselves. Their bags were, thus, liable to be pilfered while they slept. Accordingly envoys often confided their most sensitive, but less urgent, reports and messages to trusted friends, servants, relatives, or tourists, who could smuggle them, inconspicuously, beyond the reach of prying postmasters or innkeepers, to their destination. Under such circumstances codes and ciphers, which could attract attention, could even be omitted.

The messenger's life was swift-moving and often attended with risk and the badges were frequently lost or stolen: between 1732 and 1759 twelve messengers lost the badge or the greyhound attached or had the royal arms broken through having been thrown from horses (E. Hertslet, *Recollections of the Old Foreign Office* p. 161 (London, 1901)). They were well paid for their labours and were given generous expenses. They could also gain extra income in earlier centuries by carrying private letters, giving lifts to travellers in their coaches, and through smuggling. The occupation therefore became attractive to reasonably well-born gentlemen with a taste for adventure. The letters of Lieutenant-Colonel Charles Townley (Additional MS 46453) vividly convey the life of a Queen's Messenger at about the time when this badge was made.

123 Letter of William Blencowe, Official Decipherer to the British ministry, 16th October 1707, enclosing a partially deciphered transcript of an intercepted letter of 13th September 1707

Blenheim (Sunderland) Papers D 1 2

The interception of letters has regularly been practised, though exceedingly rarely acknowledged, by governments throughout the world, who have thereby obtained much precious information. Ciphers, codes and invisible ink have never provided effective protection for more than a short time. Indeed this very weakness has occasionally been utilised as an instrument of policy, and false information has been put into cipher with the expectation that it would be deciphered and the intention that it should mislead.

Most Italian states employed cipher secretaries in the fifteenth century; and the ministers of Henry VIII and Elizabeth I of England were proficient in the field (27, 45). In the seventeenth century considerable progress was made in the science of cryptology particularly by Rossignon, the chief French decipherer from 1628 to 1682. But it was only at the turn of the seventeenth and eighteenth centuries that interception and decipherment became efficiently organised. In Britain responsibility for the interception of diplomatic correspondence was formally vested in a special section of the Post Office, called the 'Secret Office', under a 'Foreign Secretary', in 1711. It was the counterpart of the *Cabinet Noir* in Paris and the *Geheime Kanzlei* in Vienna. All three had no official existence, but long series of transcripts of intercepted diplomatic correspondence in the national archives and libraries (including the British Library) bear testimony to their activity. The deciphering of despatches, whether intercepted in England or abroad (49), was from 1703 officially in the hands of a Deciphering Branch headed by an Official Decipherer who was directly responsible to the Secretary of State. John Wallis (1616–1703), the Savilian professor of geometry at Oxford (1649–1703), who had been responsible for much of this work on an ad hoc basis since 1642, was paid a regular annuity from 1701. His grandson William Blencowe (1683–1712), a promising young Oxford graduate, was the Official Decipherer until he committed suicide in 1712. From 1716 until its abolition in 1844 the Deciphering Branch was dominated by members of the Willes family, who from 1762 occupied all the positions and were rewarded with knighthoods and clerical appointments. The British Library possesses papers of Wallis, Blencowe, and the Willes family.

This letter by Blencowe reveals something of the decipherer's methods. 'There is one sentence . . . which I have not made intelligible to myself . . . The characters being all explained by what they signify in other places except one, 437, which I have ghessed at but uncertainly. The number 763 seem's (*sic*) pretty plainly to signify *le Roy de France . . .*' The enclosed transcript is of a letter [which was intercepted by a postmaster, Jaupain, in the Southern Netherlands] from a counsellor of the Hungarian rebel leader, Prince Rakoczi, to the secretary of the Elector of Bavaria (108). He expresses the hope – possibly with the intention of frightening any Austrians who intercepted the letter – that Russia and Sweden would be reconciled under French mediation since they both intended consequently to turn their arms against the Emperor. Blencowe notes in the margin 'Number 13 is in other places a nought here it seems miswritten for what should signify *en*'.

NEGOTIATION

Resident diplomats are constantly engaged in a wide variety of formal and informal negotiations at conferences and congresses or with the governments of the countries to which they are accredited. The resulting agreements can take several forms, the leading practitioner-theorist of the beginning of this century, Sir Ernest Satow, noting at least fourteen distinct types of instrument including treaties: (e.g. of peace (126, 129, 134, 135, 138), alliance (130, 131, 132), commerce (125, 126, 136), navigation, extradition, compensation (133), boundaries, arbitration), conventions, accessions, adhesions, arrangements, declarations (136), and confirmations (138). But frequently negotiations can conclude quite satisfactorily with a simple letter or an exchange of notes.

From the earliest times negotiations have normally proceeded through several clearly defined stages, associated with particular types of document. The structure and wording of these documents have remained virtually unchanged throughout Western Europe over the centuries, though their outward appearance and the language in which they are written have undergone considerable alterations.

'Full Powers' (124) formally confirm that a representative is authorised to undertake a specific negotiation on his master's behalf and that any resulting agreement (when ratified) will be accepted and abided by. They have to be issued to anyone involved in formal negotiations, foreign ministers (128, 134) as well as diplomats. While special envoys and ambassadors to congresses depart from home with them, they can be sent at any time to long-established resident diplomats. The exchange of full powers between negotiators marks the formal start of negotiations (125). At congresses, where full powers perform some of the functions of credentials, this comes at an early stage, but elsewhere it often occurs only when informal talks have reached an advanced stage. For rulers fearful of unwelcome commitments like to keep a close control over negotiations through frequent instructions to and correspondence with their representatives (127), and this total control becomes more difficult to exercise after the exchange of full powers. But valid agreements can only be concluded by properly constituted 'plenipotentiaries', that is negotiators with 'full power' (Latin 'plena potestas') to act for their masters.

Negotiations can proceed in any number of ways but the continuous exchange and amendment of drafts ('projects') and counter-drafts ('counter-projects') of the desired agreement until unity is achieved over the final text seems to have been the most frequent (126) after the initial exploratory discussions (125). The agreed text is set out in orderly fashion in the so-called 'Protocol' or 'Articles of Agreement', of which at least two examples are prepared. The plenipotentiaries then formally affix their personal seals to them (129, 130, 131), though each party does not need to seal all the examples (130); and in recent centuries plenipotentiaries have signed as well as sealed (131). The articles of agreement are then transmitted to the rulers in such a way that each receives an example sealed by the representative(s) of the other(s) if not always by their own plenipotentiaries. The articles of agreement are then ratified, usually but not invariably by the head of state (132, 133). The instruments of ratification are often the most splendid of the treaty documents, and the terms of the treaty normally come into force only after the instruments of ratification have been exchanged, each party receiving the instruments of ratification of (all) the other(s) (134, 135). A declaration or certificate of exchange is then issued (136) and is normally attached to the instruments of ratification. Until the middle of the eighteenth century hostages were on occasion given as pledges for the execution of the terms of a treaty (137).

The conclusion of one treaty often paves the way for negotiations for another (131, 136). Thus the process of negotiation becomes continuous.

124 Full Powers for Sir Isaac Wake signed by Charles I of England, Greenwich, 29th June 1631, with the second Great Seal of Charles attached to grant of special livery to Sir Giles Bray, 1629

Additional Charters 1529 and 1730

These full powers were prepared for Sir Isaac Wake (*c.*1580–1632), a lawyer by training, who had begun his diplomatic career in 1609 as secretary to Sir Dudley Carleton, James I's ambassador in Venice. Knighted in 1619, he was sent as Resident Ambassador ('morantem oratorem' in the words of this document) to France in 1631 and had his first audience with Louis XIII in May of that year. These full powers, drawn up the next month, were never issued. They have never had a Great Seal attached to them.

Their appearance is more elaborate than normal full powers of the time and would even then have seemed old-fashioned for diplomatic documents. For their particular Gothic hand and the initial C containing the King's portrait and the other embellishments – for which an additional fee was payable – reveal them as having been drawn up in the English Lord Chancellor's Office, or Chancery. The Chancery had been responsible for the execution and registration of diplomatic documents

throughout the Middle Ages but from about 1530 the Secretary of State's Office had gradually taken over most of these functions, relegating Chancery to domestic, English, transactions. By 1700 Chancery seems to have been responsible only for attaching the Great Seal to diplomatic documents and for the official enrolment of the texts of treaties. By then most full powers were unadorned and written – though still on parchment in Latin – in italic script in the Secretary of State's Office (**68**). English came into use in the nineteenth century. If necessary, full powers could – even as early as the reign of Elizabeth I (see Additional MS 24023 f.1) – take the form of a simple English letter, written on paper and signed by the monarch and normally a secretary of state, with a papered royal signet seal bearing the royal arms, rather like Queen Anne's letter of the recall for the Earl of Sunderland (**153**). The Great Seal is Charles I's second seal, showing the King enthroned in majesty on the obverse and, on the reverse, riding. It would have been the seal attached to these full powers.

The form of all full powers, regardless of their language, is similar throughout Europe. It dates back to the twelfth-century Papal court. Consequently, though taking the form of Royal Letters Patent, these full powers and almost all English

124

diplomatic Letters Patent, differ markedly in their form of wording from Letters Patent issued for domestic use. They begin with a recitation of the King's principal titles, as do all Royal Letters Patent. Charles then announces, by way of preamble, that certain difficulties and controversies remain between himself and the King of France despite their recent reconciliation. He declares his desire, for the general well-being, to remedy this unsatisfactory state of affairs, which is best achieved through negotiations between French and English commissaries. Therefore he names Sir Isaac Wake, of whose prudence, virtue, and courage he is convinced, as his 'commissarium, deputatum et procuratorem' and gives him 'plenam . . . potestatem' (full power) to negotiate with properly constituted French commissaries, and to agree and to sign an accord settling these differences and any others obstructing the full restoration of peace and trade between the British and French crowns. Finally Charles promises on his royal word to ratify and observe in future any agreement duly concluded between Wake and the French in confirmation of which he affixes his signature and English Seal.

125

125 English ambassadors, including Thomas More, report to Cardinal Wolsey, Bruges, 15th September 1521

Cotton MS Galba B. vii, ff. 125–126

More and the three other ambassadors who had gone to Bruges on a special mission describe the start of their formal negotiations with ambassadors of the Hansa, a commercial and political league of several major north European cities. First 'we shewed them the kinges benevolent mynde in forme and manner as ys conteigned in *our* Instruccions and that done dyd exhibit owre commissions [i.e. full powers] which were thowgt by eythre of bothe parties ample and sufficient'. The negotiations could thus commence though the English had a procedural trick up their sleeves. More and his colleagues explained the purpose of their mission: 'there hath bene grete and meny complaynetes made unto the kinges highnesse and youre grace of robberies and despoyles and other Iniuries doone unto the kinges subiectz which complayntes we dyd aggravate bothe bi estymaccion of grete Sommes and allso by exhibiting certaine bookes and meny billes of complayntes, saying that . . . such complaynantes doith daily desyre Justice'. Having thus used exaggeration to alarm the other ambassadors, the English suggested that these particular cases be redressed before general principles were discussed. This was a cunning ploy, for expecting the other side to make difficulties about

anything they said, they had proposed the very opposite of their real instructions. The Hansa ambassadors asked for a break to consider what the English had said and, sure enough, the next day they proposed 'that we wolde treate upon the generals and particulers togydre because meny . . . of the particulers dependeth upon the generals and this doing', the English report, 'we folow the contentes of your gracious instruccions.' The English then intentionally caused confusion among the Hansa Ambassadors by demanding a written list of the 'numbre and names of the citese [&] townes that made the body of the hanz at the first tyme of the graunt of their privileges'. For otherwise 'they colde afferme theymselves to be Oratours for the bodye of the hanz and cowde not shew what members made the saide bodye'. The startled Hansa ambassadors (this was 'nivyr put in dowte . . . before this') promised 'they would do their best to gyve us knowlege'. The English, having succeeded in cowing the other side, then agreed to begin discussions of other issues, though warning they 'wolde at tyme convenient return unto the same' subject. At the end of the letter, the ambassadors promise 'the briefe expediccion' of their business and, reminding Wolsey that they 'have bene at grete charges', they ask that 'provision . . . be made for us' until the end of their negotiations. These continued until 8th October, when More went to spend a few days with his friend Erasmus.

The letter gives a good impression of the start of formal negotiations in the early modern period, first with the checking and exchange of full powers and then the discussion of procedures which could be used by one side to place the other at a disadvantage. The next stage would be the drawing up of a draft treaty or project by one side which would probably be answered by a counter-project from the other. The final treaty would evolve from the project and counter-project in the course of negotiations.

Note how the ambassadors repeatedly refer to their instructions, which through the ages envoys have had to follow meticulously but which – as the letter demonstrates – they could execute in the most expedient manner.

126 Lord Lexington, Queen Anne's Envoy Extraordinary in Spain, notes Spanish replies to his draft proposals for treaties of peace and commerce, Madrid, March 1713. From the Lexington Papers

Additional MS 46559 B. ff.61–62

These notes seem to have been scribbled down onto scrap paper while Lexington was actually listening to the Spanish reply to his proposals being read out. In his hurry he switches from French, in which the negotiations were conducted ('accordé', 'de mesme', 'à examiner', 'comme avant la paix') to English ('to be considered'). Earlier he had scribbled aggressively 'we insist'. The notes were probably intended to remind him of points to be raised later in the discussions.

By the time of this meeting the negotiations, which had begun in October 1712, had already gone through several stages of projects and counter-projects. Beforehand the British and French had agreed in secret, informal contracts, that Britain would receive much-coveted commercial privileges in Spain and its American empire. In return it would recognise the Bourbon candidate for the Spanish throne, Philippe Duc d'Anjou, as Philip V of Spain under certain conditions, particularly his renunciation of all claims to the French throne for himself and his descendants. Nevertheless, the negotiations had proved hard – particularly for the commercial treaty.

Several of the comments here indicate the advanced stage negotiations had reached by March, when details and the wording of articles were being discussed ('7: a corriger avec le tariffe'; '14: accordé – Canarys' (i.e. Canary Islands)). On the opposite page Lexington has noted the wording for an article in the peace treaty relating to Catalan political rights, which the authorities in Madrid wished to

abolish, but which the British were pledged to make at least a show of defending. According to the article the Catalans would have 'Permissione de vivre selon leurs ancienes coutumes que ny opose ny Blesse directement L'Authorité Royale et que pouront estre Reglé par Monsieur le Marquis de Monteleon et les ministres de sa Majesté Britannick' ('permission to live according to their former customs which do not oppose or directly harm the royal authority and which the Marquess of Monteleon, [Philip V's ambassador to the English court and at Utrecht], and the ministers of Her Britannic Majesty will be able to regulate'). This type of formula was an old manoeuvre used by diplomats eager for a general agreement but confronted by a few intractable problems. While appearing to settle the problem, it can be interpreted so as to satisfy both sides and in fact leaves the issue open for the immediate future. Beneath this draft article, and reflecting the British wish to make Philip's renunciation as binding as possible, Lexington notes the need for a law to be passed by the (Castilian) parliament or Cortes to conclude ('conclure') by confirming the renunciation.

Nevertheless, despite progress on the political front, the commercial negotiations were going badly and only nine of the twenty articles of the commercial treaty had as yet been agreed. In the event, on 26th and 27th March only a contract, popularly called the 'Asiento', for the import of Africans slaves into Spanish America by the British, and a preliminary peace treaty were signed in Madrid. Four months later, when the formal peace treaty was signed at Utrecht, only a highly unsatisfactory provisional commercial treaty could be signed.

These notes illustrate the protracted haggling over apparently insignificant details and words in draft treaties that mark the later stages of most negotiations. The issues at stake, though, were clearly important.

127 Instructions from Secretary of State Windebank to Arthur Hopton, Charles I's resident in Spain, Westminster, 23rd January/2nd February 1635

Additional MS 32093, f.84

This letter well illustrates the reluctance of rulers and their ministers to relinquish control over negotiations to their diplomatic representatives, and their concern to see that their instructions were obeyed.

Windebanke writes that 'since the finishing of the dispatche herewith sent unto you, his M: hath thought fitt as well for avoyding the delayes & other adiusting it as it was sett downe in the first paper. You will therefore be carefull and wary not to binde his Ma:ty to those inconveniences as they most unreasonably desire but strictly to follow the direccions of the dispatch and to give a speedy accompt hether of your negotiations therein, considering the great weight thereof.' The tone of the letter verges on that employed by Charles II when he wrote to his independent-minded representative in the Hague, Sir George Downing, on 16th/26th January 1672 (N.S.) that 'it is your part to obey punctually my orders, instead of putting yourself to the trouble of finding reasons why you do not do so' (Stowe MS 142, f.84).

Once an envoy reached the limit of the concessions he was allowed to make, it was customary for him to frame an 'ultimatum': a final draft of the articles of the proposed treaty which the other side either had to accept (though minor modifications were usually accepted), or break off negotiations.

128 Lord Palmerston's quill pens
Additional MS 59854.B

According to the words, in a contemporary hand, on the page, they are mounted 'in his usual mode of keeping them'. Palmerston signed countless instructions and several articles of agreement, such as those for the Treaty of London, which guaranteed Belgium independence in 1839.

129 Signature of the peace treaty between France and Spain, Nijmegen, 17th September 1678. Painting by Henri Gascar, 1679
By courtesy of the Nimeegs Museum 'Commanderie van St Jan', Nijmegen

This painting has been described, in the catalogue of the exhibition '*De Vrede van Nijmegen 1678–1978*', as an interpretation of the ceremony, composed of as many realistic details as was possible in a work of art. It conveys many of the most characteristic features of such ceremonies – though many treaties (more accurately described at that stage as articles of agreement) were concluded totally without ceremony.

The treaty was signed in the house of the Dutch plenipotentiaries, out of respect for Hieronymus van Beverningk and Willen van Haren, who had acted as mediators during the last stages of these negotiations. The reception room, on the first floor, where the ceremony was held, was lined with tapestries in such a way that it appeared to be completely symmetrical – for in this way disputes

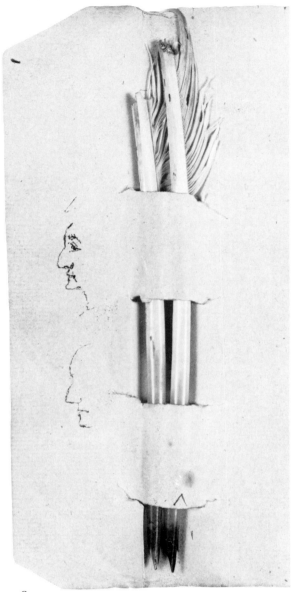

128

inconveniences of sending up & downe, as to give them [i.e. the Spaniards] assurances there of his reall intentions to the accomplishment of this treaty . . . to enable you by these powers heerwith sent unto you, to treate & conclude these articles there, according to such conditions as are expressed in the said dispatch & not otherwise. You will finde the powers very large & answerable to the trust his M: reposeth in you . . . But you are by no means to make use of them, unless they will agreee to these articles concerning the convenient tyme, as in the 3^d, the warning to be given to his M: as in the 8th and the utter cancelling of the 16th as it was last proposed concerning restitution of prizes or

129

over precedence could be avoided. For the same reason, the two antichambers prepared for the French and Spanish Ambassadors and their suites were also identical. The table, covered with a gold-fringed green velvet cloth, was placed lengthways in the room, stretching from the door, leading into a corridor, to the windows of the house. Van Beverningk, the first Dutch Ambassador, is seen in profile sitting in the place of honour, with his back to the windows and the viewer. To his left are the French and to the right, the Spaniards, while van Haren sits facing him at the other end of the table. The first French and Spanish Ambassadors, the Marshal Godefroy d'Estrades (146) and Don Paolo Spinola Doria, the Marquess de los Balbases, share equal honour in sitting nearest to van Beverningk and the windows. Next to d'Estrades sits the second French Ambassador, Charles Colbert, Marquis de Croissy, and next to him, the third French Ambassador, Jean-Antoine de Mesmes, Comte d'Avaux, perhaps the most astute French diplomat of the day. Next to the Marquess de los Balbases sit the second Spanish Ambassador, Gaspar de Trèves, the Marquess de la Fuente (see 146) and the third Spanish Ambassador, Jean-Baptiste Christyn. All the Ambassadors wear hats, but everyone else in the room, except for the priests, who occupied a special position, are hatless out of respect. The Ambassadors sit surrounded by their suites. At the front, on the French side, stand two pages, apparently in livery. Next to the Marquess de los Balbases stands his young son, the Duke of Sesto. The French Secretary of Embassy, Mignon, hands a quill pen to the Marshal d'Estrades. His Spanish counterpart Don Francesco de Urbina is probably the man whose arm is on the back of the chair of the Marquess de los Balbases. Prominent among the Spanish suite is their chaplain, a Jesuit. The French chaplain, dressed demurely in black with a simple white collar, stands behind Colbert. He may be the Abbé Jean-François d'Estrades, the son of the first Ambassador.

The Ambassadors had entered the room and seated themselves at the table at exactly the time as their counterparts, and the picture shows them just a moment before they signed the articles of agreement. D'Estrades and de los Balbases would sign and seal their respective copies on the left of the page – the place of honour – at exactly the same time, to be followed by their colleagues in precise sequence. The copies would then be exchanged and the process would be repeated on the right hand side. The mediators then signed a declaration guaranteeing the articles of agreement which were sent for ratification to Paris and Madrid (131).

Louis XIV commissioned this painting, which commemorates one of his greatest triumphs, six months after the signature of the treaty and while the participants were still in Nijmegen.

130 Articles of agreement of the Perpetual Alliance between King Richard II of England and King John I of Portugal, Windsor, 9th May 1386

Public Record Office: Exchequer, Treasury of the Receipt, Treaty Documents (E.30) 310

These articles of agreement are written in Latin on a single large parchment membrane. They are notarially attested and two armorial seals, of red wax set in natural-coloured wax, are appended on parchment tags. They have the typical appearance of medieval articles of agreement.

The text of the articles of agreement consists of three elements. First there is a preamble setting out the justification of and background to the treaty in somewhat ornate language. Then follows a list of the provisions of the treaty. These renew the perpetual offensive and defensive alliance of 1373, and provide for the marriage of King John and Phillippa, King Richard's cousin. In the previous year, with English help, John of Avis had wrenched the Portuguese throne from the Castilian King and his Portuguese wife. Through this marriage John hoped to carry the war into Castile nominally in support of his future father-in-law, John of Gaunt (8), who claimed to be rightful King of Castile. Further articles provide for security for all the subjects of the one party within the territories of the other and lay down that 'the successors of the above kings, each in their time, shall within a year of the coronation be obliged to renew and confirm the alliance under the Great Seal'. Lastly there are quotations from the ambassadors' full powers giving their names and status.

Under the articles can be seen the notarial attestation. Notaries public (international lawyers) were long involved in the treaty-making process. They knew the forms the documents had to take if they were to be internationally valid and they had the authority to declare the documents were true records in a way recognised in countries where sealing alone was not considered a sufficient guarantee. Indeed, so closely involved were notaries public that in late-thirteenth century England several of them also worked as professional scriveners. Here the notary public John Bouland (Bowland) states, that while he did not actually write the document, he was present at the whole of the proceedings and recorded and reduced the statement to the form of a 'public' instrument. He vouches for the accuracy of the text, specifying certain necessary corrections and alterations. He places his elaborate personal mark, based on a standing cross, with his name, at the left of this declaration. Frequently such a declaration would have been supported by that of another notary public (132). Notarial attestations are found on

English treaty documents as late as 1543.

The seals bear the arms of the Portuguese Ambassadors, Ferdinand, Master of the Military Order of St James (left) and John Fogaca, the Portuguese Chancellor (right). The seals of the English Ambassadors are not appended, since at this period the different parties did not generally seal the same copy of articles of agreement. Instead, each side sealed its own copy, and the various copies (if there were more than two parties to the treaty) were then exchanged, as the full powers had been (and still are) at the start of the negotiations. The seals contain the personal arms of the Ambassadors and not those of their masters who had not yet formally consented to the terms. The seals and the notarial attestation are sufficient to authenticate the articles of agreement, rendering unnecessary the signatures of the Ambassadors.

This treaty is still in force today, the oldest Alliance by which Britain is bound.

131 Marlborough's copy of the articles of agreement of the Anglo-Dutch Treaty of Alliance and Defence, The Hague, 11th November 1701 (see plate no. XIV)

Blenheim (Marlborough) Papers B II 28

This Treaty was signed two months after the conclusion of the Second Treaty of the Grand Alliance (68), by which time it had become clear that war between the Allies and the Bourbons would not be long delayed. The preamble takes the form of an impersonal declaration and states that the union of France and Spain and Louis XIV's occupation of the Southern Netherlands (Belgium) had placed Europe in imminent danger of losing its liberty and falling under the yoke of a universal monarchy. Accordingly William III and the Dutch States General had been compelled to bind themselves together as closely as possible and to agree on the means necessary to enable them to preserve the common liberty of Europe, to conserve their own trade and security and to deprive their neighbours of all hope of ever dividing them. The articles confirm previous Anglo-Dutch treaties, and define the nature of the event that would lead to the outbreak of war; it would be any enemy attack or even preparations for an attack on any of the Allies, or the continued French occupation of the Southern Netherlands. The start of hostilities would activate an offensive and defensive Anglo-Dutch alliance, and arrangements are made for close co-operation on land and at sea in wartime. Further articles stipulate that neither party should make peace unilaterally and that when peace was made particular attention would be paid to the commerce and security of both powers – particularly with regard to the Southern Netherlands. The articles are signed and sealed by William III's Ambassador Extraordinary and Plenipotentiary John Churchill, then Earl of Marlborough, and by the Dutch delegates Christiaan Karel van Lintelo, Lord of Ehse (representing the province of Guelderland); Frederik van Reede, Baron of Lier (Holland and West Friesland); Antonie Heinsius, the Grand Pensionary (also Holland and West Friesland); Willem van Nassau, Count of Odijk (Zeeland); Everard van Weede, Baron of Dijkveld (Utrecht); Willem van Haren, (Friesland); Burchard Joost van Welvelde, Baron of Zalk (Overijssel), and Wicker Wickers (Groningen).

The protocol resembles that of 1386 in having a justificatory preamble, and a description of the negotiators and their status, based on their full powers; and the treaty articles are listed in an orderly fashion. Protocols of today continue to have these features. The appearance of this protocol is however totally different from its medieval predecessor. The articles are written in French, on paper, in a book of sixteen pages bound with red and silver cord and the negotiators have signed them as well as sealing them in red shellac, otherwise known as sealing wax (resin coloured and melted into thin plates). Moreover, most examples of this protocol are signed and sealed by all the negotiators involved: in some of the copies the Dutch have the place of honour on the left, and in others (as here) Marlborough. But all are of equal status and validity.

The appearance of treaty documents, and certain diplomatic conventions, had altered considerably since the fourteenth century. From the fifteenth century the book form had gradually replaced single sheets of parchment membranes sewn together. For these, whether kept flat or in rolls, had proved extremely cumbersome and could exceed five feet in length (e.g. Additional Charter 1260 containing a ratification of the Anglo-Burgundian commercial treaty of 1496). Parchment in book form continued to be used for the more important treaties, but paper was increasingly used for lesser agreements. With the Reformation, the notarial attestation disappeared from English diplomatic documents. Catholic powers, however, continued to utilise notaries until well into the seventeenth century and perhaps later (see Additional MS 19271; Anglo-Spanish contract of marriage of 1623). A further change had occurred in the sealing and signature of protocols. For seals, other than the royal Great Seals, had grown smaller and by the seventeenth century they were no longer suspended from protocols. Instead they became flat blobs of wax or shellac on paper which received impressions of the negotiatiors' arms from their signet rings. Growing literacy also meant

that the negotiators came to sign their names as well as sealing agreements, though, in theory, the seal was sufficient.

These changes necessitated the evolution of new procedures for concluding articles of agreement, the so called 'alternat', an example of which is recorded in an Anglo-French treaty as early as 1546. This established that the place of honour was the left-hand side of a page, that where there were several plenipotentiaries employed by one power they should sign according to rank (129), and that all parties should have the right to at least one copy of the articles of agreement with the signature of their representative(s) in the place of honour.

Another important change was the replacement, from the turn of the seventeenth and eighteenth centuries, of Latin by modern French as the generally accepted diplomatic language (136). The first major treaties to be worded in French were those concluded at Utrecht in 1713, but before that there had been cases of treaties in French, as here, and often negotiations had been carried on in French, with the final draft being translated into Latin. Since the application of treaty articles often depends on interpretations of their vague wording, this new custom occasionally gave the French a diplomatic advantage.

Since the eighteenth century, the appearance of articles of agreement has not radically altered. English and other modern languages have joined French as accepted diplomatic languages, and the texts have been typed or printed since the middle of the last century. The only major change, however, has been the revision of the 'alternat'. At the Congress of Vienna in 1815 it was accepted that henceforth plenipotentiaries should sign multi-lateral articles of agreement according to the alphabetical order of their countries in French, with each party nevertheless retaining the right to one copy of the articles with the signature of their negotiator(s) in the place of honour at the head of the left-hand column. The seals and signatures at the end of protocols have thus often formed long lists, beginning on the left side of the page.

132 Ratification by the Neapolitan crown of a league between the Pope, Naples, Milan, Florence, and Siena; Naples, 13th March 1480
Additional MS 27373

King Ferdinand I (also called Ferrante) of Naples (1458–1494) ratified this Treaty between the Papacy, the Kingdom of Naples, Milan, Florence, and Siena shortly after it had been concluded in his palace, the Castello Nuovo. Negotiated after two years of warfare between Florence and Milan on one side, and the other parties, this League was the latest in a long line of such alliances which, ostensibly aspiring to reconcile and unite all the states of Italy, effectively only provided brief breathing-spaces between their internecine wars. The terms provided guarantees of the lands and rights of all the participants and made detailed provision for mutual aid on land and sea against internal rebellion or invasion by other powers. Certain favoured states were invited to join, such as Venice and the Duke of Ferrara; other cities, like Bologna, or petty rulers, like Federigo da Montefeltro, Duke of Urbino, were mentioned favourably. Certain despots in the Romagna, however, like Sigismondo Malatesta's son, Roberto, the ruler of Rimini, were expressly excluded. Pope Sixtus IV was allowed to proceed against them as he wished – though Milan and Florence were exempted from having to aid Sixtus in this. Months earlier, these same despots had been commanding Florentine troops . . . The League was to continue in operation for fifty years. Just over two years later, after months of tension, it had dissolved, Naples, Florence, and Milan going to war with Venice and the Papacy in defence of the Duke of Ferrara.

The ratification takes the form of a parchment book of twenty-four pages. It contains a preamble justifying the Treaty, a full recapitulation of the articles of agreement including the wording of the notarial attestations, a full transcription of the plenipotentiaries' full powers, and finally the ratification of the articles by King Ferdinand. Not only does Ferdinand seal the document with his Great Seal, but he also signs it and places his personal mark, comprising the arms of the Aragonese dynasty to which he belonged, on the page. Ferdinand's words of ratification in which he 'accepts, praises, approves, ratifies and confirms' the articles and affixes his great seal, are standard. The seal, of which fragments remain, was originally covered with paper, and shows the King seated on

the throne, holding orb and sceptre, and surrounded by the shields of the lands associated with his dynasty. The reverse shows him on horseback. The seal is appended to the document with a red and yellow cord, the colours traditionally associated with the Aragonese dynasty. As seems to have been the case in Catholic countries until well into the seventeenth century, the ratification is witnessed as well as being attested by the King's secretary, Antonello de Petrucci, and by Gerardo Rustico, a public notary from Piacenza. The witnesses are the ambassadors who had concluded the articles of agreement: first Ferdinand's ambassador, Lorenzo Giustino de Castello, then the Milanese, Pietro da Gallarate and Giovanni Angelo de Talentis, next the Florentines, Agostino de Billotti (significantly a former resident agent of the Medici Bank in Naples) and Niccolo Michelozzi, and finally the Sienese, Jacopo Piccolomini and Antonio Biccho. The body of the ratification is written in a very fine humanistic hand, probably by one of the scribes employed in the Neapolitan Chancery.

This ratification was acquired by the Department of Manuscripts in 1866, having passed into Spanish hands by the seventeenth century. It may earlier have been in the archives of Siena.

133 Ratification signed by Queen Victoria, Osborne, 4th January 1867 (see plate no. VI)
Additional MS 45862

The instrument ratifies the supplementary convention, signed in Mexico in October 1866 by Peter Campbell Scarlett, the British Envoy Extraordinary and Plenipotentiary in Mexico, and Don Bonifacio Gutierrez, a Mexican Councillor of State. This implemented the fifth and sixth articles of the convention of 26th June 1866 between Great Britain and Maximilian I, Emperor of Mexico, for the investigation and settlement of the claims of British subjects against the Mexican Government. It was drawn up in the Treaty and Royal Letter Department of the British Foreign Office, which had come into existence in 1813, and consists of a book of twenty paper pages bound in crimson velvet covers lined with royal blue silk and with light and dark blue, green, and red ribbons. The Great Seal, bearing impressions of Queen Victoria's second seal, is made of yellow wax and is in a case, or skippet, of silvered base-metal. This is embossed with the royal arms, supported by the crowned lion of England and the unicorn of Scotland, surrounded by the Garter with a George pendant, and surmounted by another crowned lion atop a crowned helmet. The field is interspersed with the roses and thistles of England and Scotland. The top of the skippet is encircled by a

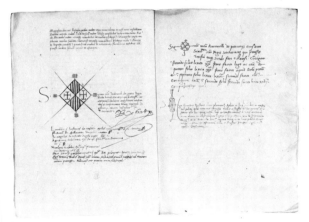

wreath of oak leaves and acorns. The seal is attached to the document by a cord of plaited red silk and silver bullion threads – apparently the standard colours for British diplomatic documents by this time – with a tassel.

The ratification takes the form of Royal Letters Patent, handwritten in English and Spanish. The text consists of a short preamble, a transcription of the articles of agreement in English and Spanish and the standard formula of ratification – in English, but virtually identical to those found in medieval ratifications: 'We having seen and considered the supplementary convention aforesaid, have approved accepted and confirmed the same in all and every one of its Articles and Clauses as we do by these Presents approve, accept, confirm and ratify it for ourselves, our Heirs and Successors: Engaging and Promising upon our Royal Word, that we will sincerely and faithfully perform and observe all and singular the things which are contained and expressed in the supplementary convention aforesaid, and that we will never suffer the same to be violated by any one, or transgressed in any manner as far as it lies in our power. – In the greater testimony and validity of all of which, We have caused the Great Seal of our United Kingdom of Great Britain and Ireland to be affixed to these Presents, which We have signed with our Royal Hand . . .'. In contrast to ratifications of earlier centuries, the plenipotentiaries' full powers are omitted. The quotation of the passage in the articles of agreement naming them and stating that they had 'communicated to each other their respective full powers, found in good and due form' was held to be sufficient.

The introduction of the book form for diplomatic documents and of skippets (initially made of wood) for Great Seals in the course of the fifteenth century presented great opportunities for decoration which came to be fully exploited. The covers of many seventeenth-, eighteenth- and nineteenth-century ratifications were magnificently embroidered and the skippets for the Great Seals on the more important ratifications were made of silver, silver gilt and even gold, which were often embossed with the royal arms. The documents and seals themselves, however, were usually plain, though some French early sixteenth-century ratifications are splendidly illuminated and have golden seals appended to them.

This ratification never became operative owing to the fall of Emperor Maximilian before the exchange of ratifications could be completed; he was executed by revolutionaries at Queretaro on 17th June 1867. President Benito Juarez subsequently refused to recognise the validity of Maximilian's acts. The ratification was presented to the Department of Manuscripts in 1942 by the British Foreign Secretary, Sir Anthony Eden (later first Earl of Avon).

See **44** for an Austrian ratification of this period.

134 The Austrian Court Chancellor, Count Philipp Ludwig von Sinzendorff, and Thomas Robinson, the British Envoy at the court of the Emperor Charles VI, arrange the exchange of ratifications for the Second Treaty of Vienna; Vienna, 1st May 1731. From the Robinson (Grantham) Papers

Additional MS 23781, f.427

As Court Chancellor, or 'Hofkanzler', Sinzendorff was in effect the Emperor's Foreign Minister. Overall control of affairs, however, at that time rested with Prince Eugene of Savoy, the Duke of Marlborough's former comrade-in-arms, who in the spring and summer months normally resided in the splendid Belvedere Palace which had been constructed for him a few years earlier just outside the walls of Vienna.

On 16th March 1731, Robinson and the leading Austrian ministers had signed and sealed a series of public, secret, and very secret articles and a variety of declarations, collectively known as the Second Treaty of Vienna, which marked the reconciliation of George II and Charles VI after years of estrangement. These had since been ratified, most recently by the Emperor on 21st April. In this note Sinzendorff asks Robinson to be 'chez le prince' at midday, 'c'est à dire à douze heures' ('that's to say at twelve o'clock') with the treaties (i.e. ratifications) in order to exchange them. Sinzendorff would have preferred an Austro-French alliance and his pique at having been excluded from much of the negotiations for this Treaty, which took place directly between Robinson and Prince Eugene, can be traced in the cool tone of the note. The ceremony of exchange itself seems to have been very simple.

More than two centuries later, on 15th May 1955, the Belvedere provided the setting for a far more significant diplomatic event when, in its great marble hall, the Foreign Ministers of Britain, France, the United States, Russia, and Austria, signed the Austrian State Treaty, which brought to an end the occupation of Austria that had followed the Second World War and restored its full independence.

135 The swearing of the Oath of Ratification of the Treaty of Münster, 15th May 1648. By Gerard Ter Borch (1617–81)

Reproduced by courtesy of the Trustees, The National Gallery, London

The Treaty of Münster brought Spain's final recognition of Dutch independence and the end of a struggle that had begun eighty years earlier. The participants in its conclusion were worthy of commemoration and between 1646, when negotiations began, and 1648, Gerard Ter Borch was in Münster, painting portraits of the plenipotentiaries. This picture immortalises the moment when Spain publicly accepted the United Provinces' right to exist and the Treaty officially came into effect.

The articles of agreement had been signed in Münster on 30th January 1648 and they were ratified by Philip IV of Spain on 1st March and by the Dutch on 18th April. According to a contemporary account of the ceremonial exchange of ratifications by Johan Cools, the plenipotentiaries seated themselves at a round table on which stood two caskets containing the treaty documents. Speeches were made and the terms of the Treaty were read out in French and Dutch. The representatives then rose and the Spanish swore by placing their right hands on the Gospels and afterwards kissing a crucifix. The Dutch followed, swearing by raising their right hands. Next the instruments of ratification were exchanged and certificates confirming the exchange were made out and signed.

Ter Borch depicts the two delegations as taking the oath simultaneously, and the suites are grouped artistically in a semicircle facing the spectator. In other respects, however, the picture accords with the description by Cools. At the left are the six Dutch delegates, dressed in black. The leader of the delegation, Barthold van Gent, representing Guelderland, holds an example of the articles of agreement in his left hand and stands in the middle of the picture. The other delegates are Johan van Mantenesse (Holland and West Friesland), Adriaen Pauw (also Holland and West Friesland), Frans van Donia (or von Dohna) (Friesland), Willem Ripperdà (Overijssel) and Adriaen Clant (Groningen). Godard van Rede, representing Utrecht, was unable to attend through illness and Johan de Knuyt was not present because his province, Zeeland, had not

ratified the Treaty. The first Spanish Ambassador, Don Gaspar de Bracamonte y Guzman, Conde de Peñaranda, stands next to Barthold van Gent. He is described by Cools as being dressed in grey with silver embroidery, and is seen wearing the high collar of the Spanish court and holding his copy of the articles of agreement. The other Spanish Ambassador, Antoine Brun, stands to Peñarada's left, dressed somewhat more colourfully and looking the prosperous Flemish administrator he was. A monk and other clerics can be seen in the throng around the table and Ter Borch has included a self-portrait of himself on the extreme left-hand side of the picture.

The exchange of treaty ratifications in Europe seems always to have been accompanied by some form of oath-taking from the earliest times, when the Greek city states sent special missions of prominent citizens to other cities to take solemn oaths of ratification of the treaties between them. Unfortunately, however, envoys have not generally described these ceremonies in detail, and in this they were followed by their staffs. Moreover, until well into the eighteenth century depictions of the exchange of ratifications of other treaties tended to be derived from this picture which was soon engraved.

The painting was owned by Talleyrand in the early nineteenth century.

136 Declaration of exchange of ratifications, Calais, 8th April 1407

Additional Charter 58 420

This parchment indenture contains an impersonal declaration in French stating that the English ambassadors Richard Aston, Lieutenant of Calais, Sir William Hoo, John Urban, Perin le Loharent and Richard Oldington, on the one side, and the Flemish commissaries, Pierre, Sire de la Viesville, Jean de Toisy, Archdeacon of Ostrevant in Hainault, Thierry Gherbode and Thierry de Heuchin, representing John ('the Fearless') Duke of Burgundy and Count of Flanders, on the other, had received from their masters the ratifications of a treaty which they had negotiated and concluded in the form of an indenture. This provided safe passage through each others' lands for merchandise and for pilgrims and clerics on their way to Rome, as well as security for fishermen in the waters of the other party. These instruments of ratification had been read and exchanged. The parties then stipulate that the Treaty will be published and executed throughout their lands, and initially in Calais and Gravelines, between April and the 15th June. Each side will check that the terms are being enforced by the

other. Finally they arrange a further meeting for 1st August to settle outstanding points such as compensation for the confiscation of and damage to goods at sea and the security of passage for ships between Boulogne, Winchelsea and other Channel ports. In testimony of this, the envoys of both parties seal the indenture with their personal arms, the English coming first. The seals are appended to the document by parchment thongs. Each party received an identical indenture (from the Latin 'dens', tooth), which came from a single sheet of parchment which had been cut in a jagged way, forming shapes, resembling teeth, across the middle. The validity of these instruments could thus be checked since the original, authentic ones would fit together if placed top to top. The ink marks across the cuts provided extra security.

The use of impersonal declarations, often in the shape of indentures, was an alternative method by which medieval negotiators could conclude agreements, diplomatic as well as domestic, if they did not wish to use personal declarations in the form of Letters Patent (130). The indenture seems to have been particularly popular with Scottish diplomats. Differing regional forms of French were used as diplomatic languages by France and the Netherlands from the late thirteenth century to the sixteenth century.

At a later period, two documents would take over the functions fulfilled by this instrument. There would be a certificate confirming the exchange of ratifications and a declaration making provision for its execution and for future negotiations. As it stands, however, this indenture serves as an admirable reminder that the ambassador is continuously engaged in negotiations, the exchange of ratifications more often than not merely marking the end of one stage and giving rise to a new series of negotiations.

This charter once formed part of the enormous manuscript collection of the wealthy antiquary Sir Thomas Phillipps (1792–1872).

136

137 Coin: Denarius of Augustus from the mint of Lugdunum, 8 BC

British Museum: Department of Coins and Medals: B.M.C. Augustus 494

The obverse of this silver denarius of Lugdunum (now Lyon in France) has a bust of Augustus in profile wearing a laurel wreath, and the legend reads AVGVSTVS DIV IMP (abbreviation of 'Divus Imperator': Sacred General). The reverse shows a distinctively cloaked barbarian chief moving forward from the left to present his child as a hostage to Augustus who is seated on a raised throne on the right, with his right arm outstretched to receive the child. The legend underneath (IMP XIIII) is a means of dating the coin, since it refers to the fourteenth year of Augustus's possession of the 'imperium', or command, over all the armed forces of the state, which he had received in 23–22 BC.

From the earliest times hostages were given by states as pledges for the execution of their treaty obligations, and as late as October 1748 Charles Cathcart, ninth Baron Cathcart, and George Yelverton, second Earl of Sussex, were sent to Paris as hostages for the return of Cap Breton to France by Great Britain in accordance with the terms of the Treaty of Aix-la-Chapelle. The province was duly surrendered and, after an enjoyable year spent being fêted in the French capital, the two aristocrats returned to London in November 1749 (Additional MSS 35355, 36592-3). Had Cap Breton not been returned, the French could have held them in gaol as prisoners of war.

137

138 Renewal and confirmation by Henry VIII of England of the Treaty of Peace and Friendship between Henry VII and King John of Denmark, London, 30th June 1523 (see plate no XII)

Additional Charter 25959

This document of confirmation and renewal takes the form of Royal Letters Patent. It was drawn up by a clerk in the English Chancery. Henry VIII announces in the preamble that he and King Christian II of Denmark and Norway had decided to confirm and renew the Treaty of Peace and Friendship concluded between their fathers. The articles of that treaty are then quoted in full. They provide for peace and friendship between the two kingdoms; for the security of English fishermen around Iceland and the Baltic; for the peaceful settlement of disputes; for the privileged position of their merchants in each other's lands and for joint action against piracy. Unlike documents of ratification, which this otherwise resembles very closely, no full powers are quoted, since the articles had not been renegotiated since their original ratification by Henry VII on 6th August 1489 at Westminster and by King John on 20th January 1490 at Copenhagen. In a few words at the end, Henry solemnly 'approves, renews, ratifies and confirms' these articles ('approbam*us*; renovam*us*; ratificam*us* et confirmam*us*'), in testimony of which he appends, with green and white ribbon, his Great Seal.

The magnificent seal of green wax bears an impression of the first seal of Henry VIII, which was used from 1509 to 1532. It shows the King in robes of majesty, crowned, holding orb and sceptres, in a carved Gothic niche ornamented with trefoiled canopy and panelled corbels. At each side is a compartment with a corbel and double arched canopy. In this is a shield of arms of France and England quartered and below a lion of England. Beyond this compartment is a smaller one, with a man-at-arms in armour, holding a javelin. In the field at the base on either side of the corbel is a rose. The legend reads HENRICVS: DEI: GRA: REX: ANGLIE: +: FRANCIE: +: DOMINVS: HIBERNIE.

The reverse has the King riding to the right, in plate armour enriched with the arms of England and France. He bears a sword and a shield with the arms of England and France. The horse is armorially caparisoned and plumed and is galloping on a mound covered with flowering plants, in which are three rabbit burrows, with one rabbit entering that on the right, another coming out of the centre burrow and a third seated at the left. The background is filled with diamond-shaped trellis work, with fleurs-de-lis at each point of intersection and a rose in each space. Above the tail of the horse is a rampant lion, and below its head, a fleur-de-lis. The legend reads: HENRICVS: :DEI: :GRACIA: :REX: :ANGLIE: :ET: :FRANCIE: :ET DOMINVS: :HIBERNIE. Each pair of colons encloses a rose. This Great Seal renders a royal signature unnecessary.

On the same day that Henry sealed this document, King Christian sealed the Danish counterpart, and the treaty was formally renewed following the exchange of the two royal confirmations.

This document was acquired by the Department of Manuscripts in Berlin in 1877. Its earlier history is uncertain, but it may have been looted by a soldier from one of the Danish royal castles in Schleswig-Holstein during the course of the war of 1864 between Denmark, Austria, and Prussia.

REPRESENTATION

The roots of the words ambassador (from the Latin 'ambactiare') and delegate or legate (from the Latin 'legare') convey the meaning of being sent as a representative, servant, vassal, or subordinate. The root of the word deputy (Latin 'deputare') means to be considered as. They testify to the antiquity of the ambassador's function as a representative. Full ambassadors however do not simply represent their masters. On official occasions the ambassador is in theory transmuted into his master. He seems frequently to have taken attributes of royalty such as canopies and robes of state with him on his mission (141). He wore his hat in the presence of other sovereigns (146), he bore his master's arms on his coach (109) and his plate (140), and made his public entry and proceeded to his audiences in almost royal state (10, 109, 144). He delivered his master's apologies (144, 146) and legally married his wife (145). When several ambassadors appeared together they had to be sensitive about their positioning relative to each other since this reflected their masters' comparative power and esteem. Thus arose the disputes over precedence and protocol that could plague the full ambassador in the execution of his duties (146).

The representative function decreased with the diplomat's grade and the roots of the words envoy (French, 'envoyer'), commissary (Latin 'committere'), and emissary (Latin 'emittere') mean simply someone 'sent' or 'charged' with a duty. Callières considered that envoys and ministers plenipotentiary represented their governments rather than their sovereigns – and they were therefore obliged to take off their hats in any sovereign's presence and did not make ceremonial entries. They were able to negotiate as authoritatively as a full ambassador but without his difficulties over protocol. Hence the prevalence of envoys rather than ambassadors between the seventeenth and early twentieth centuries. Callières stated that the lowest grades of minister, resident, and commissary had no representative function and indeed they seem rarely if ever to have been furnished with official plate for their tables. Nevertheless almost all heads of mission, even of the lowest grades, seem to have retained vestigial representative duties. They were and are still expected to commemorate national and royal events and anniversaries in a fitting manner (139, 142); to provide worthy hospitality (141); to keep order amongst their compatriots abroad; to marry them and to support their interests in all ways. This may take the form of providing them with money and passports, of securing reasonable treatment from the local authorities, or of furnishing them with introductions to court or to other places of interest (143).

139 Mathew Prior's bill of extraordinaries for representation, Paris 1714

Additional MS 15947, f.14

The diplomat and minor poet, Mathew Prior (1664–1721) served as British Plenipotentiary in France between 1712 and 1715. The bill lists the expenses incurred in the first ten months of 1714, when 16135 French livres (about £942 sterling) were spent on celebrating the Coronation anniversary of Queen Anne and the Coronation day of George I; on mourning for the deaths of the young Duc de Berri, Louis XIV's youngest legitimate grandson, who died in May following a riding accident, and of Queen Anne, who died on 1st August; and on 'My lodging at Fontainbleau during the Kings [Louis XIV's] stay there, the expense for my Table, my Family [i.e. household], Equipage; My lodging at Paris still running on'.

On important anniversaries, such as his master's birthday (or Catholic rulers' name-days) and the anniversary of coronations, the conscientious ambassador normally held a large reception to which ministers of the government to which he was accredited, other envoys, his compatriots and local notables and their ladies would be invited. The ambassador would dine in state, and the reception would often be accompanied by a firework display and a ball. The greater the occasion, the greater the festivities, and in 1688 Sir George Etherege (92) celebrated the birth of the Prince of Wales (later the 'Old Pretender') with three days of banquets and balls in Regensburg, during which the town's fountains ran with wine.

There were various degrees of mourning, the most expensive being for the ambassador's own sovereign, when the whole of the household – which could number 200 – the furniture, the coach harness and the horses, had to be dressed or draped in black for a lengthy period. Mourning for a minor member of the host royal family, on the other hand, could be brief and relatively inexpensive. Only the most important members of the household had to wear mourning and this needed only to consist of grey, white or purple suits. Mourning for Queen Anne cost Prior 3300 livres, that for the Duc de Berri only 1935.

The bulk of the expense was generally incurred in the 'normal' representation of one's master – particularly if the court to which one was accredited tended to move from palace to palace, as most major ones did. Nevertheless Prior computed that celebrating the Queen's birthday (3100 livres) cost more than one month's ordinary expenses (3000 livres).

Prior was more unlucky than most envoys. On his return from France in March 1715, he was impeached by the Whigs because of his involvement on behalf of the Tory ministry in the early negotiations with France that resulted in the Treaty of Utrecht. He was imprisoned for the next two years and never seems to have been reimbursed in full for the extraordinary expenses incurred while he was in France.

140

140 Silver-gilt dish and ewer from the ambassadorial plate of Thomas Wentworth, Lord Raby (later Earl of Strafford), 1705/1706. Silversmith's mark: Philip Rollos 1705/1706

Victoria and Albert Museum: M. 23 + a – 1963

In May 1705 Raby (**39, 40, 104**) was created Queen Anne's Ambassador Extraordinary in Berlin and this dish and ewer were among the plate ordered for his use. The centre of the dish and the area beneath the mouth of the ewer are engraved with the royal arms borne by Queen Anne before the passing of the Act of Union between England and Scotland in 1707. The arms are encircled by The Garter, supported by the crowned lion of England and unicorn of Scotland, and surmounted by the Crown. A rose and a thistle issue from the top of the strapwork behind the shield. The legend reads 'Semper Eadem' ('Always the Same').

Despite this visual evidence that the plate remained the property of the Queen, it was never returned by Lord Raby (**102**).

141 The ambassadorial table of Roger Palmer, Earl of Castlemaine, as James II's Ambassador to Pope Innocent XI, January 1687. Drawn by A. Cornelii and G.B. Lenardi; Engraved by A. van Westerhout, John Michael Wright *Ragguaglio della Solenne Comparsa fatta in Roma gli Otto di Gennaio MDCLXXXVII dall' Illustrissimo . . . Signor Conte . . . di Castlemaine, Ambasciadore Straordinario di . . . Giacomo Secondo Re d'Inghilterra . . . alla Santa Sede Apostolica in andare publicamente all' Udienza della Santita di . . . Papa Innocenzo Undecimo* **(Rome 1687) plate 9**

Department of Printed Books 603. l. 19

The engraving demonstrates the splendour of an ambassador's table of state on special occasions during the period of the Baroque. Since this ambassador was British the table is littered with statuettes of English crowned lions and Scottish unicorns interspersed with larger statuettes representing the scenes from classical mythology beloved of Roman artists and sculptors of the Baroque. To the right of the centrepiece Apollo is shown catching up with Daphne who turns into a tree – the subject of one of Bernini's most famous sculptures. Elsewhere can be seen vases, dishes, salts and, anticipating the Rococo, shells – all in gold, silver or silver-gilt. The ornate centrepiece seems to be an allegory on the truth and splendour of Roman Catholicism, to which James II was a convert. It shows a sunburst piercing the clouds with the help of the Church, shown as a veiled woman. The centrepiece is surmounted by James II's royal arms. Behind the table, and underneath the elaborate

painted ceiling of the Roman palace where Castlemaine resided, is a portrait of James II enthroned and carrying orb and sceptre. The portrait is surmounted by a canopy and underneath, during the banquet, would be placed a throne for the ambassador (147). Thus was he transmuted from the King's representative into the very King himself – a mystery which occurred wherever an ambassador appeared in state.

For Castlemaine's mission see 109.

142 Silver Medal commemorating the Franco-Dutch Treaty of Nijmegen struck by the Dutch Ambassador in Stockholm, December 1678. Engraver: Arvid Karlsten (1647–1718)

British Museum: Department of Coins and Medals: M7618

The Dutch Ambassador in Stockholm, Dr Christian Rumpf, commissioned this little medal from Arvid Karlsten, the royal Swedish medallist, to commemorate the signature of peace between France and the United Provinces under English mediation on 10th August 1678 at Nijmegen. On the obverse the arms of France, England and the United Provinces are shown suspended from a laurel wreath. The legend reads 'GALLO-BATAVA. PAX' ('French-Batavian (Netherlands) Peace'). The reverse contains a view of Nijmegen with the sun shining above. The legend reads 'PAX. OPTIMA. RERVM.' and underneath 'NOVIO-MAGI Ao. 1678' ('Peace [is] the best of things; Nijmegen, in the year 1678'). The medal was distributed on 6th December 1678 in the course of a reception held by Rumpf in his residence, the Van der Noth Palace in Stockholm.

Gestures such as the commissioning and distribution of commemorative medals in the national honour were by no means rare among ambassadors.

142

143 Note from the Viscomte de Châteaubriand, French Ambassador in London, to Henry Hobhouse, Under Secretary of State at the Home Office, 50 Portland Place, London, 8th May 1822. From the Peel Papers

Additional MS 40347, f.52

The author and diplomat, François-René Viscomte de Châteaubriand (1768–1848) then newly appointed French Ambassador to Great Britain, writing in the third person, requests Hobhouse to facilitate the visit of the Comte de Marcellus, a member of the French Chamber of Deputies, the Viscomte de Marcellus and M. Bourqueney, two of his Secretaries of Embassy, to Newgate Prison. Conditions in the prison were notoriously bad, but efforts were at that time being made to ameliorate them. Hobhouse passed the note to his political superior Sir Robert Peel (1788–1850), the Home Secretary in the Tory administration.

Ambassadors frequently provided introductions for distinguished compatriots.

144 Official account of Charles Whitworth's audience as Queen Anne's Ambassador Extraordinary with Tsar Peter I, 'The Great', of Russia, Moscow 5/16th February 1710 (N.S.). From the Strafford (Raby) Papers

Additional MS 31128, ff.208–9

In August 1709, Charles Whitworth, the British Envoy in Russia (**48**) was created Ambassador Extraordinary and was ordered to apologise formally, in the Queen's name, to Tsar Peter for the injury done to him in the person of his Ambassador to Queen Anne, Andrei Artemonovich Matveev, through Matveev's arrest and imprisonment for debt in London in July 1708 (**35**). It took many

143

weeks and the exercise of considerable finesse on Whitworth's part before the special audience of apology could be arranged. It is fully described in this newsletter, which was circulated to all British diplomatic representatives and was printed as the public report which appeared in *The London Gazette*, number 4672, nearly two months later.

At eight in the morning the British Consul, merchants, and British officers in the Tsar's service, about forty in all, assembled at Whitworth's house. Two hours later the Tsar's First Carver, Czoltikoff, a brother of the Dowager Tsarina, arrived and a ceremonial procession formed up. The first twenty-two coaches, all with six horses, carried the merchants. Whitworth's Secretary, Ludwig Christoph Weisbrod, carrying the credentials and in the company of the Tsar's Secretary, rode in the twenty-third, which was owned by Peter's favourite field marshal, Prince Menshikov ('Menschikoff'). 'Then followed 1° The Ambassador's sled carv'd and gilt, lin'd with green trim'd with gold galoons [braid], the foot cloth of the same richly lac'd and embroider'd, and drawn by six pyed Horses. 2dly a handsome Chariot painted and gilt lin'd with scarlet drawn with six black horses and the harness trim'd with silver'd plates 3°, a Chariot very richly gilt, lin'd with red velvet trim'd with silver lace, drawn with six black horses their Harness very finely gilt 4°, Twelve footmen in red liverys with broad gold galoons interwoven with green and white silk 5°, four pages on horsesback, their Coats of fine scarlet richly lac'd with gold and silver, their wa[i]stcoats and sleeves of green brocard [brocade] with gold and silver flowers. 6° The Czar's Coach of State where the Ambassador sat with Mr Czoltikoff and the Master of Ceremonies, his Gentleman of Horse riding by. The march was near an hour and a halfe, and the streets throng'd with spectators.

'At His Excellency's coming into The Castle [i.e. the Kremlin], the Gards received him with Drums beating, colours flying, the officers at the head with their swords drawn, and saluted [him] with their hats. At his lighting out of the Coach the Ambassador was complimented by a Gentleman of the Bedchamber Mr Naroskin, who is some Relation to the Czar. The Grenadiers ware [i.e. were] rang'd on both side[s] of the stairs. At the top he was received by Prince Scherbatoff, and in the antichamber by a Privy Councillor Mussin Puskin, who is one of the Chief officers of state and has the Inspection of all the Ecclesiastik affairs and revenues. His Czarish Majesty stood on the state uncover'd [i.e. in state, hatless].

'When the Ambassador came up to him, He [i.e. the Ambassador] made a speech in English, declaring Her Majesty's just concern for the affront offer'd to Mr Artemonowitz [i.e. Matveev] and the severall proceedings [taken] by Her Majesty's orders towards a full reparation which was the only end of this Embassy. His secretary read the same in High Dutch [i.e. German] and one of their's [i.e. one of the Russian secretaries] afterwards in the Russian Language. His Majesty answer'd in Russ, which Vice Chancellor Shaphiroff interpreted and was in substance that His Majesty might have very well expected those people who had violated the Law of Nations in the person of his Ambassador should have been punish'd according to his desires [Peter had wanted the malefactors executed], yet since that could not be, by the Defect of our former Constitutions, His Majesty, considering the concern the nation had shown in the act of Parliament (see 35) and the honour Her Majesty the Queen had done him by this Ambassy, was willing to accept of this satisfaction and would order his ministers to settle the other articles in a Conference.

'His Excellency was then dismiss'd from his Audience with the same Ceremonys . . . and at his coming home found three tables prepared by the Czar's officers for the Ambassador and his Company . . . Mr Czoltikoff in the Czar's name made pressing Instances to continue the same two days longer, but with much ado His Excellency got a dispense from the Civilities . . . and contented himself with six men more order'd to the gard [than was] usually given to all foreign ministers'.

In his letter to Lord Raby in Berlin which accompanied the account, Whitworth wrote that his 'was the neatest Equipage ever seen here', but he was forced to admit that it was 'small not comparable to what is used by Her Majesty's Ambassadors at other Courts . . . t'was done on good Husbandry' (Whitworth to Raby Moscow 9/20 February 1710 (N.S.) Additional MS 31128, ff.206–7). In a letter of the same date to the British Secretary of State for the North, Henry Boyle (Lord Carleton), he bluntly admitted 'it was neither so numerous or magnificent as is usuall on such solemnities' (Additional MS 37358, f.42).

This account does, however, give a good impression of the ceremonial attached to special missions of compliment and particularly significant are Peter the Great's statement about 'people who had violated the Law of Nations in the person of his Ambassador' and Whitworth's emphasis that 'full reparation . . . was the only end of this Embassy' – indeed, he left Russia for England eight weeks later. Whitworth's refusal of an additional two days of hospitality at the Tsar's expense is indicative of a growing distaste for such customs and ceremonial which led to their virtual disappearance by the end of the eighteenth century.

145 Ercole I, Duke of Ferrara, notifies the Priori of Perugia of his marriage, Ferrara, 9 November 1472
Additional MS 16163, f.11

Ercole formally announces his union with Princess Eleanor, daughter of Ferdinand I of Naples (132) following a marriage ceremony on 1st November ('*Kalendis presentis mensis*') between the Princess and '*oratorem . . . nostrum ad ea specialiter per nos constitutum nomine nostro*' (our ambassador, specially appointed by us for these purposes, in our name). The letter is sealed with a large papered seal bearing a shield with Ercole's arms, surrounded by his full titles.

Until the last century royal marriages were by proxy, with special ambassadors taking the place of, and legally, briefly, becoming, their masters.

146 Silver medallion commemorating Spain's acknowledgement of French diplomatic precedence in 1662. Engraved by Jean Mauger (1648–1722) after a design possibly by Sebastien Leclerc (1637–1714)
British Museum Department of Coins and Medals: George III Fr. m. 473

Full ambassadors, unlike diplomatic representatives of a lower grade, had to be most sensitive about where they stood or were placed on official occasions attended by other ambassadors. For their position relative to the other ambassadors reflected the comparative esteem in which their masters were held by the courts to which they were accredited. Since the pre-eminence of the Pope's representative, the Nuncio, followed by the Ambassador of the Holy Roman Emperor was accepted without dispute, at least in Catholic courts, the rivalry for position affected the ambassadors of other countries. The dispute between French and Spanish Ambassadors for third place was particularly bitter. Traditionally this had been filled by France, but during the great days of Spain in the century after about 1550, Spanish Ambassadors, like Gondomar (73) had often usurped it. As French power began to recover under Richelieu, Mazarin, and Louis XIV, French Ambassadors reasserted what they believed were their rights vis-à-vis Spain with ever greater energy. Spanish Ambassadors, however, replied with equal vigour.

One of the worst incidents occurred in London on 10th October 1661 (by the Gregorian calendar) during the public entry of the special Swedish Ambassador, Count Nils Brahe. The other ambassadors in London had, somewhat rashly, been invited to take part in the procession and the hot-blooded Spanish Ambassador, the Baron de Batteville, found himself behind the French Ambassador, the Marshal d'Estrades (128). Rather than endure this public slight, he ordered his coachmen to overtake the French Ambassador's coach. The French suite resisted and in the ensuing fray two servants were killed and many innocent bystanders were injured. Louis XIV, deeply offended at this affront, determined to establish French precedence beyond challenge. Strong pressure was put on Madrid, which had been humiliated by France only two years earlier in the Treaty of the Pyrenees. Rather than risk another armed confrontation, Philip IV recalled de Batteville and agreed to send a special mission of apology to Paris.

The formal audience of the Spanish Ambassador, the Marquess de la Fuente (129), was held in the Louvre on 24th March 1662, in the presence of the French royal family, French ministers and the eight full Ambassadors, and twenty-two other envoys who were accredited to the French court. After delivering his credentials and public instruction to Louis XIV, the Ambassador announced that in order to satisfy Louis, his master had recalled de Batteville and had instructed all Spanish Ambassadors at other courts to abstain from disputes over precedence with French diplomats at the public functions to which both were invited. In order to emphasise the significance of this step the French King then instructed the assembled diplomats to

inform their masters of de la Fuente's declaration 'affin qu'ils sachent . . . que c'est la volonté du dit Roy (d'Espagne) . . . que ses ambassadeurs cèdent en toutes occasions le rang aux miens' (so that they know . . . that it is the (Spanish) King's desire that his ambassadors should yield precedence to mine on all occasions).

This medallion indicates the importance attached to this event by the French. It was one of a series commemorating important events in Louis XIV's reign, issued as propaganda after 1677. It shows Louis XIV standing, left arm outstretched, beckoning the Spanish Ambassador to approach. The back of the chair behind the King is decorated with a shining sun befitting the Sun King ('le Roi Soleil'), as Louis was known even by his contemporaries. The Spanish Ambassador, to the right, is bowing and approaching. Behind the two men and in front of the windows of the palace stand the other Ambassadors, positioned strictly according to protocol with the Nuncio, Cardinal Coelio Piccolomini (who was expelled from France six months later) standing immediately to the King's left. All the Ambassadors wear hats in the King's presence – as no French courtiers normally could – because they represented Louis's fellow monarchs. The legend reads IUS PRAECEDENDI ASSERTUM (the right of precedence asserted) and beneath HISPANORUM EXCUSATIO CORAM XXX LEG PR MDCLXII (apology of the Spaniards in the presence of thirty princely envoys 1662). The obverse bears a portrait of the young Louis XIV.

Seemingly petty disputes over apparent trivia such as one's place in a procession or over the shape of a table have given diplomats a bad name. This is somewhat unjust, for such behaviour usually reflects differences so profound as to make negotiations – the diplomat's work – well-nigh impossible. If relations are generally good and a ruler wishes negotiations to take place such disputes can easily be avoided. Thus, before 1945, envoys were generally appointed in preference to full ambassadors, and ambassadors anxious to avoid disputes found pretexts, such as diplomatic illnesses, for absenting themselves from potentially awkward ceremonies. When disputes occurred they were almost invariably intentional and symbolic of a far deeper malaise or of an intention to avoid or delay negotiation until a time more favourable to the 'trouble-maker.'

Disputes continue to this day, but those over precedence, as illustrated here, were finally ended by the Réglement of the Congress of Vienna of 1815 by which ambassadors were ranked according to the length of their residence in the host country.

146

148

147

This contains an early suggestion for the medallion issued by the French Académie des Inscriptions et Belles Lettres to Leclerc. It contains all the basic elements in the final design, except that the main legend is much blunter, reading LOCO ET DIGNITATE CEDIT HISPANVS (the Spaniard yields [his] position and dignity). The writing around the sketch gives details of the event portrayed.

This sketch and the next come from a slim volume containing cuttings with designs for historical medals drawn by Sebastien Leclerc and other artists accompanied by descriptions and suggestions for designs transmitted to them by order of the Ministers or the Academy.

148 A later sketch for the same
Additional MS 31908, f.16ᵛ

Though this sketch is more detailed than its predecessor, there are still several differences between it and the final version of the medallion. The main legend reads, perhaps a little too vapidly, GALLVS. DIGNITATE. ANTECEDIT (the Frenchman comes first in dignity) and underneath FATENTE HISPANO CORAM XXXII PRINC LEGATIS M. DC. LXII (the Spaniard acknowledging in the presence of thirty-two [sic] envoys 1662). Note that the King's chair is surmounted by a canopy.

OTHER DUTIES

In addition to his other responsibilities, the ambassador was expected to keep a diary for his own use recording his daily activities (**149**). He might also find himself being used by leading figures at his court as a glorified postman (**150**) or as an artistic agent (**151**). Indeed he could find himself pandering to the often eccentric whims of his master, regardless of the harm this might do to diplomatic relations or the cost in embarrassment to himself (**152**). Rarely did envoys openly object – for it could be these services rather than their more official duties that brought them the rewards that they coveted.

149 Diary of Sir William Trumbull, British Ambassador in Constantinople, 31st March–23rd April 1689

Additional MS 52279, ff.128–9

These brief and abbreviated entries reflect the Ambassador's routine in a post which until then had been considered 'soe remote (from London) as any intelligence from hence thither . . . can be of little use here' (Secretary of State Nicholas to the Earl of Winchelsea, Charles II's Ambassador in Constantinople 1661). Trumbull records visiting the widowed French Ambassadress, who was responsible for French interests until the arrival of her husband's successor 'that she might not say I neglected her since ye change of affairs in Eng*land*' [i.e. James II's flight] [3rd April]. Five days later, Trumbull sends a packet of letters to the Dutch Ambassador for transportation to Venice aboard a Dutch ship – thus did envoys help one another. On the 17th, he received French gazettes from the French Ambassadress. For the rest he lists his guests at dinner, the arrival of ships in Constantinople, the holding of services in the Embassy church (31st March, 16th April), his trips to the countryside near Constantinople ('a very long days Journey; But *G*od kept us') (2nd April) and discussions with British merchants about firing of the cannon on St George's Day, (23rd April) ('I rep*lied* [I] Had no advice from Court, onely pub*lished* News L*etters*').

The even tenor of Trumbull's days are disturbed only by two events. Much the most spectacular occurred on Monday, 15th April, when 'having slept ill ye night & waking betimes, my deare [wife] rose before 6 & having gott me some prunes & sirrup of violets, shee went out & shut ye Chamber door; after w*hich* I endeavoured to sleep & ab*out* h*alf* an h*our* after 6, I (being wrapt up in Bed) heard a sudden noise: w*hich* I thought was people ru*nn*ing in ye Gallerie, till suddenly I heard ye Cabinet shake violently by ye Bed side; Upon wch I jumpt out & cryd 'L*ord* have Mercie upon us', & with my slippers got out and calling out for my deare, run in my shirt down staires. But *G*od spar*ed* us. According to my Guess [the earthquake] lasted neare 2 minutes. I dresst myself in ye kitchin'. The next day Trumbull, blandly noted a still greater event. 'In ye Evening *received* from Mr Jacob ye news of ye P*rince* & Princesse of O*range* being proclaimed K*ing* & Queen of Eng*land* etc. upon which Mr Haley [the Chaplain] alter'd his Prayers'. The accession of William and Mary totally altered the nature of the Constantinople Embassy. Trumbull was soon to be ordered to mediate between the Sultan and the Emperor who were at war with one another, in order to enable the Imperial-German troops to be turned against France. In the process the

Ambassador was transformed from being 'a commercial agent masquerading as an ambassador into a servant of the Crown sent primarily for political and diplomatic business'.

William Trumbull (1639–1716), though he belonged to a diplomatic family, worked as a lawyer until 1685, when he was sent as ambassador to France (1685–1686). Later he served elsewhere, particularly in Constantinople from 1687 to 1691, before becoming a secretary of state (1696–1697). He was a friend of the poets John Dryden and Alexander Pope.

150 Letter from Madame de Pompadour to the Duc de Mirepoix, French Ambassador to George II, 12th October 1751. From the Newcastle Papers
Additional MS 32685, f.61

This floral-edged note was written when Jeanne Antoinette Poisson (1721–1764), created Marquise de Pompadour by her lover the French King Louis XV, was at the height of her power.

She informs the French Ambassador that she is sending a box from Paris to his London address and asks him to deliver it to the Duke of Newcastle, then the most important British Secretary of State. She hopes Newcastle will find the (dried?) flowers from her garden as beautiful as the fruit which he had sent her had been excellent and that they will help to replace the natural flowers (during the coming winter). She compliments herself on having found a skilful method of making him think of her, the person in the world who values him most.

151 Letter from Henry Newton, British Envoy Extraordinary in Tuscany, to the Duke of Marlborough, Florence, 4th March 1710 (N.S.)
Blenheim (Marlborough) Papers M. 46 (previously B II 2)

Dr Henry Newton (1651–1715), a lawyer of scholarly interests, spent much of his time as Queen Anne's representative in Tuscany between 1704 and 1711 acting as an artistic agent for British leaders and aristocrats who increasingly wished to embellish their houses with works of art from Italy.

The Duke of Marlborough was anxious to acquire sculptures to adorn Blenheim Palace which was then being constructed under the direction of its architect, the playwright Sir John Vanbrugh. Newton had a difficult time executing the Duke's orders and in this letter he explains that 'ye Cavaliers to whom ye statues belong, tho they fall somewhat in their demands, yet still they aske double what they are thought to bee worth, pretending that under 12000 crowns they will not

150

part with them. Signor Soldani [Massimiliano Soldani 1658–1740] will bee very proud to doe whatever lyes in his power for your Grace's service and indeed hee has an Universall esteem, his workes in Brasse being very much prizd not onely here but at Rome, Vienna & Paris. The Grand Duke [Cosimo III reigned from 1670 to 1723] is very ready to give any orders that may tend to your Grace's satisfaction about ye Statues in his Gallery (one order at my desire has bin sent mee today . . . wch will very much expedite ye worke) . . . I have written more at large upon all matters by ys [this] post to Mr Vanbrugh . . .'.

In the previous century Sir Dudley Carleton, when the representative of James I and Charles I in the Hague, had performed a similar service for his masters and noblemen, like the Duke of Buckingham, who wished to buy paintings by Rubens.

152 Robert Earl of Salisbury, Lord Treasurer of England, to Sir Thomas Edmondes, James I's Ambassador resident in Brussels, Greenwich, 9th June 1609. From the Edmondes Papers

Stowe MS 171 f. 85

In 1609, James I of England decided to have the Latin version of his *Apologie of the Oath of Allegiance* presented to the Catholic rulers of Europe, despite its strongly Protestant tone. In this letter Salisbury – somewhat ambiguously – writes that 'when I consider what I sende you in sendinge you this booke, as well in respecte of the Author as of the Subiecte, I conclude you will neither looke for many woordes from mee to prayse that wch prayseth ytself nor that I shoulde use persuasion to you to geve yt all circumstances of advantage in the presentacon. By the enclosed copie you shall see what the Kinge hath wrytten; in conformitye whereof your Language may bee carried'. In an autograph postscript Salisbury adds 'It is not amiss yt (that) you do lett fall to ye Archduks yt ye fr[ench] k[ing] hath receaved it, yt a book is gon to ye k[ing] of Spain and to ye Emperour'.

Salisbury's apprenhensions are clearly discernible and were quite understandable for the Southern Netherlands were ruled by particularly pious Catholics. Archduke Albert (72) was a former cardinal and his wife Isabella was a daughter of Philip II of Spain. Less than a month later, on 5th July, Edmondes was forced to report to Salisbury (*Stowe MS 171 f.101*) that despite his own eloquence and the book's merits the Archdukes (as Albert and Isabella were generally styled) had refused to accept it 'in respect that there was so much spoken therein against the Pope and the doctryne of their churche'.

Also of interest in the letter is Salisbury's mention in the postscript that, though Edmonde's letter of revocation was enclosed, he could 'use it at your best Tymes'. Envoys frequently continued at their posts long after the date of their letters of revocation which only became effective once formally presented to the rulers to whom the envoys were accredited.

152

5. THE END OF THE MISSION

SUCCESSES

Before this century the close of a mission was generally marked with formalities similar to those that attended its opening. The ambassador would receive official letters of recall or revocation from his master, one addressed to himself (**153**) and others to the rulers of the state to which he had been accredited (**154**). Though normally very sober in appearance (**153**), the letters intended for non-Europeans could be ornate (**154**). The mission formally ended with a leave-taking audience, rather resembling the first public audience (**111**). The departing envoy would deliver the letters of recall addressed to his host and be handed his 'recredentials'. These took the form of a formal letter to his master allowing the envoy to depart and expressing the hope that he would give a faithful account of his host's (i.e. the writer's) sentiments. Since the letter was usually sealed, the ambassador (envoy) would receive an official copy for his own use (**161**). At the audience the ambassador or envoy was normally given a gift of regard. This varied according to his master's importance and his own grade. A distinguished ambassador might be knighted (**158**), but miniature portraits of the ruler (**156**) set in diamonds or in jewelled rings (**157**), gold medals (**159**), or golden boxes (**160**) were common diplomatic gifts (**155**). Before his departure the ambassador might also be given precious gifts for his master (**163**).

Occasionally there was no formal leave-taking audience and the new ambassador presented his predecessor's letters of recall with his own credentials (**154**). This procedure has become customary since 1900.

On his return home, the ambassador was expected to provide a detailed report on his mission and on the country where he had resided, the 'relazioni' given by Venetian ambassadors to the Doge and Senate being particularly famous (**163**). After the sixteenth century the custom of delivering these as orations at formal audiences gradually disappeared, except in Venice. A satisfied master could reward an ambassador in any way he pleased, but certain orders of chivalry have long been associated with diplomats. In Great Britain these have been the Order of the Bath (**164**) and, since 1917, the Order of St Michael and St George.

153a

153 Queen Anne's letter of revocation for the Earl of Sunderland, her Envoy Extraordinary in Vienna, Kensington Palace, 21st September 1705
Blenheim (Sunderland) Papers S2 (formerly C I 2)

This has the typical appearance of the letters of revocation sent by English rulers to their envoys when formally recalling them. It is written in English on paper and signed at the top by the monarch and countersigned at the bottom by a secretary of state, in this case Robert Harley. A papered royal signet seal bearing an impression of the royal arms is affixed to the back of the letter, officially to seal it but in reality, since the letter seems never to have been properly sealed, to provide further authentication.

The wording of this letter is fairly standard, though royal letters of revocation were often a little longer and employed more flowery language. Sunderland is informed that his presence in England is required and that he should prepare himself for his return. He should take 'the first opportunity' to deliver the Queen's letters to the Emperor, the Empress and the Empress Dowager 'whereby we give them notice of your Revocation'. He was then to return to London 'as soon as conveniently you can . . . where you shall receive the Assurances of Our Royal Favour'.

Letters of revocation for the envoy were invariably accompanied by letters for the sovereign and leading figures at the court to which he was accredited announcing his recall. In spite of the peremptory tone of most letters of revocation the envoy was normally left free to request his formal leave-taking audience when he wished (152). Sunderland received his letters of revocation in the middle of October, but waited another month before taking his formal leave of the Emperor on 20th November. He departed from Vienna three days later.

154 Letter of revocation and introduction sent by James II to the Ottoman Grand Vizier Azem, Windsor, 30th September 1685. From the Nugent-Brydges-Chandos-Grenville papers (see front cover)
Stowe MS 221

In November 1684 Charles II determined to recall his Ambassador in Constantinople, James Brydges, eighth Baron Chandos (1642–1714), whose Whiggish views he found distasteful. Charles died before any action could be taken, but his successor James II had the necessary documents recalling Chandos and introducing the new Ambassador, Sir William Soame, drawn up.

The appearance of this letter resembles other royal letters intended for non-European states (57). It is written in English on a large sheet of parchment and it is spectacularly decorated in gold leaf, red and blue. The letter is surmounted by the royal arms, crowned, supported by the English lion and the Scottish unicorn and encircled by the Garter. To the left and right are the English and Scottish lions standing on royal crowns. The first line of the letter is illuminated in gold and the initials J, S, and B are decorated with intricate ink flourishes. The left border contains the crowned arms of England and, beneath, of France. The narrower border on the right contains the crowned arms of Scotland and, beneath, of Ireland. Certain words in the text are written in gold and the letter is signed in the King's own hand 'your affectionat freind James R.'.

The main business of the letter is done in the first few lines, where James formally announces to the Vizier 'that we have thought fitt to recall the Lord Chandos Our Ambassador in ordinary at the High Port (i.e. the Ottoman Court), that he may attend Us in our Dominions And . . . Wee have supplied that place by the Bearer hereof Our Trusty and welbeloved Sir William Soame Baronet whom We have appointed to succeed and remaine as Our Ambassador at the High Port. We therefore desire you will at all times procure and grant him a favourable and easy accesse whenever he shall have

153b

occasion to address himself for our service either to your Imperiall Master (i.e. the Sultan) or Yourself, Giving full credence to whatsoever he shall deliver unto you in our Name.' The King then touches on Anglo-Turkish relations. He asks redress from the Vizier, the Sultan's 'Prime Minister of State,' on behalf of the British subjects who had been imprisoned and fined by his predecessor. He begs his 'favor and protection' for British merchants, and particularly that those in Smyrna and Aleppo may be represented in Constantinople by the ambassador or other merchants in Constantinople. 'And above all we desire that the Capitulations may be observed' (56, 59). 'And so we recommend the Person of this Our Ambassador to your benigne favour and courteous reception desiring that you would please to procure the dismission of the Lord Chandos that he may return to our Presence. And so the High illustrious and excellent Lord the One Great and Ommipotent God have you in his keeping'.

The equivalent letter for West European rulers would have been written in Latin on paper, with very little ornamentation, an impression of the royal signet seal and the countersignature of a secretary of state, like normal credentials (**100**). Its basic tenor, however, would have been the same.

Soame died in Malta on his way to Constantinople and the letter was never presented. Instead it apparently came into the hands of Lord Chandos and his heirs, only passing out of their possession in the last century. Lord Chandos was finally replaced by William Trumbull (**149**) in 1687.

155 The Lord Chamberlain confirms the purchase of gifts for foreign envoys in London, 18th December 1678
Additional MS. 32476 f.50

This letter was probably written to the Lord Treasurer, Thomas Osborne (1632–1712), then Earl of Danby and later created Duke of Leeds, by Henry Bennet, Earl of Arlington (1618–85). The writer confirms that he had 'by his Ma*jes*ties Command agreed with Mr Le Gouch His Ma*jes*ty's Jeweller, for a Jewell with his Ma*jes*ties picture of the Value of three hundred and fifty pounds, given to Mons*r* Bellow, Envoy from the Duke of Lunengbergh and other princes of Germany: And also for a Ring of the Value of three hundred pounds, w*hich* is given to Baron Swerin Envoy from the prince Elec*tour* of Brandenbergh: And also for a Jewell of the value of One Thousand pounds which was to have beene given to the Late portugall Ambassador decea*sed* and now given by His Ma*jes*tie to the Countess of Penalva his Sister.' The total value of these gifts is calculated in the margin at £1650.

'Mons*r* Bellow' or Joachim Heinrich von Bülow had been on a special mission in London since November 1677, trying to win admission for his master, the Duke of Brunswick Lüneberg-Celle, to the Congress of Nijmegen. The gift he received from the King at his final audience on 29th November 1678 seems to have been a miniature of Charles II set in diamonds – rather resembling the 'Lyte Jewel' of 1610 which forms part of the Rothschild Bequest on display in the Waddesdon Room of the British Museum. The ring given to 'Baron Swerin' (Otto, Freiherr von Schwerin), who had his final audience on 6th December 1678, was another typical gift given to diplomats at the end of a mission. The expense of the 'Jewell' given to the sister of the deceased Portuguese Ambassador, Francisco, Conde de Melo e Torres and Marques de Sende, reflects the special position he occupied. For over seven years he had resided in England as the Ambassador and representative of the brother of Charles II's Queen, Catherine of Braganza.

In addition to gifts, envoys might also receive permission to 'augment' their arms by including in them a part of the English royal arms – as did Michael Mercator, for instance (**89**).

156 Miniature portrait of Charles II by Samuel Cooper, 1665. Watercolour on vellum, rectangular
Trustees of the Goodwood Collection

This miniature was given by Charles II to his mistress Louise de Kerouaille, Duchess of Portsmouth (1649–1734), mother of Charles Lennox, first Duke of Richmond. It shows the King in his robes, wearing the sash and Order of the Garter. It is signed SC and dated 1665.

This is one of the most important miniatures of the King that Cooper (1609–72) painted and it served as the model for the later miniatures of Charles that were distributed to envoys like Joachim Heinrich von Bülow in 1678. Although the records indicate that the miniatures presented to diplomats were originally contained in jewelled frames and cases, exceedingly few miniatures still survive in such settings. It seems that, mercenary – or needy – as ever, the recipients almost invariably sold off the jewels for money as soon as they could decently do so.

157 Gold ring containing a miniature portrait of Charles II of England
British Museum: Department of Medieval and Later Antiquities: Dalton 1369

This ring, set with two diamonds, contains a miniature of Charles II in later life. The ring given to Baron Schwerin was probably similar to this, though it may have been surrounded by more jewels.

157

158 Constantijn Huygens's patent of knighthood, Westminster, 7th October 1622 (see plate no. XIII)
Additional Charter 12777

This patent of knighthood was drawn up during the course of Constantijn Huygens's mission as Dutch Ambassador to England between December 1621 and March 1623. The margin at the top and at the right is elaborately decorated in red and gold while in the wide left margin the capital J of Jacobus is painted in pink, green, and gold and contains a crowned seated lion bearing James I's English royal arms surmounted by a crown and encircled by The Garter. Beneath is a painting of Huygens's arms surmounted by a helmet. The patent takes the form of Royal Letters Patent. The preamble justifies the princely practice of rewarding meritorious individuals and, James continues, he has therefore created Huygens, who is eulogised as the worthy son of a worthy father, a knight, as is confirmed by the patent. The patent is signed by the King. The Great Seal (King James I's second Great Seal) is appended by a plaited cord of red and white silk. The seal, of bronze-green wax, shows the King enthroned wearing his coronation robes and crown and holding the orb and sceptre. On the left-hand side of the throne a crowned lion holds a standard and pennon containing the arms of Cadwallader, the last King of the Britons. On the right is a unicorn with a standard and pennon containing the arms of Edward the Confessor. On either side of the throne are the arms of James I crowned and encircled by the Garter. The legend around the seal gives James's name and his titles as King of England, Scotland, France, and Ireland, and Defender of the Faith. The reverse shows the King on horseback, galloping, with a greyhound – possibly the origin of the Royal Messenger's symbol – running in front.

Constantijn Huygens, Lord of Zuylichem (1596–1687) was a member of one of the leading Dutch families and his father, Christiaan, had been Secretary to the Dutch Council of State. Constantijn was one of the foremost men of his age. He was outstanding both as a diplomat-politician and as a poet, but he was also extremely capable as an artist, as a musician – and as a gymnast who when in his twenties scaled the spire of Strasbourg Cathedral. In the course of his career he was appointed as Dutch Ambassador at Venice, in France and England – where he met and became a firm friend and admirer of John Donne – and at other leading European courts. As this document shows, his talents were obvious enough to win him a foreign knighthood at the age of twenty-six. For a letter addressed to Huygens see **87**.

Another capable artist-diplomat to be awarded a knighthood during the course of a diplomatic mission (in 1630) was Rubens.

159 Golden medal of Johann Philipp von Gebsattel, Prince Bishop of Bamberg, 1601
Victoria and Albert Museum: 66–1867 (Tross Collection)

The oval medal is cast and chased and set in an ornate frame suspended from a chain. The obverse shows the Prince Bishop, who reigned from 1599 to 1609, in profile. The legend reads . 1601 + IOAN: PHILIP. EPS. BAMBER. ETATIS. 44 + (1601, Johann Philipp, Bishop of Bamberg, 44 years of age). The reverse shows two shields: of Bamberg (left) and of the Gebsattel family (right) surmounted by the German Imperial Crown, with the crossed staff and episcopal crozier behind them. The inscription reads DOMINE NOLO VIVERE NISI MORIAR TECUM (O Lord, I do not wish to live unless I may die with you).

Before the proliferation of orders of chivalry, envoys who did not merit full knighthood but were worthy of special reward were often presented on taking their leave with medals, called 'Gnadenpfennige' (pennies of grace) in German, by the rulers to whom they had been accredited. The custom survives in the semi-official orders, often containing miniatures of members of the royal family, which are still bestowed on meritorious courtiers by royalty.

159a 159b

160 A gold box made in Paris in 1763–4. Maker: D.F. Poitreau
Victoria and Albert Museum: m.120–1917

The top and sides of the box are decorated with embossed groups of drums, clarinets, and trophies of war.

Small gold boxes like this were another common farewell present for worthy envoys particularly in the eighteenth century. All too often, however, they seem only to have been regarded by the recipient as a means of recouping at least some of the expenses incurred during his mission.

161 The Earl of Sunderland's copy of his recredentials, Vienna, 20th November 1705

Blenheim (Sunderland) Papers S 2 (formerly C 12)

Recredentials take the form of a letter, signed by the ruler to whom the envoy is accredited, formally commenting on the outcome of the mission; notifying the envoy's master that in response to the letters of recall or revocation he has, with regret, allowed the envoy to depart furnished with this testimonial; and expressing confidence that the envoy will give a truthful account of his mission. It is normal too to stress the writer's amiable sentiments. Recredentials, like credentials, have the usual appearance of official royal letters.

The Emperor Joseph commences these re-credentials by thanking the Queen for the letter brought to Vienna by the Earl of Sunderland, her Envoy Extraordinary and Plenipotentiary. It, the mourning worn by him and his expressions of condolence, confirming the Queen's message, had proved a great solace and had greatly increased the new Emperor's obligations towards her. Joseph's fixed and immutable intention is to join the strength of his provinces to the Queen's for the common benefit and security.

Acknowledging Anne's assistance, he stresses that one of his principal concerns will be to convince the disaffected Hungarians of his goodwill and clemency so that their rebellion may cease and their leaders may look to their country's true peace and happiness and not to the blandishments of French emissaries. Praising the help already given by Sunderland, Joseph says he had hoped he would stay in Vienna longer, for Sunderland had from the start been executing his duty in a most praiseworthy manner. Since the Queen's wishes and the pressure of his own private affairs necessitate his recall without further delay, however, Joseph releases

him, with this testimonial, not doubting that on his return he will inform the Queen of Joseph's fraternal love and constant concern for the public good.

The actual letter contained Joseph's full titles at the head and was signed by the Emperor, countersigned by his secretary and his Hofkanzler Count Sinzendorff (134) and sealed with a papered impression of his arms (98), but the original and Sunderland's copy were written by the same scribe.

Marlborough shared Sunderland's farewell audience since the Emperor – in fulfilment of the Duke's secret request conveyed by Sunderland (99) – had invited him to Vienna a few weeks earlier. Marlborough's copy of his own recredentials are still among his papers (M. 94). The two men arrived back in England shortly before Christmas.

162 Esperanza Malchi, the Grand Sultana's maidservant, writes to Elizabeth I, Constantinople, 16th November 1599

Cotton Charter XXVII.8

Writing in a form of Italian on behalf of her mistress, the Sultan's mother, Esperanza begins the letter by comparing Elizabeth's virtue and greatness to the rays of the sun which spread throughout the universe and make people of different nations, living under different laws, want to serve her. Esperanza, a Jewess, had wished to do so from the very moment she entered the service of the Grand Sultana. Now that Elizabeth had sent an ambassador to Turkey with a present for the Grand Sultana, and the Sultana had asked Esperanza's help in order to reciprocate, Esperenza had her opportunity. Since the ambassador was departing, the Grand Sultana wanted to show her love for Queen Elizabeth by sending her, by way of the ambassador, a gown, a belt, two strips of cloth worked in gold, and three in silk in the Ottoman manner, and a collar of pearls and rubies ('una veste et una cintura et doi faciolli lavorati de horo et tre lavorati di seta al usanza di questo Regno et un collar' di perle et Rubbini'). This was being conveyed to the ambassador by Bostanggi Basi, but the Sultana had got Esperanza to give the ambassador one of her diamond crowns (and) a precious stone which the Sultana wants Elizabeth to wear for love of her ('una corona di diamanti gioia di sua ser*en*ita qualli dice piacera a sua maesta portar p*er* amor' di lei'). Elizabeth is not a prude ('p*er* esser sua maesta donna senza vergogna alcuna') and Esperanza wants a favour of her. She hears that there are all sorts of fine distilled waters for the face ('aque destillati di hogne sorti p*er* la facia') and perfume for the hands ('hogli hodoriffere p*er* le mani') in her kingdom. Could Elizabeth send her some of these for her mistress, the Sultana? Being

160

135

womanish matters, she does not want them to pass through other hands ('per esser cosa di donne non volle che passa per altra mano'). Similarly if there is excellent woollen or silk cloth in England, suitable for a Queen or Sultana, and if Elizabeth could send some, the Sultana would prize it more than any precious stone she might send Elizabeth ('panini di seta ho di lana cosse stravaganti et convenienti per una tanta alta Reggina como lei sua maesta potra mandarli che piu avera lei caro questo che qual si voglia gioia che sua maesta gli posia mandar').

One of the most important gifts ever made to an ambassador for his master was the Codex Alexandrinus, given by Cyril Lucar, Patriarch of Constantinople, to Sir Thomas Roe while Roe was Charles I's ambassador in Constantinople. It is on permanent display in the British Library's galleries.

163 Copy of the 'relazione' delivered by Giovanni Sagredo on his return from acting as Venetian Ambassador in London, 1656

Additional MS 36679

This final report contains a description of the geography, economy, social and political structure, court and leading personalities of the country where Sagredo had resided. But he concentrates on the history of the Civil War, since, as he explains, this had not been covered in any previous relazione (final report).

Sagredo's bias is royalist and Roman Catholic. Nowhere does this appear more clearly than in his description of the creeds to be found in the London of Oliver Cromwell (ff.16–17). Having abandoned Roman Catholicism, he writes, the English have become divided into no less than 246 different sects, including Adamists, Anabaptists, Lutherans, Calvinists, and Quakers. 'Quakers meet in a large room and begin to tremble and shake until they fall to the ground in what they call ecstasy, but which really resembles sleep. After a while they rise and pray for the most extravagant and ridiculous of things.' He illustrates the religious diversity by mentioning his neighbour in London, a leading English peer with six sons. All belonged to different sects and quarrelled and fought among themselves so much that their father was incessantly having to separate and pacify them. Cromwell's government was frequently denounced in the churches – and there were even women preachers whose eccentric interpretation of the holy scriptures caused mirth rather than devotion.

This manuscript dates from 1690 and seems to have been given as a present by one Venetian to another in 1698. The text, with that of Sagredo's relazioni of Germany and the Ottoman Empire, was first printed in 1844.

The final report or relazione seems to have originated in Venice, where it was originally a report delivered to the Doge and Senate within fifteen days of an ambassador's return from a special mission. From 1268 the relazione became obligatory for Venetian diplomats, but as special missions gave way to resident missions the nature of the relazione altered. Since the course of a mission could be followed from the normal despatches (119), relazioni became devoted to broader analyses of the country and its people. Ambassadors often devoted considerable time and skill to the preparation of the relazioni which, although officially confidential, were frequently copied and circulated among the ambassador's contemporaries. The official copies, which were meticulously preserved in the Venetian archives, were undoubtedly utilised in the formulation of Venetian foreign policy. They also constitute an extremely important source for historians of Europe and Asia.

Venice retained its pre-eminence in this field, with much of the old ceremonial, until the end of the Republic in 1797, but the practice of delivering final reports was copied throughout Europe, even in England (48, 98). By the eighteenth century, however, non-Venetian relazioni were no longer delivered as orations by ambassadors at a formal audience.

164 Golden Pendant Badge of the Order of the Bath. Early eighteenth century (see plate no. X)

British Museum: Department of Medieval and Later Antiquities: 1978, 1–4, 1

The badge of enamelled gold, with diamonds, rubies and an emerald, has the Order's device of three crowns, grouped around a central staff, with a rose and thistle springing from stems, all enclosed within a frame bearing the Order's motto 'TRIA JUNCTA IN UNO' (three joined in one: a reference to the union of England, Scotland and Ireland).

Between 1725, when the Order of the Bath was re-instituted after a lapse of seventy-five years, and 1917, successful British diplomats were regularly created Knights of the Bath. Before this date the rewards received by diplomats conformed to no fixed pattern. Some might be awarded offices of profit at home, or be given pensions. Others, like Sunderland, who was created Secretary of State for the South in the year following his return from Vienna, might be given offices of state. Others still were ennobled, while the more humble might have been satisfied with the grant of the 'park or domycile about London' so ardently desired by Thomas Spinelly in 1518 (25). Nor did the award of a Knighthood of the

Bath exclude these additional rewards after 1725. Since 1917 the Order of St Michael and St George has taken the place of the Order of the Bath as the diplomat's order. Founded in 1818 for the natives of the Ionian Islands, which had come under British rule in 1814, it was extended in 1864 (when the islands were ceded to Greece) to all British subjects serving beyond the seas, particularly in the Colonial or Foreign Services. Following the disappearance of the obsolescent Order of the Star of India, the Order of St Michael and St George will come to rank immediately after the Order of the Bath.

164

FAILURES

This little section serves as a reminder that diplomatic missions have not always ended happily. Some have not officially started at all (**165**), while in other cases political changes at home have brought the long-serving ambassador an abrupt recall or forced his resignation and even exile (**166**). Many worthy ambassadors and envoys of lower grades have died before the official termination of their missions (**167**), and still more have had after their return to spend years in petitioning their masters – often in vain – for their pay (**168**).

165 Letter from the Emperor of China to the Prince Regent of Great Britain, Kea-King, 11th September 1816 (20th day of the 7th moon of the 21st year)

Public Record Office: Foreign Office, Protocols of Treaties (F.O.93) 23/10

The letter takes the form of an Imperial mandate, issued by the Emperor to his vassals, consisting of a single sheet of yellow painted paper, decorated with a border of Imperial Dragons, with the texts in Manchu, Latin, and Chinese. An ink stamp seal is applied to each of the three versions.

The occasion of the despatch of this letter was the unsuccessful mission of Lord Amherst, who refused to kneel and bow his head to the ground in a kowtow when in the Emperor's presence as Macartney had done in 1792 (**60**). The Emperor explains that the Ambassador had been repeatedly told that he would have to make the kowtow and that he had agreed to do so. On the day of the audience, 29th August, however, just as the Emperor was about to enter the Hall of Audience, Amherst 'suddenly affirmed that he was exceedingly ill and could not move a step. I [the Emperor] thought that the Ambassador had suddenly been taken ill, and therefore ordered the Assistant Ambassador to enter and see me: but both the Assistant Ambassadors also affirmed that they were ill. This was rudeness which was never exceeded. I . . . sent them away the same day with an order to return to their country.' Nor did the Emperor accept the Prince Regent's letter which was returned unopened.

The Emperor reassures the Regent, however, 'that your Ambassador's inability to communicate on your behalf with profound veneration and sincere devotedness is his fault. The disposition of profound respect and obedience felt by you . . . I indeed really perceive. I took from amongst the articles of tribute only maps, landscape prints, portraits and highly commend your feelings of sincere devotedness just the same as if I had received them all. There were conferred upon you . . . a white corundum Jooee (an emblem of prosperity), a string of court beads, two large purses and eight small ones.'

'Your country is too remotely distant from the Central and Flourishing Empire [China] . . . Further your Ambassador cannot understand and practice the rites and ceremonies of China. The subject involves a severe labour of the lips and tongue, to hear which is by no means pleasant. The Celestial Empire does not value things brought from a distance. All the extraordinary and ingenious productions of your country also it does not look upon as rare pearls. I, the Emperor, highly commend that you . . . should preserve your people in peace and be attentive to strengthen the limits of your territory, that no separation of that which is distant from that which is near should take place.

'Hereafter there is no occasion for you to send an Ambassador so far and to be at the trouble of passing over mountains and crossing seas. If you can but pour out the heart in dutiful obedience, it is not necessary at stated times, to come to court . . . this Imperial Mandate is now given that you may for ever obey it.'

166 The Comte de Choiseul-Gouffier transfers his responsibilities as French Ambassador in Constantinople to the Ottoman Authorities, French Palace, Constantinople, 24th September 1792
Additional Ms 41567, ff. 185–6

Marie Gabriel Florent Auguste de Choiseul-Beaupré (1752–1817), Comte de Choiseul-Gouffier, wrote this note shortly after hearing the 'affreuses nouvelles' (frightful news) of the storming of the Tuileries Palace in Paris and the imprisonment of the French King and his family (10th August 1792) and of the 'September Massacre' of aristocrats. Choiseul-Gouffier foresaw that these events would soon lead to the declaration of a French Republic and the execution of the King by the new government, which he brands as a horde of villains ('horde de scélérats').

He announces that his unalterable attachment to his unfortunate master and the former constitution of the French Empire ('empire françois') prevents him from recognising for a moment ('pour un moment') the new government's usurpation of the sovereign power. He therefore feels unable to continue to hold a position, as French Ambassador in charge of the administration of French establishments in the Levant, which he had received from a sovereign who was then free and all-powerful. Since, in this momentary state of anarchy ('cet état momentanée d'anarchie') he is no longer able to take responsibility for the conduct of the individuals involved in policing the Turkish commercial ports ('Echelles') or for the maintenance of the Capitulations, he transfers his functions to the Turkish government. He asks in particular that it protect Roman Catholic priests, who have been protected since time immemorial by the French crown, and royalist Frenchmen. He requests a reply and concludes by expressing his profound sorrow ('profonde douleur') and at the same time gratitude to the Ottoman administration for the esteem and kindness with which he had been treated during his eight years as French Ambassador. The letter is signed by Choiseul-Gouffier and sealed with his arms.

Choiseul-Gouffier came of a family closely associated with the French royal administration (46). A man of scholarly tastes, with a particular interest in ancient Greece, he had been involved in some of the earliest scientific excavations in Greece before being sent as ambassador to Turkey in the autumn of 1784. He performed his duties most effectively in the political and commercial fields, and as a protector of the Catholics in the Ottoman Empire. He also secured the services of French instructors to improve the efficiency of the Ottoman army. Initially he supported the reforms that were introduced in France after 1789, even donating 12,000 Francs to the National Assembly, and in 1791 was offered the French Embassy in Rome or London. Already alarmed at the turn events were taking in France, however, he refused to return to Paris. In June 1792 he received letters of revocation (dated 12th June) which he refused to heed, formally announcing his resignation in August. He daily expected the Allied armies to inflict a crushing defeat on the new French government and found himself in difficulties when this failed to happen. Although appointed the personal representative of the Comte de Provence (later Louis XVIII), he had to flee from Constantinople to St Petersburg in 1793 following the seizure of his papers by the authorities. He returned to France in 1802.

It was rare for ambassadors to resign after a change of government; normally they seem to have waited until they were officially recalled.

167 Tomb of George Stepney, Westminster Abbey
Photograph by the British Library

George Stepney (1663–1707) was one of the most able British diplomats of his time, though his relative poverty prevented him from ever attaining the grade of ambassador. He was educated at Westminster School and Trinity College, Cambridge, where he made a name for himself as a poet and was, in 1687, elected a major fellow. He began his diplomatic career, under the patronage of his friend Charles Montague, Earl of Halifax (94), as a Secretary of Embassy, first to Sir Cyril Wych in Hamburg and later (1690–2) to James Johnston in Berlin. Over the following years he served as British representative in the grades of agent, minister, and envoy extraordinary and plenipotentiary in Vienna (1693, 1701–5), Hesse-Cassel (1694–7, 1706–7), Cologne (1695–6), Mainz (1695–6), the Palatinate (1695–7; 1701), Saxony (1693–4, 1695, 1698), Trier (1695–7), Poland (1698), Sweden (1702), and Bavaria (1704). Finally, in 1706, his long-standing wish to be transferred to the Netherlands – where he hoped to play a leading part in a forthcoming peace congress – was met (**99**). Nine months after his arrival, however, he fell ill of 'the bloody flux' and returned to England in the hope that the change might benefit him. He died unmarried in Paradise Row, Chelsea, on the 15th September 1707 (Julian calendar). In the words of Joseph Addison to Christian Cole, in a letter written the next day, he died 'lamented by everybody. He has left Mr Prior (**139**) a legacy of £50, to my Lord Halifax a gold cup and 100 tomes of his library and the rest of it is to go to Mr Lewis and a silver ewer and basin to Mr Cardonell. His estate is divided between his two sisters. The best part of it lies in the Treasury which owes him £7000.' Thus ended the last mission of 'a thorough statesman', in the words of a contemporary, who spoke 'all the modern languages, as well as ancient, perfectly well . . . No Englishmen ever understood the affairs of Germany so well, and few Germans better'. He was buried in great state on 22nd September 1707 in Westminster Abbey, the pall being carried by two dukes, two earls, and two barons.

An elaborate monument, with a long and complimentary epitaph, surmounted by his bust, was subsequently erected to his memory in the south aisle of Westminster Abbey.

For a letter written by him see **47**. His papers now form part of the collections of the Department of Manuscripts.

Many diplomats, particularly of the lower grades, were even less fortunate than Stepney. Thomas Spinelly (**25**) died in Spain in 1522 before he could retire to the 'lytel hol' near London of which he had been dreaming. The fate of Philip II's Ambassador to London, Bishop Quadra, was more gruesome. He fell so heavily into debt during the course of his mission that after his death in 1563 his creditors seized his body and kept it rotting by a London quayside for two years until their demands were satisfied.

168 Sir William Temple's petition to James II for payment of outstanding debts, *c.* **1685. From the Temple Papers**
Additional MS 9800, f.155

Writing more than six years after his return from the Hague and the Congress of Nijmegen in July 1679, Sir William Temple (**103**) requests payment of the £2140 that was still owed him from that mission.

167

Suggestions for further reading

The literature on the theory and practice of diplomacy is vast and growing so rapidly that it would be impossible in the space available to produce even a representative short bibliography. This list therefore contains a few of the works which have been found invaluable, enlightening, or simply enjoyable. Several contain good bibliographies.

I. General Histories of International Relations

New Cambridge Modern History Vols. I–XII (Cambridge, 1957–71)

P. Renouvin (ed.) *Histoire des Relations Internationales* Vols. I–VIII (Paris, 1953–8)

II. The Theory and Practice of Diplomacy

E.A. Adair. *The Exterritoriality of Ambassadors in the sixteenth and seventeenth centuries* (London, 1929)

Sir F. Adcock and D.J. Mosley. *Diplomacy in Ancient Greece* (London, 1975)

B. Behrens. 'Origins of the Office of English Resident Ambassador in Rome', *English Historical Review* XLIX (1934) pp.650–56

B. Behrens. 'Treatises on the Ambassador written in the fifteenth and early sixteenth centuries', *English Historical Review*, LI (1936) pp.616–27

R.P. Bond. *Queen Anne's American Kings* (Oxford, 1952)

Sir G. Butler and S. Maccoby. *The Development of International Law* (London, 1928)

C.H. Carter. 'The Ambassadors of Early Modern Europe: Patterns of Diplomatic Representation in the early seventeenth century', *From the Renaissance to the Counter-Reformation. Essays in Honour of Garrett Mattingly* (ed. C.H. Carter) (London, 1966)

C.H. Carter. *The Secret Diplomacy of the Habsburgs 1598–1625* (New York, 1964)

L.G. Durrell. *Esprit de Corps, Sketches of Diplomatic Life* (London, 1957)

K.L. Ellis. 'British communications and diplomacy in the eighteenth century', *Bulletin of the Institute of Historical Research*, XXXI (London, 1958) pp.159–167

K.L. Ellis. *The Post Office in the Eighteenth Century. A study in administrative history* (London, 1958)

C. Gladwyn. *The Paris Embassy* (London, 1976)

R.A. Graham. *Vatican Diplomacy: A Study of Church and State on the International Plane* (Princeton, 1959)

R.M. Hatton. *War and Peace 1680–1720* (London, 1969)

R.M. Hatton and J.S. Bromley (eds). *William III and Louis XIV: Essays 1680–1720 by and for Mark A. Thomson* (Liverpool and Toronto, 1968)

R.M. Hatton and M.S. Anderson. *Studies in Diplomatic History. Essays in memory of D.B. Horn* (London, 1970)

E. Hertslet. *Recollections of the Old Foreign Office* (London, 1901)

F.H. Hinsley. *Power and the Pursuit of Peace, Theory and Practice in the History of Relations between States* (Cambridge, 1963)

D.B. Horn. *The British Diplomatic Service, 1689–1789* (Oxford, 1961)

R. Jones. *The Nineteenth Century Foreign Office: An Administrative History* (London, 1971)

D. Kahn. *The Codebreakers* (London, 1966)

P.S. Lachs. *The Diplomatic Corps under Charles II and James II* (New Brunswick, 1966)

M. Lee. 'The Jacobean Diplomatic Service', *American Historical Review*, LXXVII (1967), pp.1264–82

L. Lewis. *Connoisseurs and Secret Agents in Eighteenth Century Rome* (London, 1961)

(London. Public Record Office) *Treaties: Catalogue of an Exhibition at the Public Record Office* (London, 1948)

(London. Public Record Office) *The Records of the Foreign Office 1782–1939* (London, 1969)

F. Masson. *Le Département des Affaires Etrangères pendant la Révolution 1787–1804* (Paris, 1897)

G. Mattingly. *Renaissance Diplomacy* (London, 1955)

G. Mattingly. *The Defeat of the Spanish Armada* (London, 1959)

G. Mattingly. *Catherine of Aragon* (London, 1942)

G. Mattingly. 'No Peace beyond what Line?' *Transactions of the Royal Historical Society*, 5th series, XIII (1963), pp.145–62

F. Moussa. *Le Service diplomatique des États arabes* (Geneva, 1960)

J.E. Neale. 'The Diplomatic Envoy' *History* XIII (1928) pp.204–18

H. Nicolson. *The Evolution of Diplomatic Method* (London, 1954)

(Nijmegen. Nijmeegs Museum) *De Vrede van Nijmegen* (Exhibition Catalogue) (Nijmegen, 1978)

B. Picard. *Das Gesandtschaftswesen Ostmitteleuropas in der frühen Neuzeit* (Graz, Vienna, Cologne, 1967)

C. Picavet. *La Diplomatie Française au Temps de Louis XIV* (Paris, 1930)

C. Piccioni. *Les premiers commis des Affaires Etrangères au XVIIe et au XVIIIe siècles* (Paris, 1928)

E.A. Pritchard. *Anglo-Chinese Relations during seventeenth and eighteenth centuries* (London 1929)

D.E. Queller. *The Office of Ambassador in the Middle Ages* (Princeton, 1967)

J. Rives Child. 'The Evolution of British Diplomatic Representation in the Middle East', *Royal Central Asian Society Journal* 26 (1939) pp.634–47

Sir E. Satow. *Guide to Diplomatic Practice* (London, 1917)

W. Strang. *The Foreign Office* (London and New York, 1955)

M.A. Thomson. *The Secretaries of State 1681–1782* (Oxford, 1932)

H. Trevelyan. *Diplomatic Channels* (London, 1973)

(Vienna, Bundesministerium für Unterricht and Verein der Museumfreunde). *Der Wiener Kongress 1 September 1814 bis 9 Juni 1815* (Exhibition Catalogue, Vienna, 1965)

D. Vital. *The Making of British Foreign Policy* (London 1968)

M. Wight. *Power Politics* (London, 1946; expanded: Leicester and Harmondsworth, 1979)

M. Wight. *Systems of States* (ed. H. Bull) (Leicester, 1977)

M. Wight and H. Butterfield (eds). *Diplomatic Investigations* (London, 1963)

A.C. Wood. *History of the Levant Company* (London, 1935)

Acknowledgements

The exhibition which complemented this study was organised by the Department of Manuscripts. Its preparation was the work of Peter Barber who also compiled the study. The design of the exhibition was undertaken by Richard Fowler.

The British Library Board wishes to thank those institutions and individuals who have generously lent to this exhibition: Sir James Bowker, GBE, KCMG; the Trustees of the British Museum; the Trustees of the Goodwood Collections; the Public Record Office, London; Mr D.H. Turner; the Departments of Metalwork, and of Prints and Drawings and Paintings, Victoria and Albert Museum.

Photographs in the exhibition and book are reproduced by kind permission of: the Accademia Gallery Venice; City of Birmingham Museums and Art Gallery; Sir James Bowker GBE, KCMG; the Trustees of the British Museum; British Museum Publications Ltd; the Department of the Environment; the Freer Gallery of Art, Smithsonian Institution, Washington; the Groeninge Museum, Bruges; the National Gallery, London; the Nijmeegs Museum, Nijmegen; the Opera del Duomo, Siena; the Victoria and Albert Museum; Chatto and Windus Ltd are thanked for permission to utilise plate 21 from R.C. Welch, *Imperial Mughal Painting* (1978).

The compiler's great debt to Professors Ragnhild Hatton, David Bayne Horn, Garrett Mattingly and Martin Wight will be plain to all specialists in the field of early modern and modern international history. The following individuals have provided especially valuable assistance in the preparation of the book and the exhibition: C.D. Black-Hawkins, Vic Carter and the British Library Conservation Section, the late G.C. Darlaston, Mrs Nina Evans and the British Library typists who worked on the copy, Mrs Winnie Fleming, Dr Edward Gregg, Carol Illingworth, R. Lees, Dr Derek McKay, Graham Marsh and the photographers of the British Library's Photographic Section, Eric Marston, John Murdoch, Dr Julian Reade, Dr E. Sollberger, Mrs Anne Somers-Cocks, Professor Christopher Thorne and the Department of International Relations, University of Sussex 1967–70, and Mr C. Vogel. Lastly the compiler would like to thank his wife, parents and family.